Employment, Growth and Basic Needs:
A One-World Problem

Employment, Growth and Basic Needs:
A One-World Problem

The international "basic-needs strategy" against chronic poverty
Prepared by the
ILO International Labour Office
and the decisions of the 1976 World Employment Conference

With an Introduction by
James P. Grant

Published for the Overseas Development Council
in cooperation with the International Labour Office
PRAEGER PUBLISHERS
NEW YORK/LONDON

The designations employed in ILO studies, which are in conformity with United Nations practice, and the presentation of material therein do not imply the expression of any opinion whatsoever on the part of the International Labour Office concerning the legal status of any country or territory or of its authorities or concerning the delimitation of its frontiers.

The responsibility for opinions expressed in the contributions to this volume rests solely with their authors, and publication does not necessarily constitute an endorsement of the views expressed in them by the International Labour Office, or by the Overseas Development Council's directors, officers or staff.

PRAEGER PUBLISHERS
200 Park Avenue, New York, N.Y. 10017, U.S.A.

Published in the United States of America in 1977
by Praeger Publishers, Inc.

Library of Congress Catalog Card No. 77-70278
ISBN 0-03-021601-X (hardback)
ISBN 0-03-021601-O (paperback)

Printed in the United States of America

FOREWORD

One of the most important and complex questions facing the world today is that of how development can be carried out in a way which can satisfy the most basic needs of all people in the shortest possible time. The basic-needs strategy outlined in *Employment, Growth and Basic Needs: A One-World Problem*, the Report of the Director-General of the International Labour Office (ILO)—prepared for the June 1976 World Employment Conference[1]—makes a major intellectual contribution to the resolution of this question. The endorsement of the basic-needs strategy by the Conference marked a major step forward in the world-wide acceptance of this new developmental concept. The ILO Director-General's Report and the far-reaching Declaration of Principles and Programme of Action of the Conference are brought together in this publication to present to American readers this important advance in thinking and action on the critical issue of addressing absolute poverty and meeting minimum human needs.

An unusual aspect of the World Employment Conference was this international meeting's parallel emphasis on the internal policies that must be followed by the developing countries and the reforms in the international order—both of which are required if there is to be a serious attack on absolute poverty. Other international meetings, such as the Sixth and Seventh Special Sessions of the UN General Assembly and the fourth UN Conference on Trade and Development (UNCTAD), have concentrated almost exclusively on the issues *between* countries. For the first time, an international forum with a majority of participants from developing countries has insisted on the necessity of *internal* as well as inter-state reforms. This approach at last acknowledges the fact that *people*, not countries, are central to the development process.

---

[1]The Conference, formally called the Tripartite World Conference on Employment, Income Distribution and Social Progress and the International Division of Labour, was held in Geneva under ILO auspices, June 4-17, 1976.

The era since World War II has witnessed unprecedented increases in output, with gross global output increasing (in constant dollars) from some $1 trillion in the late 1940s to more than $3 trillion in the early 1970s. The expectation of the 1950s and of the 1960s (the First UN Development Decade) was that, with sufficient increase in output, there would be—admittedly with some lag—a "trickle down" sharing of benefits for all. The increasing affluence of a relative few in the developing countries was initially treated as a necessary pre-condition for the savings that would lead to the more rapid growth which ultimately should be of benefit to all. Or, as Mahbub ul Haq—a prominent development expert from the Third World—expressed the prospect in 1963, "The road to eventual equalities may inevitably lie through initial inequalities".[2] By the late 1960s and the early 1970s, however, it had become increasingly clear that a great proportion of the poor in most developing countries were not benefiting significantly from this pattern of development and that there was little prospect of an early, major improvement in their lot. In the early 1970s, approximately one billion people remained desperately poor, with some 400-500 million (according to the UN Food and Agriculture Organization) falling within the category of malnourished or hungry. Moreover, despite the unprecedented increases in output achieved in the 1960s, unemployment and underemployment in absolute numbers has been increasing in most developing countries in recent years, clearly illustrating the failure of most developing countries to mobilize their single greatest asset—their people. Projections of current trends indicate that by the mid-1980s there will be an even larger number of underemployed people living in absolute poverty.

By the early 1970s, new labor-intensive approaches to development—emphasizing "growth from below", "participation" and "employment-oriented" strategies—were being advocated. Research was indicating, moreover, that in those people-plentiful, land- and capital-short societies where the "poor majority" were effectively sharing in the work of building a nation, growth had not come to a stop; on the contrary, greater equity and greater participation seemed to be capable of supporting and reinforcing growth. In such countries, farmers with small plots of two or three acres who were effectively supported by low-cost delivery systems for services such as credit, health and education were producing more per unit of land than were the farmers practicing extensive, mechanized agriculture on larger farms. In other words, there was evidence that earlier strategies had been weak not only on humanitarian and social grounds but on economic grounds as well. The alternative, labor-intensive approach to development—designed to overcome these shortcomings of past strategies

---

[2]For an absorbing account of the evolution of Mr. Haq's own thinking on this issue since then, see his new book, *The Poverty Curtain* (New York, Columbia University Press, 1976).

—underlies (a) the "new directions" bilateral development aid legislation enacted by the US Congress in 1973 and reinforced in 1975, (b) the strategy changes advocated in recent years by World Bank President Robert McNamara and (c) the policies of an increasing number of OECD donor governments.

The basic-needs strategy articulated by the ILO builds on this labor-intensive, more effective approach to development *with* growth and extends it in two important ways: (1) it incorporates into the development strategy a far more direct and accelerated program to meet basic human needs—without assuming that this goal will be achieved automatically as a *by-product* of a more labor-intensive growth strategy; (2) it proposes the year 2000 as a target date by which the most essential basic needs should be met in all societies. The ILO Director-General's Report for the World Employment Conference not only represents the most detailed articulation of this concept by an international agency but also details the national and international strategies required to make it possible.

The 1976 World Employment Conference endorsed the basic-needs strategy—although without agreeing to set a uniform minimum standard for basic needs or to set a specific date by which these needs should be met in all countries. It called on the UN General Assembly to make the policies required to meet basic needs "an essential part of the United Nations Second Development Decade Strategy" and "the core of Third Development Decade Strategy".

The decisions of the Conference reproduced in the annexes to this volume are prefaced by a brief analysis by Charles Paolillo on the debate and actions taken at the Conference; this analysis is excerpted and adapted from a staff report on the Conference initially prepared for the House International Relations Committee of the US Congress.[3] Mr. Paolillo, now a Staff Consultant to the House International Relations Committee, is a former Visiting Fellow of the Overseas Development Council. His analysis of the Conference proceedings and their implications for implementation of a basic-needs strategy draws heavily both on his attendance at the Conference on a study mission for the Committee and on his close association over the past three years with the evolution of the "new directions" aid legislation in the US Congress. It should be noted, however, that Mr. Paolillo's comments, like those contained in any such study mission report, formally represent his own views.

Since the World Employment Conference took place in June 1976, the concept of a more targeted approach to meeting basic needs within this century has acquired increased legitimacy in a growing number of international forums. Thus leaders of the non-aligned nations, meeting in Colombo, Sri Lanka, in

---

[3] *A Basic Human Needs Strategy of Development: Staff Report on the World Employment Conference* (Washington, D.C., US Government Printing Office, 1976).

August 1976, called for the "eradication of unemployment and poverty" through the implementation of a policy for "satisfying the basic human needs of the population".[4] In October, the United Nations' inter-secretariat Committee on Co-ordination, chaired by Secretary-General Waldheim, set up a group to analyze the implications of the conclusions of the World Employment Conference for the activities of all the organizations of the United Nations system. Robert McNamara, President of the World Bank, in his address to the Board of Governors of the Bank in Manila on October 4, 1976, called for "a basic understanding", a kind of "global compact", which would

> make clear in overall terms both the additional trade and aid support to be provided by the developed nations and the policy reforms and structural changes to be undertaken by the developing nations. These should have as one of their major objectives the meeting of the basic human needs of the absolute poor in both the poor and middle income countries within a reasonable period of time, say by the end of the century.[5]

Later in the same month, a team of twenty international experts directed by Nobel Prize winner Professor Jan Tinbergen also embraced the basic-needs concept in their report to the Club of Rome, *Reshaping the International Order*. The "Tinbergen Group", as they are known, also called for a "global compact on poverty" between rich and poor nations and for the attainment of "the following national objectives for all countries by the end of this century": life expectancy, 65 years or more; literacy, 75 per cent or more; infant mortality, 50 or less per thousand; birth rate, 25 or less per thousand.[6] The Tinbergen Group estimated that the total investment required to alleviate the worst forms of poverty by the mid-1980s would be $15-$20 billion annually over the next decade, with some $10-$12 billion a year of this total coming from the developed countries.

Thus the concept of greatly increased and accelerated attention to addressing basic physical needs of humans is one that is rapidly gathering support in the late 1970s. Whether it is a concept that will become a focus of international

---

[4]"Economic Declaration," Fifth Conference of Heads of State or Government of Non-Aligned Countries, Colombo, Sri Lanka, August 1976, Document NAC/Conf. 5/S.3, p. 13.

[5]Robert S. McNamara, *Address to the Board of Governors*, Manila, October 4, 1976 (Washington, D.C., World Bank, 1976), p. 23.

[6]Jan Tinbergen, *Reshaping the International Order: A Report to the Club of Rome* (New York, E. P. Dutton, 1976), p. 130. Comparable figures in the early 1970s for the approximately 50 countries (with a total population of over 1,300 million) having per capita incomes under $300 were: life expectancy, 48 years; literacy, 33 per cent; infant mortality, 136 per thousand; and birth rate, 40 per thousand.

cooperation for the last quarter of this century, beginning in the late 1970s, depends very much on the leadership taken by key individuals in the developing as well as developed countries and in international institutions to bring about the actual launching and implementation of such an effort. The stakes are huge. If the poorer developing countries today were able to achieve death rates and birth rates comparable to those of Sri Lanka, Taiwan and China—all of which (from very different ideological-political bases) implemented basic-needs strategies in the 1950s and the 1960s—this could mean over 10 million fewer deaths a year and an even larger number of births avoided each year.

The ILO Report that comprises most of this volume makes clear, of course, the need for more effective international trade and aid policies, with the latter targeted more directly toward meeting basic needs. The Report stops short, however, of providing explicit discussion of *how* developed and developing countries alike might develop the political will and determination to initiate and implement the changes that are part of a basic-needs strategy—changes ranging from land-tenure reform in many developing countries to increased aid and improved trade policies in most developed countries. With respect to the developing countries, the Report lets the matter rest with the single comment that "there might be great difficulties, political and other, in implementing policies for redistribution". The few extremely poor countries which have to date addressed the basic needs of their poor majorities with relative success, notably China, Sri Lanka, Taiwan and both North and South Korea, have all accomplished this under very special circumstances which, for a great variety of reasons, are either not reproducible or not acceptable elsewhere. For example, the reforms in the East Asian countries (including, notably, the redistribution of land and other productive assets) that initially led to increased equity with growth were in good part the consequences of twenty years of major civil and international wars which led to millions of deaths. And in Sri Lanka—though not in the other countries mentioned—one cost of the income-redistribution measures that were especially emphasized in that country was a major slowing of growth in national output.

What is becoming increasingly clear (although it is admittedly still difficult to assert in any official international document) is that the leaders of developed and developing countries need to take *parallel* actions—on the reform of *international* systems and on *internal* reform—to create the political environment necessary to bring about any major changes on either front. This explains, in part at least, the references in Robert McNamara's already-mentioned Manila speech and in the Tinbergen Group's report to the need for a "global compact" under which significantly increased aid resources would go to the poorest countries to support greatly increased efforts on their own part to meet the basic needs of their poor majorities.

Several other points about the World Employment Conference and the ILO Report invite comment in this Foreword. At the Conference, the United States was one of the last to support the new basic-needs concept, having stood virtually alone in its broad opposition to the approach through much of the Conference. This may seem odd in light of the existing US congressional mandate to favor bilateral aid programs that will benefit the "poor majority" in the developing countries, but a number of complicating factors led to this US stance at the Conference. Notable among these were the many other differences between the United States and the ILO, the fact that the delegation was led by representatives of the US Labor Department (which has not been involved in the redirection of US aid programs) and the general weakness in recent years of policy co-ordination within the US government on issues related to many aspects of the wide-ranging basic-needs approach to development.

A further point that merits comment is the suspicion of some in the developing countries that a basic-needs strategy is a formula for keeping the poor countries as the world's "hewers of wood and drawers of water". The fact that the United States opposed the strategy during so much of the Conference should at least make it clear that the new concept is not a US government strategy to "keep the developing countries in their place". Properly implemented, as has been demonstrated in such places as Taiwan, a basic-needs strategy can accelerate growth and industrial development. This predictable complaint, however, does increase the importance of making any expanded development assistance program to support basic-needs programs an integral part of a much more *comprehensive* global strategy that enhances and accelerates the industrialization of the developing countries. This more comprehensive approach also calls for, among other components, greater access by developing countries to the markets of the more advanced industrial states and the implementation of measures by the developing countries that strengthen a non-autarkic "collective self-reliance" among themselves in appropriate sectors of economic activity.

Finally, reference needs to be made to the fact that the ILO's excellent articulation of a basic-needs strategy—while focusing most specifically on fulfilling the economic/physical aspects of humanity's basic needs—is clearly, though briefly, placed within the broader framework of attaining human freedom, physical security and the range of factors which contribute to the individual's sense of "identity", achievement and satisfaction. True development to meet basic needs must ultimately encompass progress in all these areas of concern. Under such an appropriately broader definition of "basic needs", *all* countries must still be considered "underdeveloped" today—a reality which most Americans acknowledge far more willingly in the mid-1970s than they would have ten years ago. Much more work is required in the years ahead on a comprehensive strategy which reflects an integrated approach to these various categories of individual basic needs and which takes into account the needs of all countries.

James P. Grant

Washington, D.C.   *President*
January 1977   *Overseas Development Council*

CONTENTS

Part Three   International Strategies

INTRODUCTION

INTRODUCTION

The fight against unemployment and poverty has been the main concern of the ILO throughout its 57 years of existence.

It was the central preoccupation of the founding fathers of the ILO in 1919, who stressed the need to attack conditions of labour involving such " injustice, hardship and privation to large numbers of people as to produce unrest so great that the peace and harmony of the world are imperilled ".

It was at the centre of the ILO's efforts in the years of the Great Depression in the 1930s.

It has been the driving force behind the ILO's attempts to set internationally agreed minimum standards governing conditions of employment.

It was stressed in unequivocal terms in the Declaration of Philadelphia which marked the first 25 years of the ILO's existence by a forceful statement of the aims and objectives of the ILO. The Declaration proclaimed that " poverty anywhere constitutes a danger to prosperity everywhere "; and that " the war against want requires to be carried on with unrelenting vigour ". It entrusted to the ILO responsibility for promoting among the nations of the world programmes to achieve " full employment and the raising of standards of living " and a " just share of the fruits of progress to all ".

This concern found expression in the rapid expansion of ILO activities in the postwar years, and its participation in a broad international effort of technical assistance to raise standards of living through rapid economic growth in the less developed nations.

In those early years of international co-operation for development it was assumed that the widespread poverty and employment problems in developing countries would be rapidly overcome by measures to accelerate economic growth. This was the central thesis of the First Development Decade in the 1960s, when the efforts of the entire United Nations system, and of its member States, were geared to raising productivity and removing the obstacles to

1

growth in developing countries. The ILO's main contribution to that effort was the training of workers and managers in an attempt to overcome the shortage of skills which were—and to some extent still are—among the main bottlenecks impeding growth and development.

However, already in the 1960s the ILO began to question the conventional wisdom that higher levels of employment and improved living standards for all would automatically result from growth, irrespective of the pattern pursued. This first found expression in the Employment Policy Convention and Recommendation (No. 122) adopted by the International Labour Conference in 1964. The Convention requires ratifying States to declare and pursue *as a major goal* an active policy designed to promote full, productive and freely chosen employment. The Recommendation and an Annex thereto containing suggestions concerning methods of application set out the policy measures by which this could be achieved. Already in 1964, therefore, the ILO's membership considered that employment was an objective to be pursued in its own right.

Five years later, in 1969, on the occasion of its fiftieth anniversary, the ILO launched the World Employment Programme, in response to a resolution presented by the Workers at the 51st Session (1967) of the International Labour Conference.[1] This Programme has been at the centre of ILO action for the past six years and has been its main contribution to the International Development Strategy for the Second United Nations Development Decade, which lays some emphasis (although not in terms of specific and explicit objectives) on employment.[2]

Under the mandate entrusted to it by the International Labour Conference and by its Governing Body, the ILO has, in the past six years, attempted to pioneer a new, employment-oriented approach to development. These efforts have been carried on with the active participation and support of many other organisations inside and outside the United Nations system and with the full backing of the United Nations General Assembly, ECOSOC and other policy-making organs of the United Nations system.

One major emphasis of the World Employment Programme has been on fact-finding and analysis—an attempt to throw new light on the complex inter-relationships between employment on the one hand and other aspects of economic and social development on the other. Thus, policy research has been carried out, both at ILO Headquarters and at the country level, on the link

---

[1] Resolution concerning international co-operation for economic and social development, as unanimously adopted by the Conference in its final form.

[2] For an evaluation of the Strategy at mid-point in the Second Development Decade from the point of view of employment and income distribution considerations, see ILO: *Time for transition; a mid-term review of the Second United Nations Development Decade* (Geneva, 1975).

between income distribution and employment, choice of technologies, labour-intensive public works, population policies, the relevance of education and training, international trade and migration, specific rural and urban employment and poverty problems, multinational enterprises and their impact on employment, etc.[1]

The other major emphasis of the World Employment Programme has been on applying these findings by providing advice to governments. For example, comprehensive employment strategy missions have visited seven countries in order to work out employment-oriented development policies.[2]

They have shown how these differ from the tried approaches and what major changes in development priorities are required. All mission reports, but particularly the one on Kenya, have brought out the link between employment, poverty and income distribution, as has much of the work of the World Employment Programme country teams and regional teams—the Regional Employment Programme for Latin America and the Caribbean (PREALC), the Asian Regional Team for Employment Promotion (ARTEP) and the Jobs and Skills Programme for Africa (JASPA).

Today, in spite of the immense efforts that have been made, both at the national and at the international levels, a significant proportion of mankind continues to eke out an existence in the most abject conditions of material deprivation. More than 700 million people live in acute poverty and are destitute. At least 460 million persons were estimated to suffer from a severe degree of protein-energy malnutrition even before the recent food crisis. Scores of millions live constantly under a threat of starvation. Countless millions suffer from debilitating diseases of various sorts and lack access to the most basic medical services. The squalor of urban slums is too well known to need further emphasis. The number of illiterate adults has been estimated to have grown from 700 million in 1960 to 760 million towards 1970. The tragic waste of human resources in the Third World is symbolised by nearly 300 million persons unemployed or underemployed in the mid-1970s.

---

[1] For further details, see ILO: *World Employment Programme—research in retrospect and prospect* (Geneva, 1976) (in preparation).

[2] ILO: *Towards full employment: a programme for Colombia, prepared by an inter-agency team organised by the International Labour Office* (Geneva, 1970); idem: *Matching employment opportunities and expectations: a programme of action for Ceylon,* report and technical papers in two volumes (Geneva, 1971); idem: *Employment, incomes and equality: a strategy for increasing productive employment in Kenya* (Geneva, 1972); idem: *Employment and income policies for Iran* (Geneva, 1973); idem: *Sharing in development: a programme of employment, equity and growth for the Philippines* (Geneva, 1974); idem: *Generación de empleo productivo y crecimiento económico: el caso de la República Dominicana* (Geneva, 1975); idem: *Growth, employment and equity: a comprehensive strategy for Sudan* (Geneva, 1976) (provisional edition).

The situation portrayed—however inadequately—by these figures has persisted, or even in some respects worsened, over the years, despite impressive rates of growth in many developing countries. Sharp inequalities in the distribution of income and wealth within and between countries have only served to highlight the depths of impoverishment of large sections of mankind.

In most developing countries the richest 10 per cent of households typically receive about 40 per cent of personal income, whereas the poorest 40 per cent of households receive 15 per cent or less.

Inequalities exist also at the international level. The postwar period has been marked by growing gaps in income and wealth between a small number of industrialised countries and the bulk of the other countries. In 1972 the industrial market economies, with less than one-fifth of world population, accounted for two-thirds of world output. At the other extreme, a quarter of the world's population lived in countries with average per head incomes of less than US$200 and whose total output was under 3 per cent of global output. If China were included in these figures, nearly half of the world's population received less than 7 per cent of the world's income. Adjustment of these figures to take account of differences in purchasing power would modify the above picture, but industrial market economies would still account for about half of world output.

Contrary to earlier expectations, the experience of the past two decades has shown that rapid growth of aggregate output does not by itself reduce poverty and inequality or provide sufficient productive employment within acceptable periods of time. This does not mean that the traditional approach could not achieve these results in the longer term. But it is no longer acceptable in human terms or responsible in political terms to wait several generations for the benefits of development to trickle down until they finally reach the poorest groups.

This situation prompted the International Labour Conference at its 59th Session (1974) to adopt unanimously a resolution concerning the convocation by the ILO of a tripartite world conference on employment, income distribution and social progress and the international division of labour. In response to that resolution, the decision to hold this Conference was taken by the Governing Body of the ILO at its 194th Session in November 1974.

This Conference provides an opportunity to reappraise the dimensions of the problem, to take stock of the work done so far and to distil from this work some policy conclusions to guide the ILO and its States Members, as well as the international community, in their further efforts to overcome unemployment and poverty.

As already indicated, the ILO is not acting alone in this endeavour. Indeed, in its 1974 resolution, the International Labour Conference had envisaged the

World Employment Conference as being " a specific contribution by the ILO towards assessing the progress of the Second United Nations Development Decade ".[1]

At mid-point of the Decade, it is evident that a much greater determination to achieve the social aims of the International Development Strategy—which called for more equitable distribution of income and wealth, substantial increases in employment, better nutrition and housing, especially for the low income groups of the population—is urgently required.

The economic paragraphs of the International Development Strategy have now been supplemented by the Conclusions of the Sixth and Seventh Special Sessions of the United Nations General Assembly, and particularly by the resolution concerning development and international economic co-operation, adopted unanimously by the Seventh Special Session in September 1975.[2]

This text reflects an emerging consensus on the future of economic relations between States and on new types of economic co-operation for development. Most of these matters (for instance, commodity trade, transfer of rural resources, international monetary reform) are further developed in other international bodies.

While the resolution adopted by the Seventh Special Session confirms the General Assembly's determination " to implement the targets and policy measures contained in the International Development Strategy ", it makes little explicit reference to the latter. Furthermore, being concerned mainly with international economic relations and co-operation, it does not deal with national policies for development. But the Strategy is to be reviewed at this year's session of the General Assembly. *A first important objective for the World Employment Conference could, therefore, be to reach a consensus on an approach, more effective than that of the present International Development Strategy, for achieving social objectives of development. This new approach would concern both national and international policies. It would be designed to ensure that the emerging patterns of economic relations effectively contribute to greater social progress for the scores of millions of people who continue to live in conditions of deepest poverty, squalor and deprivation.*

Other parts of the Seventh Special Session resolution also have a bearing on ILO concerns, for instance, certain parts of the chapter on industrialisation[3], which calls for labour-market policies and structural adjustments in developed

---

[1] It will be recalled that the United Nations General Assembly adopted in October 1970 an International Development Strategy for that decade. See Resolution 2626 (XXV).

[2] Resolution 3362 (S-VII).

[3] This chapter of the resolution concludes: " In view of the importance of the forthcoming World Employment Conference, governments should undertake adequate preparations and consultations ".

countries so as to lead to a higher degree of utilisation of material and human resources in developing countries.

Another important objective of the present Conference, therefore, could also be to reach a consensus on ways in which active manpower policies and adjustment assistance are best implemented in mutually satisfactory ways and in the light of the goals for industrialisation and for increasing the agricultural exports of developing countries.

The agenda of the Conference as determined by the Governing Body at its 196th (May 1975) Session, consists of the following items:

1. National employment strategies and policies with particular reference to developing countries.

2. International manpower movements and employment.

3. Technologies for productive employment creation in developing countries.

4. The role of multinational enterprises in employment creation in the developing countries.

5. Active manpower policies and adjustment assistance in developed countries.

These items are all inter-related. To look at any one of them in isolation from the others would be to lose sight of the interactions between various national and international measures. They have therefore all been covered in this one report, which is the basic document for the Conference's discussions.

The main proposal in this report is for adoption by each country of a basic-needs approach, aiming at the achievement of a certain specific minimum standard of living before the end of the century. The main instruments for attaining this goal would be increasing the volume and productivity of employment and taking the national and international measures of economic and social policy needed to bring this about.

The basic employment policy would be extended in two ways: first, by directing and supplementing it so that the ultimate result would be adequate levels of consumption of certain essential goods and services; and secondly, by taking steps to achieve this ultimate result by the year 2000.

In view of the tremendous adjustments and changes needed in existing policies and trends, this target date is very near, at least as far as developing countries are concerned. Great efforts would have to be made in most of these countries as from now, and be maintained throughout the coming 25 years, if the objective suggested here is to be achieved.

For purposes of this discussion, basic needs are defined as the minimum standard of living which a society should set for the poorest groups of its people. The satisfaction of basic needs means meeting the minimum requirements of a family for personal consumption: food, shelter, clothing; it implies access to essential services, such as safe drinking-water, sanitation, transport, health and education; it implies that each person available for and willing to work should have an adequately remunerated job. It should further imply the satisfaction of needs of a more qualitative nature: a healthy, humane and satisfying environment, and popular participation in the making of decisions that affect the lives and livelihood of the people and individual freedoms.

The satisfaction of an absolute level of basic needs as so defined should be placed within a broader framework, namely the fulfilment of basic human rights, which are not only ends in themselves but also contribute to the attainment of other goals.

The concept of basic needs is of universal applicability. The objectives to be set will naturally vary according to levels of development, climatic conditions, social and cultural values. Basic needs are therefore in large part a relative concept; but there are also certain minimum levels of personal consumption and access to social services which should be universally regarded as essential to a decent life, and which should therefore be looked upon as minimum targets for raising the living standards of the very poor for the entire international community.

The basic-needs approach suggested here implies some broadening of the scope of the World Employment Programme. That Programme has focused on the creation of more productive and remunerative jobs. This is an essential means of achieving the objectives of a basic-needs approach.

But creating more and better jobs on a scale large enough to make an impact on mass poverty requires difficult political and economic decisions. This was already recognised in 1969, when the Director-General's Report introducing the World Employment Programme stressed the need for, for instance, agrarian reform (possibly including land redistribution) and various shifts in investment: from physical to human capital, from urban to rural development, from capital-intensive to labour-intensive activities, and from the production of non-essential consumer goods to essential ones.[1]

Subsequent experience and research have confirmed how essential it is for employment policies in developing countries that some redirection or redistribution of investment over time, and a redistribution of the ownership or the utilisation of land, be brought about. Experience has also shown how great the

---

[1] ILO: *The World Employment Programme* (Geneva, 1969), pp. 68 and 81 ff.

political obstacles to such shifts usually are and how difficult it often is to secure a firm and lasting government commitment to these measures of an anti-poverty policy. These findings have been one of the reasons for increasing interest in the organisation of poverty groups, which led the International Labour Conference to adopt last year a Convention and Recommendation concerning the organisation of rural workers in trade unions and similar organisations.[1]

The need for redirection of investment and for other measures to increase opportunities for the working poor to raise their productivity and incomes—including some redistribution of productive resources and of income—obviously increases with the scale or the speed of the intended results of the anti-poverty policy. The more ambitious the employment target, and the sooner it is to be attained, the more drastic the measures that will be needed. The need for redistributive measures and for redirection of investment increases further if the targets are not only for higher employment and the output of marketable goods which it must entail but also extend to other basic needs such as public health and general education of adequate quality.

Thus, a combination of these measures together with more equitable access to public services is needed if underemployment, inequality and poverty are to be significantly reduced. Such measures need not imply a slower growth of output. They place greater emphasis on patterns of growth leading to a more equitable distribution of the gains from growth, and they may well lead to increasing growth rates as well.

In such approaches, employment policy must necessarily play a central role. Employment productive enough and well enough remunerated to allow individuals to meet their basic personal consumption needs is a fundamental requirement. Without it there is no feasible way to achieve adequate expansion of the output of such goods and services. Even if there were, in the absence of full productive employment the poorest people of the developing countries would not be able to meet their needs because of lack of purchasing power, and would continue to lack an opportunity of participating in development.

In many ways the environment for development over the next 25 years is likely to be more difficult than in the past three decades. The marked slow-down in world economic growth and trade in 1974-76 has been a severe setback. Even if there is a rapid recovery, it seems unlikely that the industrialised market countries will be able to attain and sustain growth rates in the 1970s and 1980s comparable to those of the 1950s and 1960s. Between the early 1970s and the year 2000 the labour force and the population of developing

---

[1] Convention (No. 141) and Recommendation (No. 149) concerning organisations of rural workers and their role in economic and social development.

countries, excluding China, will approximately double. Productive employment opportunities must be found not only for the approximately 300 million people at present unemployed or inadequately employed, but for a total of 1,000 million if those who will be entering the employment markets of the Third World over the next 25 years are included. The pressure on natural resources, including land, and on the environment will further intensify and may constitute additional obstacles to economic growth.

It therefore seems clear that major efforts will be required and major changes will need to be made in national development strategies and in the international economy if the world employment situation is to be improved within a generation and a substantial amelioration brought about in the standards of living of the working masses.

This report is concerned with both national and international aspects of a basic-needs strategy. International measures are essential to support the efforts of developing countries; but they are no substitute for a full commitment by those countries to the implementation of appropriate policies and reforms to satisfy the basic needs of their poorest citizens.

The report is also concerned with the situation in industrialised countries. The industrialised market-economy countries are currently suffering from high levels of unemployment, and even the most affluent of them have pockets of relative poverty and deprivation. The rapid attainment of full employment in these countries is essential not only to alleviate the hardships of the unemployed and their dependants, now totalling nearly 45 million, but also to restore a world economic environment conducive to international reforms and to the satisfaction of basic needs in the developing countries. Nor, given the interdependence of the world, are the socialist countries wholly unaffected by developments elsewhere. A consideration of the strategies pursued in the socialist countries of Eastern Europe to attain and maintain full employment should also help in discussing what contribution they could make to an attack on poverty in developing countries. The World Employment Conference provides an opportunity to examine the inter-relationships between employment and manpower problems in the industrialised market-economy countries and development strategies and problems in the socialist countries, on the one hand, and the basic-needs-oriented strategy for developing countries, on the other.

This report is divided into three parts. Part One (Chapter 1) provides some background information on employment, income distribution and poverty in the world. It then (in Chapter 2) proceeds to outline the rationale, targets and broad approach of the proposed basic-needs strategy.

Part Two reviews the national strategies of developing countries (Chapter 3), European socialist countries (Chapter 4) and industrialised market-economy countries (Chapter 5).

Part Three of the report deals with international strategies. After a short discussion of the international setting (Chapter 6), it deals with adjustment-assistance policies and measures (Chapter 7), international migration and the brain drain (Chapter 8), the international aspects of technology (Chapter 9) and multinational enterprises (Chapter 10). These are all means through which the international division of labour is being constantly affected.

The term " international division of labour " which appears in the title of this Conference may require a few words of explanation. It refers to the geographical location of economic activities in the world, in other words to " what is being produced where ". Some people associate the term with a static redistributive device which implies a shift of existing factories from one country to another. The expression " international division of labour " is used here in a much more dynamic sense. The report examines the policies which would encourage a progressive shift in the pattern of production between regions and countries over time, so that all will benefit from changing comparative advantages and specialisation. The report looks at this issue in the light of the contribution which a new approach to the international division of labour could make to a strategy aiming at increasing employment and reducing mass poverty, and its possible policy implications for adjustment assistance, international migration, technology and multinational enterprises. The related issues of aid, international monetary reform and trade and commercial policies are being considered in more detail in other international forums.

This report therefore covers a very broad canvas, as indeed is demanded by the breadth and scope of the subject matter before the Conference. Its aim is to help the Conference reach a world-wide, tripartite consensus on the directions and emphases of a new approach to achieve the goals assigned to the ILO in its Constitutional texts.

The report represents a relatively brief distillation of the main conclusions which emerge from six years of intensive work by the ILO and several other agencies. It represents a first, but bold, attempt to come to grips with the formidable problems of unemployment, underemployment, inequitable income distribution and mass poverty in the world. Clearly, it cannot claim to present final solutions, nor can the Conference be envisaged as a one-time operation, either for the ILO or for the countries in the world community which take up this challenge.

The Report does, however, endeavour to formulate new policy insights to deal with the related issues of employment, growth and social progress. It is my sincere expectation that it will be instrumental in furthering international dialogue and solidarity on these complex and controversial issues. It is accordingly with humility but with a sense of hope that I now submit it for the appraisal of the Conference.

Francis Blanchard
Director-General
International Labour Office
Geneva   *Secretary-General*
March 1976   *1976 World Employment Conference*

PART ONE

SIZE AND CHARACTERISTICS
OF WORLD EMPLOYMENT AND
INCOME DISTRIBUTION PROBLEMS

EMPLOYMENT, POVERTY AND INCOME DISTRIBUTION

1

During the three decades since the Second World War, most governments have relied primarily on over-all economic growth backed by high investment to reduce poverty and inequality, and in the industrialised countries to avoid serious cyclical unemployment. This policy has led to rapid and sustained growth in national output and investment in both developed and developing countries. However, it has become increasingly evident, particularly from the experience of the developing countries, that rapid growth at the national level does not automatically reduce poverty and inequality or provide sufficient productive employment.

There are employment problems in all economic systems, but their precise manifestation varies from non-socialist to socialist and from more to less developed countries. Different forms of institutional organisation and different ways of reacting to economic events make it difficult to show the precise importance of these problems in various areas. In almost all countries, however, insufficient and unequal access to employment rank high among the major causes of poverty and inequality. This is especially true if the term employment is interpreted, as it is here, in the widest sense to include adequately remunerated self-employment, which may demand access to land or capital, as well as wage employment.

Even in industrialised countries it is an over-simplification to think of people as being either employed or not. Some people will seek work only when suitable jobs are conveniently available. Some systems will sack workers when there is an economic downturn, others may keep them unproductively on the payroll. Blue-collar workers may be laid off more quickly than white-collar workers. Where the family is still the production unit (as in a large part of the agricultural sector of most developing countries), even such concepts as the labour force cease to be very meaningful, since family members work when they are needed. Definitions of who is employed, of what is an economic activity (these generally exclude household work by women), and even more of who is unemployed are necessarily arbitrary and often not comparable. Countries collect such statistics by different methods, and this introduces a bias that is often unknown.

EMPLOYMENT IN DEVELOPING COUNTRIES

During the 1960s national income per head grew exceptionally fast by historical standards in most developing countries. The growth rates exceeded those obtained during the development phase of the countries that are now industrialised. However, the recent growth in the developing countries has often tended to be concentrated in relatively limited parts of the economy, mostly those using capital-intensive techniques and having few linkages with the traditional rural sector or the informal urban sector, which between them account for by far the greater part of the total employment in most developing countries. As a result, the benefits of growth, and in particular opportunities for productive employment, have mainly gone to a very small part of the total population.

Several factors have contributed to this uneven pattern of development, in addition to the basic inadequacy of the development model itself. The structure of production and the distribution of wealth have often originated under colonial or other alien régimes. The pursuit or application of foreign patterns has often led to inappropriate systems in such fields as education and health. Government policies have frequently been ill adapted to the circumstances of an independent nation in which the reduction of poverty ought to be the major objective of economic policy.

Even since independence, however, inappropriate institutions and policies have continued to lead to a poor allocation of investment resources, the selection of economically inefficient methods of production in relation to factor endowments, the underutilisation not only of labour but also of capital and land, and an increasing concentration of income and wealth. Very high and sustained rates of population growth have compounded these problems. These interlocking factors have combined to keep vast numbers of people in abject poverty, deprived of any share of the benefits of the increase in total output.

By the end of the 1960s it was clear that in most developing countries following conventional patterns, growth was not leading to a reduction of poverty. On the contrary, the numbers of the very poor were rising, the degree of inequality was only rarely improving and the employment problem remained largely unresolved.

The employment problem in developing countries is one on which the ILO can speak with some authority, because of its experience gained through its research and field work. But that experience shows that attempting to aggregate the problem and produce comparable statistics for different countries can be done only at the cost of great over-simplification.

Open unemployment in developing countries can be measured fairly accurately. It frequently reflects, to a greater extent than in the industrialised countries, more the problem of young dependants seeking employment than that of experienced workers losing their jobs. Despite very high rates of open unemployment for some areas and some age-groups, and much higher rates in urban than in rural areas, it is not generally a large fraction of the total labour force. Nor do the statistics of open unemployment give any real guide to the over-all poverty situation. The unemployed, although including some people, such as landless rural workers, who are certainly in desperate straits, also include—as ILO research in several countries has shown—a large number of people who are not heads of households and who therefore have some other means of support. The unemployed in many developing countries are disproportionately concentrated among the youth, first-time jobseekers, women and the relatively better educated.

Other dimensions of the employment problem in the developing countries are of much greater importance. Seasonal unemployment is often extreme. Visible underemployment (working short hours and wanting more work) is widespread, but except for certain groups it is not usually severe. The most widespread and critical phenomenon is simply that work of various kinds (especially self-employment) yields an income inadequate for the working poor to meet their basic needs. In countries without unemployment compensation, those in the most desperate need (particularly heads of households with dependants) can spend little time looking for the kind of work they prefer. They must find something even if it yields only a pittance. Thus heads of households are more likely to be bound among the inadequately employed or underemployed, for example in precarious low-productivity self-employment, than among the unemployed.

The crux of the employment problem in the developing world thus lies in the high proportion of the labour force earning inadequate incomes. These persons are classified as underemployed in table 1. As will be seen, the proportion of the labour force classified as underemployed is approximately the same as the proportion of the population classified as " destitute " (see table 2 below). Thus, problems of employment and poverty are inseparable.

The labour force of the developing market economy countries is now around 700 million. Table 1 indicates that about 5 per cent of this labour force is openly unemployed. It also suggests that about 36 per cent is underemployed, the proportion being less in urban and more in rural areas. Of the total of unemployed and underemployed, about 80 per cent are rural. Thus the employment problem, like the poverty problem, is largely a rural phenomenon.

Table 1. Preliminary estimates of unemployment and underemployment in developing countries, by region, 1975 (in millions)

Region	Unemployment [1]				Underemployment [2]				Total			
	Total		Urban		Total		Urban		Total		Urban	
	Nos.	%	Nos.	%	Nos.	%	Nos.	%	Nos.	%	Nos.	%
Asia [3]	18	3.9	6	6.9	168	36.4	20	23.2	186	40.3	26	30.1
Africa	10	7.1	3	10.8	53	37.9	7	25.1	63	45.0	10	35.9
Latin America	5	5.1	5	6.5	28	28.9	14	22.8	33	34.0	19	29.3
Oceania	—	—	—	—	1	49.0	—	—	1	49.0	—	—
Total	33	4.7	14	8.0	250	35.7	41	23.3	283	40.4	55	31.3

[1] Defined as " persons without a job and looking for work ". [2] Defined as " persons who are in employment of less than normal duration and who are seeking or would accept additional work " and " persons with a job yielding inadequate income ". [3] Excluding China and other Asian centrally planned economies.
Source: ILO Bureau of Statistics.

It is necessary to comment on the quality of the available data. The data in table 1 on open unemployment are relatively unequivocal. The main problem in measuring open unemployment concerns the borderline between those in and out of the labour force, and the conditions under which those not normally in it would want work. The reference period over which unemployment is measured can also have a significant effect.

However, the estimates of underemployment are much more open to question. Underemployment can in the first place be measured as those working part-time (generally under 40 hours per week) who want additional work. More important is the underemployment of those working over 40 hours a week but at low levels of productivity, as indicated by their income levels. Incomes may not always be a good guide to productivity, but they are the best general indicator available. The data in table 1 on underemployment essentially reflect national concepts of inadequate incomes and productivity. They were taken from a variety of national sources, and the same ratios were assumed to apply in otherwise comparable countries for which no data were available. The data must be interpreted with the very basic qualification that what counts as " inadequate " in one country (and hence as underemployment) may count as " adequate " and hence as full employment in another.

As will be seen below, it is estimated that the poor people of the developing market economies amount to about 1,200 million, of whom about 700 million are destitute or in acute poverty. Given that many of the unemployed have no dependants and that nearly two dependants per labour force member may be usual, it is clear that the total of 283 million in table 1 is consistent with estimates of acute poverty but understates the magnitude of the total poverty problem.

The growth of the labour force in the developing market economies has accelerated in recent years. From an annual rate of 0.6 per cent in 1900-30, it rose to 2.0 per cent a year in 1960-70. It is likely that these rapid rates of growth will accelerate still further, and that the acceleration will continue for some time after the over-all rate of population growth has finally begun to slow down. The United Nations medium population variant (which assumes quite substantial reductions in fertility) suggests that between 1975 and the year 2000 the labour force of all the developing countries (including China) will rise by some 75 per cent. Excluding the socialist countries, the labour force would grow by 2.7 per cent a year over the 25-year period. By the year 2000 the total labour force of the countries shown in table 1 would have reached nearly 1,400 million, with a further 600 million in the socialist developing countries.

The rate of growth of the total labour force depends on the growth of the total population, its age and sex distribution, and the participation rates of the various groups in the labour force. The sectoral distribution of this labour force between agriculture and the rest of the economy depends mainly on the rate at which employment opportunities in the non-agricultural sectors can be increased. In the developed countries the agricultural labour force has long been decreasing not only as a proportion of the total labour force but also in absolute terms, whereas in the developing countries it continues to increase in absolute terms. FAO projections, made on the basis of the United Nations medium population variant and a continuation of recent trends in the growth of non-agricultural employment, suggest that this state of affairs is likely to continue in the developing countries as a whole until the beginning of the second decade of the next century. This broad conclusion is likely to remain true even if non-agricultural employment were to expand much more rapidly, as it should and could if the policies recommended in this report were adopted. Thus agriculture, in addition to absorbing a substantial backlog of under-employment, will have to continue to provide employment for new entrants to the labour force for a long time to come if rural-urban migration is to be slowed to a rate commensurate with the creation of non-agricultural jobs.

That the incomes of so many of the working poor are inadequate does not mean that, like the unemployed, their labour is totally unused. Some of them are no doubt very fully occupied. However, they are available for more productive and better paid work when it becomes available. Which strategies might be followed to make full use of these labour resources and to allow the working poor to meet their basic needs is the theme of later chapters. However, a few points may be made here.

There are still many areas where factual knowledge is far from complete. More information is needed on the relation of unemployment and under-employment to poverty. What are the employment characteristics of the poor? Are they available for rural works programmes, would they migrate to seek work or do they find security in their home villages? How many of the poor are sick or old? Without such knowledge it is impossible to tell what kind of government programmes are needed to reduce poverty.

Regular household surveys, promptly published, are required to monitor the open unemployment situation. Are school leavers finding jobs more quickly than in the past? Has the unemployment situation reacted perversely to faster rates of growth? Such surveys can identify more clearly who are the unem-ployed. Are they from low-income households, are they the school leavers who passed their examinations or those who failed? The Conference might wish to consider whether the ILO should not promote the collection of such statistical information on a regular and systematic basis.

It has already been stressed that, from nearly every point of view, inadequate employment in the traditional rural and informal urban sectors is usually more critical than open unemployment in the developing countries. Creating the conditions where the former disappears will make it very much easier to deal with the latter. Measures aimed solely at reducing open unemployment, on the other hand, will worsen the basic problems of under-employment and poverty. Either additional waves of seekers of jobs in the modern sectors will appear, or even more resources will be used for the interests of the few and thereby perpetuate the poverty of the many.

POVERTY AND INEQUALITY IN DEVELOPING COUNTRIES

Poverty in the world today must be mainly understood in an absolute sense. Very large numbers of people throughout the developing world are absolutely poor, subsisting at a level shared by few people in the industrialised countries. They fall very far short of the target level of basic needs presented in the next chapter. But poverty is also socially defined and relative. Our notion of what it is to be poor, or of the minimum income required to lead a decent and respectable life, depends partly on the level of consumption of those around us.

It is very difficult to determine just how many people in the developing countries are poor. The World Bank estimates that about 650 million persons have incomes per head of less than US$50. Such a figure is incomprehensible to most people, and taken at its face value it is meaningless. The reality behind the figure, however, can perhaps be grasped when one recalls the FAO estimates presented to the World Food Conference indicating that at least 460 million people (about 430 million in the developing market economies and about half of them young children) suffered from a severe degree of protein-energy malnutrition in 1969-71.[1]

It seems certain that the true number of the poor is very much greater. Table 2 represents an attempt to assess these numbers in relation to certain criteria. It suggests that in 1972 some 1,200 million people in the developing market economies (67 per cent of their population) were " seriously poor ", and 700 million (39 per cent) were " destitute " and suffering from severe malnutrition. By each of these standards, the proportion of the poor in the total population is greatest in Asia (although Africa comes a close second), and some 70 per cent of the total are in Asia.

Before going any further it is necessary to explain some of the problems of making such calculations and of the methodology used in constructing the table.[2] In addition to the need to determine somewhat arbitrary " standards ", estimates of poverty in principle require information on the relative purchasing power of different currencies, since foreign exchange rates give a very distorted picture; on the distribution of income before tax; and on the extent to which taxation and the provision of public services improve the real distribution of income.

The two " standards " or " poverty lines " in the table are based respectively on the average earnings of unskilled labour in large-scale manufacturing enterprises in India (the " seriously poor ") and on the equivalent of 1 rupee per person per day in Indian terms (the " destitute ").[3] These, together with the income data, were then converted to " purchasing power parity ".

This was done on the assumption that a typical basket of goods consumed by the poor costing US$1 in Western Europe could be obtained for 20 cents in Asia, 23 cents in Africa and 36 cents in Latin America.[4] Thus the use of these coefficients enables one to avoid the distortions associated with conversions

---

[1] These numbers have undoubtedly increased as a result of the difficult world food situation that has developed since 1972. It is estimated that, even if the projected increase in the effective demand for food (assuming no measures of income redistribution) can be met, they will increase to 750 million by 1985. Moreover, the standard of a " severe degree " of protein-energy malnutrition is a very low one, and many more people suffer from some degree of hunger and malnutrition.

[2] The details are presented in ILO: *Poverty, unemployment and underemployment* (document for limited distribution).

[3] A conceivable universal standard might be a " Western European standard " (equivalent to the basic unemployment benefit for a single person with no dependants in France and the United Kingdom). By this standard, some 1,500 million people (84 per cent of the population of developing countries) were poor in 1972.

[4] These conversion ratios are based on estimates made by the Fundación Bariloche, Argentina. See M. Hopkins and Hugo Scolnik: *Basic needs, growth and redistribution: a quantitative approach* (Geneva, ILO, 1975; document for limited distribution). The Conference might wish to consider whether the ILO should be encouraged to collect statistical data on which more refined estimates of this type could be based.

Table 2. Estimated numbers of people in developing market economies living in poverty, 1972

Region	Total population	Seriously poor	Destitute	Seriously poor	Destitute
		(millions of people)		(percentage of population)	
Asia	1 196	853	499	71	42
Africa	345	239	134	69	39
Latin America	274	118	73	43	27
Total [1]	1 815	1 210	706	67	39

[1] Excluding developing countries in Europe and Oceania, with a total population of about 25 million.

based on exchange rates and to reflect more accurately the fact that many of the items consumed by the poor do not enter into international commerce.

On this basis, the poverty line of the " seriously poor " is equivalent to an income per head of US$500 in Western Europe, US$180 in Latin America, US$115 in Africa and US$100 in Asia. Similarly, the " destitute " comprise those with an income equivalent to US$250 in Western Europe, US$90 in Latin America, US$59 in Africa and US$50 in Asia. The last number thus coincides with the standard of the World Bank mentioned earlier. The effect of these adjustments is to reduce the income disparities between rich and poor countries to more realistic levels. The use of these coefficients suggests that the average inhabitant of a developed market economy country is not 13 times as rich as the average inhabitant of a developing country, but some four times as well off.

Within developing countries the degree of inequality is often high, and consumption patterns of the rich may make it appear even higher than it really is. Statistically, incomes are more unequally distributed in most developing countries than in most industrialised market economies, while government social programmes also usually have a wider and more effective coverage in the latter. In most developing countries the richest 10 per cent of households typically receive about 40 per cent of personal income whereas the poorest 40 per cent receive 15 per cent or less, and the poorest 20 per cent receive about 5 per cent. Reliable data on income distribution are, however, available for relatively few individual developing countries.[1] The table does not take account of the effect on the real distribution of income of the availability of cheap or free social services.

---

[1] The data on income distribution used in preparing table 2 were taken from Hollis Chenery et al.: Redistribution with growth (London, Oxford University Press, 1974).

Table 3.   Increase in poverty, 1963-72
            (millions of persons)

Region	Total population	Seriously poor	Destitute
Asia	195	92	34
Africa	68	26	5
Latin America	62	1	4
Total	325	119	43

Thus the estimates in table 2 are to some extent arbitrary, and are based on data that are far from sufficient. However, the numbers that result are so large that, even if they are considerably overestimated, it is clear that the problem of poverty is of appalling magnitude.

What is more, there is no doubt that the numbers of the poor have increased, in spite of the rapid economic growth in most developing countries. The calculations shown in table 2 were made for 1963 as well as 1972, using the same income distribution. These indicate that, whereas the proportion of the population in each category declined slightly in each region, this was offset by demographic expansion, so that they increased in absolute numbers. While the increase in the number of " destitute " was small in Africa and Latin America, it nevertheless rose by some 40 million over-all. The figures for the three main regions are presented in table 3. If one examines the 32 individual countries for which data are available, it will be found that the number of " destitute " people increased in 17 countries in 1963-72 and the number of persons suffering from " serious poverty " increased in 14. Among other indicators of deprivation, UNESCO estimates that the number of illiterate adults rose from 700 million in 1960 to 760 million in 1970.

Whether in addition income distribution has in fact worsened in most developing countries is difficult to determine. There are very few studies of changes in income distribution in individual developing countries over time. The limited available studies indicate that income distribution has become more equal in recent years in some developing countries but has worsened in a number of others. No general relationship with such factors as the rate of economic growth is discernible.

There is also considerable evidence, although often fragmentary or circum-stantial, that the material conditions of life for large numbers of people are worse today than they were one or two decades ago. In a very few countries average levels of living have fallen.

INEQUALITY AND GROWTH

It is sometimes claimed that redistribution in favour of the poor will automatically reduce savings, weaken incentives and impair the rate of growth. However, despite the existence, on the one hand, of some fast-growing countries with an undoubted worsening of income distribution and, on the other, of some slow-growing countries with an equitable income distribution, there is no real evidence of a general conflict between growth and equity. A statistical exercise drawing on data from 66 countries suggests in fact a slight tendency for the share of income accruing to the poorest 40 per cent to be higher in countries which had grown more quickly.[1] There is of course no presumption that there is a causal connection either way. In the long run the rate of growth probably is independent of the distribution of income, while in the short run the effect of redistribution on growth will naturally depend to a considerable extent on how the redistribution is carried out. It is much more a question of the specific policies followed than of any inherent relationship between equity and growth.

It is often claimed that a more equal distribution of income would result in lower savings. There is, however, no empirical support for this contention. Moreover, even if redistribution did affect savings, its effects are likely to be confined to household savings, which in most countries are a small proportion of the total. There is the further consideration that too small a fraction of the savings of the rich are channelled into investments designed to produce goods and services for the poor. One important reason for this is that, as a consequence of the unequal distribution of income, the poor have little purchasing power and hence there is little incentive to produce for them. Finally, the savings potential of the poor has probably been underestimated, and such saving and investments as they do undertake have the virtue of being directed toward the production of commodities which satisfy their basic needs.

But even to talk of conflicts between growth and income equality implies that US$1 accruing to the poor is worth no more than US$1 accruing to the rich. Conventional national income accounting looks only at the total value of output, and not at the current living levels of the income recipients. A better measure of social and economic performance might be an index of welfare which gave a higher weight to increases in the income of the poor. Countries with a slow growth of output but with an improving distribution of income would then be evaluated more favourably than by the traditional system of

---

[1] Chenery *et al.*, op. cit., p. 29.

statistical measurement. Conversely, fast-growing countries in which the poor had a declining share of total incomes would be evaluated less favourably.

Countries could usefully experiment with the construction of a welfare index of this kind to evaluate the effects of their development programmes. Such programmes as road construction and the expansion of education and health services could all be evaluated according to the income group of the beneficiaries. It should be reiterated, however, that redistribution together with growth is the aim.

INDUSTRIAL MARKET ECONOMIES

Until recently the industrial market economies enjoyed unprecedented rates of growth combined with generally high levels of employment and, in some countries, diminished inequality. At the moment, however, unemployment rates in most of the advanced market economies are the highest they have been in four decades.

Poverty has by no means been totally eliminated in these countries, and in some of them significant numbers of people remain relatively poor, at least in comparison with their own country's average levels of income and consumption. The aged, the sick, the displaced, households headed by a woman, minority groups, residents of declining or stagnant regions and employees in certain service sectors are the majority of the poor in these countries. Transfer payments, regional policies and programmes to guarantee rights or provide assistance to minorities have met at least part of the needs of these categories. Some, however, have not been eligible for help despite their poverty.

In developed market economies unemployment data give a fairly meaningful indication of the underutilisation of labour. Nevertheless, there are problems in their interpretation. Different policies and systems of industrial relations in different countries naturally affect employers' willingness to discharge or lay off rather than hoard labour. Many countries construct their unemployment returns from employment office data and not from household surveys. Countries such as the United States, which use household survey data, invariably record higher unemployment rates, as a result of the more thorough coverage of part-time and secondary workers, etc. Thus international comparisons based on the data in table 4 should be made with great caution.

Between 1965 and 1973 most developed market economies maintained relatively stable unemployment levels, with peaks of 5-6 per cent in North America and somewhat lower elsewhere. However, there was a fairly general although very slight upward movement from 1965 to 1973. In certain countries migrant workers were steadily increasing as a proportion of the labour force. Other countries, such as Ireland, Italy and Finland, were net labour exporters.

Table 4. Estimates of unemployment, September 1975

Major regions	Numbers of unemployed persons (millions)	Unemployment as percentage of total labour force
Asia and Oceania [1]	1.3	2.0
Northern Europe [2]	2.1	5.7
Western Europe [3]	2.9	4.4
Southern Europe [4]	2.7	4.0
North America [5]	8.1	8.1
Total	17.1	5.2

[1] Australia, Japan, New Zealand. [2] Denmark, Finland, Ireland, Norway, Sweden, United Kingdom. [3] Austria, Belgium, France, Federal Republic of Germany, Netherlands, Switzerland. [4] Greece, Italy, Portugal, Spain, Turkey and Yugoslavia. [5] Canada, United States.
Source: ILO Bureau of Statistics.

The years 1974 and 1975 were crisis years for the industrial market economies. Unemployment rose sharply. In North America unemployment rates were above 8 per cent. Most European countries, Australia and Japan managed to keep unemployment rates below 5 per cent, although Ireland and more recently the United Kingdom, for example, were badly hit. In most countries unemployment rates reached a peak in late 1975, and in some of them these rates were declining by the end of that year. However, the slow recovery of demand and output suggests that, at least throughout 1976, unemployment will remain significantly above the levels of the 1960s and early 1970s.

Part of the unemployment burden has inevitably been passed to the migrant groups, and growing restrictions on their admission has restricted the job opportunities of many workers. However, unemployment is concentrated disproportionately in certain regions and occupational groups, and thus selective measures of manpower policy directed towards solving specific structural problems have an important role to play in solving the employment problem.

Two important issues raised by recent experience are the role of stimulating demand in averting unemployment and the alleged "trade-off" between unemployment and inflation. The absence of the 8-10 year trade cycle after the Second World War was a major factor in the improved economic performance of the developed market countries from 1948 to 1973. There were some cyclical fluctuations, particularly in North America, but the cycle was shorter and less marked and, moreover, until the 1970s the timing was different in different countries. But 1970 and 1971 were years of slow growth in nearly all the major developed countries. These were years of low capital investment. Low rates of interest and abundant national and international liquidity subsequently gave a sharp stimulus to investment and led to a simultaneous but short-lived boom in world demand from mid-1972 to mid-1973. During this period the real output of the main developed countries grew at an annual rate of 7.5 per cent. The increase in demand, coupled with bad harvests on a world scale and other supply limitations that were partly the result of the low level of investment in 1970 and 1971, led to the steepest rise in commodity prices since 1950. This was exacerbated by the increase in oil prices at the end of 1973.

Government-induced changes in the level of aggregate demand have played an important role in this recent record. Supply limitations affected agricultural products and petroleum, but aggregate demand has been a much more critical source of generalised inflationary pressures. It has been suggested that governments over-reacted to slow growth and rising unemployment in 1970 and 1971 by increasing the money supply too much, generating the alarming inflation that began in 1972. Over-reaction to this combined with the deflationary effects of the oil crisis to plunge the world into its present recession.

The relationship between inflation and unemployment is a complex one. Until a few years ago it was widely believed that a modest increase in the level of unemployment would lead to a reasonable degree of price stability. Recent experience has cast serious doubts on this view. High rates of unemployment have failed to bring inflation down to acceptable levels. Undoubtedly the creation of massive unemployment could dampen inflationary pressures, but such policies are hardly acceptable politically. This gives increased urgency to the search for policies which can ensure a return to reasonable price stability with high levels of employment.

In the longer-term perspective for the developed market economies (and this applies also to the European socialist countries) there are questions of whether and how changing attitudes to work and leisure can be made to complement and harmonise with the need to increase the proportion of the world's industrial output produced in developing countries. This does not mean that large numbers of jobs should be transferred from one set of countries to the other. It would mainly mean that, with the passage of time, a larger share of the growing world demand (including that from developed countries) for products that intensively use labour should be met by developing countries. Exports from industrialised to developing economies of products that intensively use capital and skill would also rise. Thus new employment opportunities would be created in both rich and poor countries.

A related issue is that the developed market economies seem to have reached, or to be quickly approaching, a " post-industrial " stage of development, with the services sector making an increasing contribution to national output and employment. This interacts with the reluctance of a more highly educated labour force to accept unskilled, dirty or routine jobs. It raises problems of striking the best balance between private services, public services and leisure, and of reconciling a growing demand for public services with a growing unwillingness to pay the taxes necessary for their non-inflationary financing.

EUROPEAN SOCIALIST COUNTRIES

The employment problems of the socialist countries are different from those of the industrialised market economies. The social and economic system is so organised that unemployment as such, except in Yugoslavia, hardly exists any longer.

As a group the socialist countries have enjoyed sustained rapid growth of productivity and income per head for about two decades. The consequence has been growing labour scarcity and an increasing recognition of the need to reduce the high rates of labour turnover and increase efficiency at the enterprise level. There have also been significant differences in productivity between the agricultural and industrial sectors. The need to increase the availability of a wide range of consumer goods as well as to make additional labour available to the expanding industrial and services sectors both point to the desirability of increases in investment and greater efficiency in the agricultural sector.

Although the socialist countries do not have a well organised labour market, an employment exchange has been established in several of the larger cities in order to improve the allocation of human resources. In spite of the differences between socialist and industrialised market economies, there could be scope for a fruitful exchange of experience in the operation of employment services—possibly through the ILO.

Until recently investment in the socialist countries was largely of the capital-widening type. One way to alleviate labour scarcity, raise productivity and reduce costs—and perhaps improve the quality of output as well—would be to switch to a pattern of investment which is capital-deepening. This process has already begun and can be expected to accelerate in future.

An opportunity exists for solving part of the employment problem of the socialist countries by expanding their trade with the rest of the world. At present they are not deeply engaged in international commerce, although their trade is increasing rapidly, albeit from a small base. Additional imports of labour-intensive goods from the developing countries would ease the employment problem in both groups of countries and perhaps contribute to a reduction in world inequality.

INEQUALITY BETWEEN RICH AND POOR COUNTRIES

Income is very unequally distributed between, as well as within, countries. The increasing differences between the incomes, wealth and control over world resources of the developed and the developing countries has become a central issue. In 1972 the industrial market economy countries, with only 17 per cent of the world population, accounted for 67 per cent of total world output (using ordinary exchange rates to calculate national totals on a common basis). At the other extreme, 26 per cent of the world's population lived in countries whose total output accounted for under 3 per cent of the world total.[1]

Such data can, however, be criticised. If, as was argued above, exchange rates give a distorted picture of the real value of national production, then the correct figures would probably not be so extreme. The 17 per cent of the world's population living in the richest countries may still nevertheless produce and consume 40 to 50 per cent of world output. They control, of course, an even larger share of the world's manufacturing, research and scientific capacity.

In absolute terms differentials are widening rapidly. This is because, say, an annual growth rate of 2 per cent per head in a very rich country such as Sweden or the United States is virtually equal to the total product per head of a very poor country. Relatively also, the inequality has continued to increase. The developing countries as a group achieved average growth rates somewhat above those of developed countries in 1960-74, but because of their higher population growth the rate of increase of income per head was less rapid. The most dramatic increase in international inequality, however, is within the group of developing countries: there has been a very noticeable tendency in recent years for the poorest of the developing countries to grow less rapidly than the less poor.

Wide income differences between rich and poor countries must be expected to remain for some time, although the position of individual countries on the spectrum from riches to poverty will continue to change. What is most important about these differences is that the rich countries have more than enough, and the poor less than enough, to ensure the satisfaction of the basic needs of all families. While problems of poverty have to be resolved mainly at the national level, international action can facilitate a solution.

The current stagnation in the industrial economies and the recent changes in relative commodity prices have had complex effects on the global distribution of income. Increases in petroleum and phosphate prices have redistributed income to developing countries as a group. However, only about one-eighth of

---

[1] These figures do not include China. If China were included, the data suggest that 47 per cent of the population received less than 7 per cent of the world's income.

the population of the Third World live in countries which have gained significantly from this. About one-half live in countries that were adversely affected by high import costs for fertiliser and petroleum. Developed countries meanwhile have often managed to pass on their higher costs in the export prices of their manufactures, which has again worsened the position of the poorer developing countries.

BASIC NEEDS

2

The arguments for the adoption of new approaches to development arise from the record of the last quarter-century and from the prospects for the next quarter-century. As seen in the previous chapter, the conventional development strategies have not succeeded in reducing the numbers of poor and inadequately employed people. It was the awareness of this problem which inspired the ILO to launch the World Employment Programme in 1969.

The focus of that Programme has been on employment, the implicit assumption being that the creation of additional jobs, more productive and adequately remunerated, had an important role to play in the attack on world poverty and in furthering social progress. Nothing that has happened since has invalidated that assumption. It has become apparent to the ILO, however, as a result of its research, and from the practical experience it has acquired in the field and in its employment missions to various countries, that an employment-oriented strategy, by itself, will not suffice. The creation of more and better jobs is not enough; employment issues are intimately connected to the wider issues of poverty and inequality, and it is in this context that they need to be examined.

The approach which is now proposed to this Conference is that development planning should include, as an explicit goal, the satisfaction of an absolute level of basic needs. This proposal goes somewhat further than the intention, already expressed by many governments, to concentrate development measures more directly on the poorest groups of the population. The definition of a set of basic needs, together constituting a minimum standard of living, would at one and the same time assist in the identification of these groups and provide concrete targets against which to measure progress.

This chapter describes, in a short and simplified way, the broad notion of basic needs. It comprises two parts.

The first part provides a definition of the concept and mentions a few of the principal instruments of economic policy which are available for trying to satisfy these needs within a given time-horizon. It then presents some observations on target setting.

The second part reviews three approaches to expressing in quantitative terms the dimensions of a poverty-oriented development strategy in the developing countries. These three approaches—which involve the utilisation of complex models and calculations—have but one objective: to enable an understanding of the perspectives open to these countries, whether or not they decide to adopt a development strategy aiming at the satisfaction of basic needs within a period of time fixed in advance. These approaches—whatever may be their imperfections—shed new light on the inter-relationships between growth, employment, income distribution and poverty. The conclusions which can be drawn suggest that development strategies must be substantially reoriented if appreciable social progress is to be achieved between now and the end of the century. The proposal which is submitted for the appraisal of the Conference as a result of this analysis is that a strategy based on the satisfaction of basic needs *can* enable the taking up of such a challenge.

THE CONCEPT

Basic needs, as understood in this report, include two elements.

First, they include certain minimum requirements of a family for private consumption: adequate food, shelter and clothing are obviously included, as would be certain household equipment and furniture.

Second, they include essential services provided by and for the community at large, such as safe drinking water, sanitation, public transport, and health and educational facilities.

A basic-needs oriented policy implies the participation of the people in making the decisions which affect them. Participation interacts with the two main elements of a basic-needs strategy. For example, education and good health will facilitate participation, and participation in turn will strengthen the claim for the material basic needs.

The satisfaction of an absolute level of basic needs as so defined should be placed within a broader framework—namely the fulfilment of basic human rights, which are not only ends in themselves but also contribute to the attainment of other goals.

In all countries employment enters into a basic-needs strategy both as a means and as an end. Employment yields an output. It provides an income to the employed. And it gives a person the recognition of being engaged in something worth his while.

The fulfilment of physical basic-needs targets in the poorer countries of the world certainly cannot be achieved by a redistribution of goods currently produced. Not only must the structure of production change, but the total amount produced must also rise over time. For this reason, it should be stressed that a rapid rate of economic growth is an essential part of a basic-needs strategy. As will be discussed in Chapter 3, part of the necessary increase in output would come from making use of currently underemployed and unemployed labour resources and linking them with a better allocation of capital, and partly through the redistribution of productive resources. Fuller employment would thus be a means of producing more goods and simultaneously of acquiring the purchasing power to gain access to them. More adequate employment would also be the first essential step towards fuller participation in society.

Improvements in the quality of employment or conditions of work should be another important objective, and one that is of particular interest to the ILO. Many people's work at present is demoralising, undignified, inconvenient, or even dangerous (to health if not to life). There is also the special aspect of the drudgery of women's work, particularly household work in rural areas, that is discussed in Chapter 3. Since most people must work in order to participate in the economy, it is naturally desirable that they should be able to take pride in their work. Thus making employment more humane and satisfying is also an element of a basic-needs strategy.

The basic-needs concept is of universal applicability, although the relative importance of its components will vary with the level of development and from one nation to another.

Basic needs constitute the minimum objective of society, not the full range of desirable attributes, many of which will inevitably take longer to attain. To determine the actual levels at which basic-needs targets should be set requires much further analysis and discussion, and some value judgements. Basic needs for health and the closely related field of nutrition can be set on the basis of scientific findings, although these are still being constantly improved. In such fields as housing and education the targets are bound to be more subjective. Climatic and other differences between countries must also play a part in determining the level of basic needs. Moreover, just as there is relative poverty (relative to the levels of living of others in the same society), as well as absolute poverty, basic needs can be relative as well as absolute. In the present situation, however, it is both legitimate and prudent to concentrate first on meeting basic needs in the absolute sense.

Alternative policies

There are several ways in which the basic needs of the poor could be satisfied within a given time-horizon. One approach is through more rapid over-all growth alone, leaving the income distribution to market forces. Under this approach, which implies high rates of investment, redistribution could occur as a by-product of over-all increased output.

There are at least three reasons why this approach may be questioned: first, it is doubtful whether the majority of developing countries will be able to achieve and sustain the very high rates of growth required; second, in certain countries a substantial portion of the population or entire regions have not automatically benefited from over-all rapid growth; third, the very high levels of investment required may lead, in an initial period, to maintaining, if not worsening, sub-standard levels of living that are unacceptable from a social or political point of view.

The second approach is to raise the incomes of the poverty groups faster than the average by a redistribution of income as well as growth. The growth rates required under this second approach would be less high and would normally be more realistic than in the first approach, but there might be great difficulties, political and other, in implementing policies for redistribution.

Such redistribution could be brought about through a combination of (i) changing the relative prices of the products and labour services which the poor provide compared with the prices of things they buy, (ii) introducing consumption transfers which benefit the poor, (iii) introducing investment transfers to the poor and (iv) redistributing part of the existing stock of capital to the poor, e.g. by such measures as land reform.

These methods of redistribution are not mutually exclusive. Indeed, unless the first three are combined both with progressive taxation and a redistribution of assets they may be ineffective. Changes in relative prices alone are unable to alter more than marginally the share of income received by the poor and some price changes lead to secondary effects which neutralise the initial impact. Higher rural minimum wages, for example, may increase the cost and price of food consumed by the poor and thereby leave the distribution of income essentially unchanged. Both consumption and investment transfers can rarely be limited only to the poor. Subsidised education, in the absence of a severe means test, benefits virtually everyone; similarly, investment in rural roads benefits all cultivators, particularly the largest farmers who have most to sell.

Target setting

A most important attribute of any worthwhile targets is credibility. If they are set too high, their attainment is likely to be too far in the future to be either morally or politically acceptable, or even of much interest to the present society. If they are too low, they are equally unacceptable; while they are more easily and quickly attainable, people may not feel it worth striving for so small an improvement.

The level at which the basic-needs targets might be established by a single country will naturally vary with the stage of development it has reached. It will also depend on the value set by the people of a country on equality of incomes and consumption. There are indeed certain minimum levels of personal consumption and access to social services which are universally regarded as essential to a decent life. But basic needs are also socially determined and few societies can be content with a situation where the bare subsistence needs of the masses are met in a context of sharp differences in material welfare and access to communal services.

Governments wishing to embark on a basic-needs strategy may find it useful as a first step to establish suitable machinery to determine a national set of basic-needs targets or minimum standard of living. These will generally be more elaborate than those discussed below, but this should not be carried too far. Simplicity in this case is probably an important aspect of credibility. It is certainly better to concentrate the country's planning expertise on the next stage of devising the policies and measures required to implement the basic-needs strategy than on the preparation of a highly sophisticated and detailed set of targets.

But the target-setting stage is nevertheless of crucial importance. It is essential that the people whose basic needs have to be met should participate in the determination of these needs, rather than having them handed down from above. In many countries it will probably be found that such participation is severely hampered by the lack of organisations that can express the views and aspirations of the poorest population groups, especially those in rural areas. It may well be, therefore, that an attempt to involve the people in the setting of basic-needs targets will provide a welcome stimulus to the establishment of such organisations.

The point of departure of any development strategy oriented toward the reduction of unemployment and poverty is the initial level of income and its distribution. The desired path of development subsequently followed by the economy then depends upon (i) the target level of income that is set, (ii) the time-period in which it is proposed to achieve the target, (iii) the extent to which it is possible to redistribute income and wealth, whether initially or over time, (iv) the speed at which output increases and (v) the rate of growth of the population. Numerous permutations of these elements are possible and by examining them interesting perspectives on the future are opened up.

ACHIEVING BASIC NEEDS

Until very recently it was common merely to set a target of development policy, often expressed in terms of a desired aggregate rate of growth, without inquiring deeply into what its attainment would imply in terms of the alleviation of poverty.

Increased concern with issues of poverty and inequality has led several institutions to try to estimate in quantitative terms the likely impact of alternative development policies on particular social groups over a given period of time. This can be done by building mathematical " models " which illustrate in a simplified form how an economy functions. These models can be of greater or less complexity but all are based upon explicit assumptions about some key economic relationships and variables. As far as possible these assumptions are based upon empirical evidence on the structure and behaviour of economies in the real world. The models can then be used to simulate what might happen if one or more policy changes are introduced, either on the assumption that all other variables remain constant or will react in specific, defined ways as indicated by real-life experience.

One example of such a model was developed for the World Bank. This model focuses on poverty incomes in general rather than target goods in particular. The findings are presented in the report of a study conducted jointly by the World Bank and the Institute of Development Studies at the University of Sussex.[1] Both institutions have made important contributions to the ILO comprehensive employment missions. The detailed specifications of the model are given in the publication cited in the footnote. The main elements and findings can be summarised as follows.

First, the skeletal framework of a " typical " developing country at the present time was established. It does not reflect the structure of any particular country, but the figures used do take into account empirical data on different types of country, especially Latin American countries. For simplicity, the households are divided into three groups, rich, middle, and poor, corresponding to the top 20 per cent, middle 40 per cent and the lower 40 per cent of the population ranked by income levels. The incomes received by individual households and groups come from two sources: the ownership of productive capital assets and from wage employment. Estimates for the existing levels of capital stock owned by each group, the productivity of that capital and the relative share of wages and profits in those sectors which employ hired labour are then used to obtain figures for per head income in each group and for their shares of the total national income.

It is assumed initially that the poorest 40 per cent of the population receive US$34 per head and 12.6 per cent of disposable income compared with US$303 per head and 56.5 per cent received by the richest 20 per cent of the

---

[1] Montek S. Ahluwalia and Hollis Chenery: " A model of distribution and growth ", in Hollis Chenery et al., op. cit.

population. This corresponds with a moderately high income inequality as revealed by the income distribution data for a number of countries.

The second stage was then to examine what would happen to income levels and shares should a " normal " growth pattern be continued for the next few decades, assuming more or less a continuance of the existing policy mix. For this purpose it was assumed that the poor would save a smaller proportion of their incomes than the rich, but their saving propensity would increase as their incomes grew. Their own capital stock (used for self-employment) would increase correspondingly. It was also assumed that the population growth rate would be higher among the poor (3 per cent per annum) than among the middle and higher income groups which would be 2.5 per cent and 2 per cent respectively. Furthermore, a small increase in the productivity of capital was anticipated in the sectors with hired labour, reflecting better nutrition, health and access to education opportunities, but the productivity of the capital owned by the poor would remain static.

On these assumptions, over the next 30 years the average per head income of the " typical " developing country would rise from US$107 to US$241, i.e. it would grow at a rate of 2.7 per cent per annum (compared with a target of 3.5 per cent in the Strategy for the Second Development Decade) and the per head incomes of the lower 40 per cent would increase from US$34 to US$74 but their share would decline from 12.6 per cent to 12.3 per cent. The model further specifies that if, however, the rate of population increase were reduced to 2 per cent in all socio-economic groups, and all other things remained the same, the average income of the poor would rise to US$109 and their share to 14.4 per cent.

The final stage in the use of the model was to examine effects of three major policy changes on the growth pattern over the same period of time.

The first consists of a policy of *wage restraint*, lowering the share of wages paid to the middle and poor income groups in order to increase the share of profits. The objective is to raise the rate of growth in total income by increasing the investment ratio. Given the magnitudes used in the model, the policy appears to be successful in that respect but at the expense of greater inequality and a substantially slower increase in the incomes of the poor.

The next two policies consist of *transferring resources, either for consumption or investment*, to the poor. It is assumed that there is an annual transfer from the rich to the poor of 2 per cent of total income. This redistribution is assumed to be achieved at the cost of reducing savings and investment by the rich without lowering their current consumption level.

The policy of *consumption transfers* raises the incomes of the poor initially. But because these transfers have an adverse effect on the rate of capital accumulation the average rate of growth of incomes slows down in all sectors.

After 30 years the poor, and everyone else, would appear to be worse off than they would be if a " normal " growth pattern were maintained.

The third policy option considered is a *redirection of investment flows*. In this variant, 2 per cent of the GNP is transferred to the poor each year not for consumption but for investment in various forms of capital assets so as to raise production and incomes of the poor directly and exclusively. Various instruments could be used for this purpose: provisions of credit and physical inputs, access to physical infrastructure (roads, irrigation, drainage, etc.), investment in human capital, etc. The model assumes that this redirected capital investment would be used less efficiently than elsewhere. Nevertheless, the effect is to accelerate significantly the rate of income growth among the poor. After 30 years the average per head income of the poorest 40 per cent in the " typical " developing country would appear to reach US$104, i.e. it would triple compared with the base year. Their share would rise from 12.6 per cent to 19.4 per cent.

Although this model does not include any initial measure of redistribution, the authors of the World Bank study believe that, because land is the main capital asset available to the rural poor, an initial redistribution through land reform or improved tenancy systems may be a necessary first step in those countries where land ownership remains highly concentrated. In others, the elimination of acute poverty may be accelerated by incremental investment reallocations at a higher level (e.g. 3 instead of 2 per cent of the GNP per annum). The main policy implications derived from the model place the emphasis on a shift in the pattern and structure of income growth and asset ownership over time. This could be achieved by redirecting part of the addition to total investment funds which becomes available each year as a result of growth. This " investment transfer " could be brought about by fiscal and other policies by governments, by changes in the credit policies of financial institutions, and by a reorientation of foreign aid towards the poorest groups.

An alternative model concentrates not on income but on achieving a set of targets, expressed in physical units, for the " hard-core " of the poor, which is taken to be the poorest *20 per cent* of the population

In an attempt to determine the feasibility of reaching a set of basic-needs targets within a certain time-period, such targets have been set for food, for housing and for education. There is also an implied health target resulting from the maximisation of life expectancy at birth through the achievement of the food, housing and education targets. The models used are constructed on the assumption that the proportion of national income devoted to the production of these three items remains more or less constant, so that, for example, the target level for food is not reached at the expense of the production of some other items like clothing

Table 5 shows basic-needs target levels compiled by the Fundación Bariloche in Argentina. The target for food is set in terms of the average daily per head intake of dietary energy, and is based on estimates of nutritional requirements arrived at by the FAO and the WHO.[1] The latest knowledge assumes that protein needs are generally met when dietary energy needs are met, so that the food target can be set in terms of this single parameter. The housing target is in terms of square metres per person, and based on United Nations standards. The education target is the percentage enrolment of children aged 7-16 in school. This involves nine years of education for the young, and corresponds to the duration of compulsory schooling which many developing countries and most developed countries have already passed into law.

The data in the table are all averages, and thus represent only a first step. Some regions, of course, are more developed than others and hence have less far to go to meet the minimum targets specified. For example, in 1970 the medium-income countries of Latin America had already attained 81 per cent of the education target whereas, at the other extreme, the arid regions of Africa had met only 38 per cent of the target. Similarly, as regards housing, only 60 per cent of the basic-needs standard had been achieved in Asia, while the low-income countries of Latin America had reached 80 per cent of the standard. The achievement of the dietary energy target was already over 90 per cent of the average in all regions.

There is, however, no guarantee or even likelihood that the needs of the poor are satisfied when average needs are met. Furthermore, any shortfall in achieving average basic needs targets will mainly hit the poor. Thus the fact, for instance, that Asia as a whole had only an 8 per cent shortfall in dietary energy is perfectly compatible with large numbers in the poorer population groups not meeting their food requirements even in years of good harvests.

Further calculations were therefore made within the ILO taking the poorest 20 per cent of families as the target group. Under this model, if the targets for this group are achieved on average, virtually all households will have satisfied their basic needs. Some families—the number depending on the distribution of income—will, of course, have exceeded the standards, while the few with incomes below the average of the lowest quintile will still have fallen short.

It is assumed that the objective is to meet basic needs within one generation, which for the purposes of calculation is taken to be the year 2000.

---

[1] A special characteristic of the food target is that it has to be sustained in years of local and national production shortfalls resulting from climatic fluctuations and other factors. Thus the proposals agreed by the World Food Conference concerning world food security, based on an internationally co-ordinated system of nationally held food stocks, are an important aspect of a basic-needs strategy.

Table 5.   Basic-needs targets in developing countries

Region	Dietary energy [1] (kilocalories per head per day)	Education (percentage enrolment of children aged 7-16)	Housing (m² per person)
Africa (arid)	2 360	98	5.25
Africa (tropical)	2 240	98	5.25
Asia [2] (medium and low income)	2 216	98	5.25
Asia (China)	2 180	98	5.25
Latin America (low income)	2 380	98	7.50
Latin America (medium income)	2 380	98	7.50

[1] Targets from FAO: *Provisional Indicative World Plan for Agricultural Development* (Rome, 1969).   [2] Excluding China.

There is therefore a production target (basic-needs), a target group (the poorest 20 per cent of households) and a time-horizon (one generation).

The model calculates an income level at which basic-needs targets are met, and compares that income level with the existing income of the poorest 20 per cent. In the illustrative examples presented below, it is assumed that the population follows the United Nations' low projection, implying a rapid decline in the rate of demographic expansion. The model then enables the twin roles of redistribution and growth in reaching the target income for the poor to be shown. The aim is to meet the basic needs of that group by the year 2000, or within a single generation.

One way to achieve basic needs within the postulated time-horizon, as has already been indicated, would be through rapid growth alone. This policy represents a continuation of the status quo as regards the distribution of income and evidently is more feasible the higher is the initial level of consumption of the poor. The latter, in turn, depends upon the average level of income and its distribution.

The second column of table 6 indicates the required rates of growth in seven developing regions. These rates range from 6 per cent in China to 11.3 per cent in the oil-producing countries of the Middle East and Africa. In the other five regions the required rates of growth cluster around 9 to 11 per cent.

Unless income distribution changes significantly, the basic needs of the target group can only be met, according to the model, within one generation by rates of growth of output which are nearly double the already rapid rates achieved in recent years. There are two major exceptions to this generalisation: China and the oil-producing countries. In the rest of the developing world the achievement of basic needs would demand, under the model, a combination of

Table 6. Alternative development policies to achieve basic needs by the year 2000

Region	Rapid growth policy (per cent per annum)	Income redistribution policy (per cent per annum)
Africa (arid)	11.2	8.8
Africa (tropical)	11.1	8.4
Asia [1] (medium and low income)	9.7	7.2
Asia (China)	6.0	6.0
Latin America (low income)	9.4	6.8
Latin America (medium income)	8.7	6.7
Middle East/Africa (oil)	11.3	11.3

[1] Excluding China.

Source: Joseph J. Stern: *Growth and redistribution*, preliminary report prepared for the ILO by Harvard University, Dec. 1975.

roughly doubling the rate of growth of output and rapidly reducing the rate of growth of the population. It is unlikely that either, let alone both, of these conditions could be achieved.

The figures in the table are merely a first approximation and the above calculations give no more than orders of magnitude. It must be recognised, however, that the calculations do not allow for any spontaneous improvements in income distribution. If, for example, more use were made of existing improved traditional technology, then the basic-needs targets would be met sooner. The calculations also probably understate the value of housing and food produced by households for their own consumption (and thus include no costs for processing, transport and marketing), nor do they take into account the stimulus that a basic-needs strategy is likely to give to the satisfaction of needs in this way. They do not allow for the fact that the poor will certainly devote a higher proportion of their income to the satisfaction of their basic needs than the proportion of national average per head income that is so used. Finally, they assume that the present highly unequal pattern of access to public services will not change.

Nevertheless, on balance, the projections may be too optimistic rather than too pessimistic in their assumptions. The model uses the low variant of the United Nations population projections, which implies an early and substantial reduction in fertility. On the other hand, it is probably reasonable to assume that the early satisfaction of the basic needs of the poor, and the consequent raising of aspirations, will itself contribute to the reduction of fertility. Without a shift to a basic-needs strategy traditional technology will probably continue to be neglected, the rural areas will continue to stagnate, and the pattern of the

Table 7.   Basic needs, 6 per cent growth and income distribution

Region	Percentage share of the poorest 20 per cent of households in the year	
	1970	2000
Africa (arid)	5.5	12.4
Africa (tropical)	4.9	16.5
Asia [1] (medium and low income)	5.3	14.3
Asia (China)	11.3	11.3
Latin America (low income)	4.3	11.9
Latin America (medium income)	4.5	9.7

[1] Excluding China.

Source: M. Hopkins and Hugo Scolnik: *Basic needs, growth and redistribution : a quantitative approach* (Geneva, ILO, 1975, document for limited distribution), op. cit.

provision of public services will continue to exacerbate rather than redress inequalities in earned incomes. Reliance on rapid growth on its own, under the model, is quite likely to worsen the pattern of income distribution, and still further delay the meeting of the basic-needs targets of the poor.

Another way of meeting basic needs was therefore examined, namely by combining rapid growth with substantial redistribution. In making the calculations reported in the third column of table 6, it was assumed that the rate of growth would not fall below the average of recent years. A lower limit was also set to the extent to which reduction in the inequality of income distribution is feasible. Since the model on which the calculations are based specifies only the distribution at the terminal year, i.e. the year 2000, it makes no difference to the outcome whether there is an initial, once-for-all redistribution at the beginning of the period or a smaller redistribution in each of the 30 years between 1970 and 2000.

The figures in the third column of the table indicate that if substantial income redistribution policies were introduced, most developing countries would appear to achieve the basic-needs objectives by growth at an annual rate of approximately 7 to 8 per cent. The required rates of growth still would be higher than those currently experienced in the majority of countries, but they would not be markedly higher. Indeed, the oil-exporting countries would need only continue at their present rate of growth to meet the targets; no redistributive measures would be necessary.

Yet another way of visualising the relationship between basic needs, growth and income distribution, using a different model, is to estimate what changes would be necessary in the distribution of income if the rate of growth were limited to 6 per cent per annum, the goal of the International Strategy adopted for the Second Development Decade. The figures are reported in table 7.

In every region except Asia (China) the share of the poorest 20 per cent of households would have to more than double and in one instance—tropical Africa—the share would have to increase more than three times. Moreover, in every region except the medium-income countries of Latin America, the extent of redistribution that would be required would be such that social changes of this order of magnitude are unlikely to occur. One would therefore be forced reluctantly to conclude, from this model, that the growth target of the Second Development Decade is not consistent with the proposed objective of fulfilling basic needs within one generation.

CONCLUSIONS

All these calculations, tentative though they be, strongly suggest that in many countries minimum income and standards of living for the poor cannot be achieved, even by the year 2000, without some acceleration of present average rates of growth, accompanied by a number of measures aiming at changing the pattern of growth and use of productive resources by the various income groups; in a number of cases these measures would probably have to include an initial redistribution of resources, in particular, land. The policy package to be adopted will obviously depend on the situation of each country.

To achieve the satisfaction of basic needs within a generation will therefore require action on all fronts, both redistribution and growth together. To be of use, this redistribution must result in the production of more basic goods and services. The provision of adequate employment opportunities is an essential ingredient in this strategy. The productive mobilisation of the unemployed, the seasonally unemployed and the underemployed, plus higher productivity by the working poor, are essential means of ensuring both a level of output high enough to meet basic-needs targets, and its proper distribution. Redistribution of the ownership of or access to land and other productive resources and stimulating the introduction of the right kind of technology are also likely to be, in a number of countries, a major means of raising the level of productivity of the working poor. When combined with the reorientation of public services, it should bring about an improved distribution of income. The sooner any necessary redistribution occurs, the shorter would be the period required to meet basic needs targets and the higher the living levels of the poor in every intermediate year. But it should be pointed out that in any case, the proposed strategy implies quite high levels of investment, without which there would be neither growth nor meaningful redistribution.

These main elements of possible basic-needs strategies for developing countries are analysed in more detail in the following chapter.

PART TWO

NATIONAL STRATEGIES

DEVELOPING COUNTRIES

3

The previous chapters have outlined the dimensions and characteristics of employment problems and of poverty in the world. They have suggested that traditional approaches to economic and social development have been unable to prevent these problems from increasing still further in the developing countries. They have drawn attention to the challenge of providing additional productive employment opportunities for 1,000 million people in the developing market economies by the end of the century—for 700 million new entrants to the labour force, and for a further 300 million who are at present unemployed or inadequately employed. They have also proposed the reorientation of development strategies and policies in order to meet the minimum basic needs of the poor within the same time period of approximately a generation.

This is not intended to suggest that a reorientation of development strategies in this way could work miracles. Even if such strategies were pursued with complete success, there is no likelihood that they could entirely eliminate employment problems and poverty within so short a period of human history. The basic-needs targets discussed earlier are set at minimum levels. It is suggested, however, that if the political will exists for a really determined effort to reach such targets, a great deal of progress could be achieved in improving the levels of living of the world's poor. The striking progress that has been made in the roughly similar period since the Second World War in several countries, developed and developing, socialist and market economy, bears witness to what might be achieved. Many other countries have already made good progress towards meeting one or other of the basic needs, without much impact, however, on the over-all levels of living of the poorest groups of their populations.

In recent years, there has already been a considerable evolution in approaches to development. Thus there would probably be little disagreement that, notwithstanding the importance of economic growth, meeting basic human needs is the primary aim of development. What is proposed here is that this generally accepted aim should be translated into specific targets, comprehensible and relevant to most of the world's people and to decision makers, against which development performance could be measured. Such an approach would concentrate attention on the critical issues surrounding access to productive employment, the distribution of income and the availability of public services. It emphasises in a concrete way that the objective of development is to serve human beings and places growth in the more meaningful context of the distribution of consumption over time. Economic growth would be seen as a means of meeting basic needs, and particular patterns of growth evaluated in terms of their efficiency in this regard.

However, although there is likely to be fairly general agreement on these fundamental principles, there is room for discussion and for considerable national differences concerning the level of basic-needs targets, the time period for meeting them and above all the national policies that are required to attain them. A main purpose of this report is to promote the necessary discussion and comparison of national experiences, aspirations and policy preferences. The present chapter discusses some of the major national policies and measures that would need to be considered by developing countries for a basic-needs strategy to be successfully pursued.

As with all aspects of development, there is of course no unique set of policies for this purpose. What is certain is that a coherent package of mutually reinforcing policies would be required in each individual country. The setting of specific basic-needs targets should in fact make it easier to determine whether the policies adopted in different fields actually reinforce one another or conflict. But although there will usually be some common elements, the components of the packages suitable for different countries will obviously vary in accordance with their economic and social conditions, as well as political choice.

Every country embarking on a strategy of development aimed at meeting the basic needs of the poor starts from a unique set of conditions. There are great variations not only in respect of given factors such as geographical size and resource endowment, but also in respect of the incidence of poverty, the distribution of income and wealth, and the degree of success already achieved in economic growth and in raising levels of living. The countries of Asia in general have further to go than those in the other developing regions in order to meet the basic needs specified in Chapter 2, although Africa has to go the furthest in terms of literacy and manpower development. Present and prospective rates of population growth and population densities differ considerably from country to country. Many developing countries, especially in Asia, are characterised by abundant labour and scarce land, while in other countries, especially in parts of Africa and Latin America, the situation is the opposite. Even among the labour-abundant countries, employment problems appear in different forms. While high levels of urban unemployment are common to almost all of them, rural unemployment is also high in plantation economies, but in peasant economies much of the rural employment problem is generally " hidden " in the form of work sharing.

The projection models presented for illustrative purposes in Chapter 2 show that the achievement within a generation of the basic-needs targets proposed there requires very high rates of growth if they are to be reached without any change in the distribution of income. A few developing countries, such as some of the petroleum producers, may be able to sustain for some time such rates of growth without running into severe balance-of-payments problems. In the great majority of developing countries, however, reliance on growth alone is likely to postpone the meeting of basic needs until well into the next century.

The magnitude of the redistribution that is required will depend mainly on the rate of growth that can be achieved and on the distribution of income at the outset. The redistribution may be obtained entirely through redistribution from growth, through an initial redistribution of productive resources, or through a combination of the two. The appropriate combination will depend partly on the magnitude of the required redistribution, partly on the degree to which the fiscal and administrative system can be relied on to redistribute from growth, and partly on political choice. In many cases, at least some initial redistribution of productive resources, particularly land, is likely to be found necessary, even in order to provide the basis for future redistribution from growth. However, the redistribution of land by agrarian reform may lead either to public ownership or to continued private ownership.

Before discussing some of the main relevant areas of specific policy in more detail, it may be useful to set out some further general characteristics of strategies aiming to satisfy the basic needs of the poor as quickly as possible. Most current or proposed development strategies could probably find a place in a threefold classification into " conventional high-growth ", " employment-oriented ", and " poverty- or needs-oriented " strategies. There are similarities as well as differences between them. The need for growth and capital accumulation is common to all three. In fact, passing from one strategy to the next, the main differences consist of additions and changes in emphasis. The emphasis of the first is almost solely on growth and capital formation. Distribution receives some attention through the emphasis on employment creation in the second, and moves up alongside growth and capital formation in the third.

Producing the goods and services and providing the productive employment required to meet the basic needs of the poor involves changes in production patterns as well as in the distribution of income and wealth. These two requirements are inter-related. High and growing inequality of income generates rapidly increased demand for luxury goods (in particular, expensive consumer durables) but relatively sluggish growth of effective demand for basic foodstuffs and consumer goods. Increased productive employment and higher incomes for the poor will change both the level and rate of growth of demand for basic consumer goods and public services. This shift in the composition of demand should induce a shift in the pattern of production towards goods which in many cases are more suitable for production on a relatively small scale. This may tend in turn to generate higher levels of productive employment, to the extent that the new output mix is characterised by greater labour intensity. Moreover, the new conditions should increase the incentive to search for and use more appropriate technologies.

Thus a pattern of production which is efficient in meeting basic needs is likely to lead to increased integration of the national economy and to greater self-reliance. Basic services such as education and health, and some basic goods such as housing and urban and rural infrastructure, are obviously not tradeable. But it is also likely that in most developing countries a strategy of the kind outlined here would require substantial increases in the domestic production of essential food and consumer goods. Many countries have in recent years become increasingly dependent on imports of cereals and other basic foods, and a central part of the new approach would be a massive acceleration in the increase in food and agricultural production in the developing countries as a whole to at least the average annual rate of 4 per cent that is called for in the Strategy for the Second United Nations Development Decade and was re-affirmed by the World Food Conference. Meeting basic needs, rather than just the increases in effective demand that occur without changes in income distribution, will probably entail still greater increases in food production.

The arguments for greater self-reliance, in the context of meeting basic needs as in other contexts, are based on the efficient use of local resources and do not imply local or national autarky. Both locally and nationally there are natural and acquired differences which afford the possibility of gains from specialisation. In the case of a small country, both the limited variety of resources and economies of scale will increase the relative importance and potential gains from international trade as a means of meeting basic needs. Furthermore, because of the changes to be expected in the pattern of supply and demand, the adoption of a basic-needs strategy should increase the opportunities for trade among countries pursuing similar strategies but with different resource endowments. Semi-industrialised countries such as Brazil, India, the Republic of Korea and Mexico should be in a position to export increasing quantities of the capital goods needed for the production of basic goods. In general, foreign trade is unlikely to be less important than under more conventional development strategies. Indeed, the proposed new approach may lead to the elimination of many arbitrary restrictions on trade that at present protect and otherwise favour large-scale manufacture.

Trade and other international aspects of basic-needs strategies are dealt with in Part Three of this report. The remainder of this chapter is concerned with national policies in developing countries. Various policy areas (macro-economic, institutional, technological and social) and specific policy measures are discussed separately, but it is believed that partial or piecemeal measures are likely to be ineffective and may even prove to be contradictory. The different policies and measures proposed are of an interlocking nature and should as far as possible be introduced jointly.

MACRO-ECONOMIC POLICIES

Even in economies that rely primarily on the market mechanism, government policies have a substantial influence, both direct and indirect, on prices, and especially on relative prices. There is widespread agreement that in many developing countries the prevailing set of relative prices has contributed not only to inefficiency in the allocation of resources but also to growing inequality in income distribution. In particular, private entrepreneurs have often been able to obtain capital or foreign exchange considerably more cheaply than its real cost to the economy as a whole. In most countries relative prices, combined with the prevailing power structure, tend to favour large industrial and agricultural enterprises, which also have privileged access to the formal credit market that is not available to small producers.

Exchange rates have often been overvalued, thereby discouraging exports and allowing those who obtain import licences to reap monopoly rents. Interest rates have been kept low (often negative in real terms in conditions of rapid inflation), thus further encouraging the adoption of capital-intensive methods of production. High levels of protection for industrial goods, often combined with artificially low food prices in the interest of urban consumers, have turned the terms of trade against agriculture and thus bear some of the responsibility for food shortages. A strong case was made by the ILO employment mission [1] to the Philippines for reforming the price system so that it reflects better the real costs of productive resources.

The distributional effects of price policies are discussed at length in the report of the mission to Sudan.[2] Changes in exchange rates, interest rates and

---

[1] ILO: *Sharing in development: a programme of employment, equity and growth for the Philippines* (Geneva, 1974).

[2] Idem: *Growth, employment and equity: a comprehensive strategy for Sudan* (Geneva, 1976). (Document for limited distribution.)

tariffs can lead to important benefits for the poor, especially in mixed economies. They can be used to correct biases against agriculture and the rural sector, to readjust the internal terms of trade, and to promote a more efficient utilisation of both domestic and imported resources.

Changes in price systems may need to be accompanied by appropriate institutional changes to ensure that their benefits are equitably shared and that they lead to better resource utilisation. For example, an increase in the relative price of capital is unlikely to induce the adoption of efficient, more labour-intensive techniques of production, unless there are suitable institutions for developing alternative techniques and disseminating information on them. Other necessary accompanying changes may include the redistribution of access to land.

The choice between meeting basic needs through expanding productive employment or through transfer payments is rarely available to a developing country, although several of the most prosperous OPEC members are obviously exceptions. Neither fiscal mobilisation, because of its limits, nor the administrative capacity of most countries are likely to be adequate for a transfer system to work satisfactorily. Moreover, even if significant transfers can be achieved they may not be able to substitute fully for a more rapid increase in employment and labour productivity, particularly among the rural poor. If the output and consumption of basic goods, especially food, is to be increased, additional productive employment is required and, in particular, higher output and incomes for the poor.

The more unequal the distribution of income and wealth, the more important will be tax policies and consumption transfers. The combination of a progressive tax system (including differentiated taxes on consumer goods) and an expansion of public financing of basic services, such as health and education, can have a significant redistributive impact, especially in relatively more developed countries.

The danger of concentrating on consumption transfers, however, is that investment will be neglected. The mobilisation and productive investment of an economic surplus is basic to any development strategy. In addition to the usual ways of accelerating capital accumulation, it may be useful to devote special attention to opportunities for using profitably local resources which remain unutilised because of the lack of complementary inputs or because of deficiencies in local organisation. The potential surpluses for investment of low-income and low-productivity groups are often specific to a locality, and must be complemented by other inputs if they are to be realised. If this is done, the savings rates of small farmers and shopkeepers can be remarkably high.

It is sometimes claimed that a more equal distribution of income is likely to result in a low rate of voluntary household saving and investment. As noted in

Chapter 1, however, the available evidence does not support this, and national savings rates do not appear to be closely correlated with the degree of inequality.

The quantity of resources that can be mobilised for investment from upper-income individuals and from high-productivity units will vary with the degree of inequality in incomes, the share of public-sector ownership, and the institutional pattern of financial flows and uses. In all cases, however, it is likely to be desirable to prevent exorbitant increases in luxury consumption, through such measures as high import and excise duties on luxury goods and restrictions on the size of homes and motor cars. The achievement of the " social minimum " implied by basic-needs targets may be accelerated by some kind of " social maximum " to divert resources from the production and import of luxury goods.

Other measures may also be necessary to ensure that revenues generated through taxation are channelled to increasing the production of basic goods and services. One key instrument is the organised financial sector, which can be used to implement allocational guidelines and co-ordinate decentralised decisions.

INSTITUTIONAL POLICIES

A major strategic choice is that between an essentially public and an essentially private productive sector. It should be noted, however, that this has little to do with the controversy between planning and the price mechanism.

It is likely that in most countries the adoption of the proposed new strategy will lead to an increased role for government planning and possibly for the public sector as well. Structural changes in such areas as the financial system, land tenure and the education system require direct government intervention. Such policies cannot be implemented simply by influencing market prices. On the other hand, the correction of market distortions and market failures can provide an appropriate framework for decentralised decision making. This framework is as relevant to an economy in which the means of production are publicly owned as it is to a predominantly private-enterprise economy.

Obviously, it is not an all-or-nothing choice. In a given country some sectors, such as finance, may be in the public sector, while others, such as small-scale agriculture and commerce, may be privately or co-operatively organised. The governments of many countries already have concluded that the foreign ownership of public utilities, land and the most valuable mineral and energy resources is incompatible with their strategy of national development. The choice between private and public ownership will affect the allocation of investible surpluses, the choice of technologies and of the goods that are produced, and the manner in which incomes are redistributed. The use of detailed, centralised instructions is unlikely to lead to efficient planning under either system. Centralised decision makers, using direct controls, are often biased in favour of large projects requiring specialised knowledge and against the use of simple technologies based on local information and resources, against small-scale production, and consequently against the self-employed, small urban entrepreneurs and farmers. Decentralisation, combined with the systematic use of prices to guide decisions, may therefore be particularly important for implementing development strategies focused on the basic needs of the poor.

Decentralisation poses special difficulties in the rural sector, where it is also especially important because of the highly local nature of rural potentials, resources and problems. For the poorest farmers and landless labourers to be able to raise their productivity and incomes requires access to land and complementary resources. Otherwise, both decentralisation and the injection of centrally funded complementary resources are likely to reinforce existing inequalities. Agrarian reform (which is dealt with more fully below in discussing the rural sector) is thus likely to be a necessary first step in many countries. It should be noted, however, that it can imply either public or private ownership, or even a mixture of the two.

Redistribution in the urban and non-agricultural rural sectors poses different problems. Medium to large-scale enterprises often enjoy easier access to markets, knowledge and finance, partly through being largely controlled by the public sector or by larger enterprises. In some cases smaller enterprises are even denied access to these resources by various inhibiting regulations.[1] Redistribution of the ownership of large units is useful only to the extent that it leads to greater ability to control the choice of products and technologies and the over-all pattern of economic activity. Whether large-scale enterprises are in the public or private sector, an appropriate price and fiscal system is likely to be more efficient than detailed regulations in influencing their decisions.

TECHNOLOGICAL POLICIES

Technology is discussed in some detail in Chapter 9, but it must be briefly mentioned here as well because of its close links with many of the national policies under discussion. The price policies and investment patterns discussed here not only affect the fulfilment of basic needs but also contribute to determining the technology that is used. Because the latter is linked with the types of goods produced as well as with the labour and skill requirements for their production, it is also a direct determinant of the level of productive

---

[1] For a detailed treatment of such questions, see ILO: *Employment incomes and equality: a strategy for increasing productive employment in Kenya*, op. cit)

employment and the distribution of income. Many of the products associated with technologies borrowed from high-income countries are inappropriate for developing countries because their high cost precludes their purchase by low-income consumers. At the same time, the costly labour, abundant capital and technical skills, and large markets in the technology-initiating countries mean that the embodiment of modern scientific knowledge in specific production techniques is often unsuitable for the conditions prevailing in developing countries. At least in the short run, a considerable part of modern technology is available only in the form of expensive labour-saving equipment. Its adoption necessarily results in investing a large part of national savings in capital equipment and infrastructure for a privileged few, leaving the greater proportion of the labour force with only the most rudimentary tools to work with.

Moving towards a technology that is capital saving and generates an appropriate product mix first of all entails research and development aimed at upgrading the productivity and quality of traditional craft production and at re-embodying modern scientific knowledge in forms more suitable to developing economies. The dissemination of information on new (or existing but unfamiliar) products and processes is a necessary complement. Specific arrangements may also have to be made for appropriate training and retraining. It is in this area that international co-operation, as discussed in Chapter 9, has a particularly significant role to play.

While research and development can widen the range of the " supply " of technological choices, " demand " factors may also be influenced so as to shift technology in the direction required for the satisfaction of basic needs. Technology is much influenced by the allocational policies, already discussed, relating to the interest rates, tariffs, licences, foreign exchange, profit taxation and wages which define the parameters within which entrepreneurs calculate profit and loss. By adjusting these policies to remove the under-pricing of capital and the monopolistic distortions that favour certain groups, competitive pressures to use more labour and less capital can be brought to bear on all producers in the modern sector. Technology is also influenced by the distribution of investment. Because various categories of investors differ in their access to capital and technical knowledge and are subject to different types of pressure, there are systematic differences in the production methods they adopt. Thus policies which encourage investment by private domestic entrepreneurs will generally tend to shift the technology in the desired direction, while (as discussed in Chapter 10) actions which favour multinational enterprises may tend to have the contrary effect.

In general, the most appropriate technology for developing countries is one that is both efficient and labour-intensive. Nevertheless, the implementation of a basic-needs strategy calls for a combination of capital-intensive and labour-intensive technologies. For example, the production of fertilisers is generally capital-intensive, yet they are essential for generating employment and incomes in the rural sector. Similarly, the total employment effects of capital-intensive technologies may be much higher than their direct effects alone.

SOCIAL POLICIES AND SERVICES

A number of policy areas that may be roughly grouped under the broad heading of social policies are highly relevant to strategies aimed at meeting the basic needs of the poor. This particularly applies to education and health policies and services and to the provision of housing and related infrastructure. Reference is also made under this heading to population policies and to policies relating to women.

Education is an especially striking example of the importance of viewing policies not in isolation but in the context of supporting or competing activities. A large number of countries in Africa and Asia, for example, have dramatically expanded their educational systems in the past two decades. Yet the initial hope that this would contribute substantially to the reduction of poverty and inequality has been largely frustrated. One reason may be that nutritional and environmental factors affect the capacity to learn. There is increasing evidence that severe protein malnutrition of infants impairs mental development, that hungry children learn less well, and that an impoverished and unhealthy environment fails to provide sufficient stimulus to the curiosity and imagination of children.

Even where such obstacles are absent, it does not appear that an increase in the supply of educational services and an improvement in their distribution leads automatically to an increase either in total income or in the equality of its distribution. All that may sometimes happen, as is indicated in the World Employment Programme report on Sri Lanka [1], is that the formal educational requirements for a given job may be raised, or that some school leavers may be openly unemployed.

It is often anticipated that, by adding to the stock of " human capital ", education and training will increase the productivity and hence the incomes of workers. It is probable, however, that in many cases productivity is more a characteristic of a job than of a person, depending more on technology than on the formal educational attainments of the worker. The distribution of wages then depends on the distribution of jobs and their associated productivity, and

---

[1] ILO: *Matching employment opportunities and expectations: a programme of action for Ceylon*, op. cit.

these in turn reflect the productive structure of the economy. Education is of course one of the determinants of who has access to jobs. It acts as one of a series of screening devices for sorting out job applicants, allowing those who pass through to occupy the best paid jobs in the large enterprises of the modern sector and in the public administration.

The educational implications of the proposed new approach relate to three major functions of education: building a capacity to learn, analyse and apply; transmitting specific knowledge and skills; and integrating the student into society and its goals. Many existing educational systems appear to fail in each of these functions. They are largely focused on a continuous education process so that, although very few students will ever complete this process, the knowledge transmitted, the context in which learning and analysis are presented and the values and goals embodied in the system at all levels are really aimed at the prospective university graduate rather than at the majority who complete only the primary or secondary phases. Thus, the employment mission to Kenya recommended the creation of a series of second-chance institutions for recuperating early school leavers and preparing them for employment and income-earning opportunities.

Education is itself a basic need, and equality of access to educational services, particularly in rural areas, is therefore an important ingredient of a basic-needs strategy. Lack of access to education denies many people, and particularly women, the opportunity to participate fully in the social, cultural and political life of the community. The education of women merits special attention, as was discussed in the ILO Kenya report.

In several cases, notably Israel, Japan, the Republic of Korea and Singapore, the improvement of educational levels appears to have made a significant contribution to equitable growth.[1] Particularly in Japan and the Republic of Korea, however, this involved substantial changes in the system of education. Indeed it seems likely that in most developing countries major changes will be needed if education is to make its full contribution to the satisfaction of basic needs. In many cases more attention needs to be devoted to improving the quality of teachers, as well as expanding their numbers. Imaginative use of non-formal and recurrent systems of education can make the available supply of trained teachers go further. Changes in curricula and in examination and selection systems are required. The necessary changes will of course vary from country to country, depending on the nature of the present system and the level of literacy. When half or more of the adult population is illiterate, an important objective may be to give mass adult education equal priority with

---

[1] Irma Adelman: "Strategies for equitable growth", in *Challenge* (New York, International Arts and Science Press, 1974).

primary education for children. It will generally be important to ensure that any educational programme of any level or kind is complete and of value in itself, instead of being mainly oriented to preparation for a subsequent course. Another important requirement in many countries is for rural education to shed its predominantly urban bias.

Health occupies much the same position as education in relation to basic-needs strategies. A decent level of health is itself a basic need. At the same time, improvements in health can contribute substantially to increased productivity and to fuller participation in society.

The WHO has proposed a " primary health care programme ", which is specifically oriented to meeting basic needs in the field of health. The main thrust of the programme is directed towards urban slum dwellers, nomadic populations and others in remote regions, and in general towards rural areas, where only about 15 to 20 per cent of the population have access to health services. Many developing countries have modelled their health services on those of developed countries, and they have consequently not been conducive to providing such basic needs as protection against communicable diseases, assistance to mothers during pregnancy and delivery, family-planning advice, safe water and sanitation, health and nutritional education, treatment for simple diseases, and first-aid and emergency treatment. In a number of countries, however, modifications are already taking place through the use of simplified, low-cost technologies, simply but adequately trained workers from the community and selected by it, and in general a multisectoral approach to health. Use is being made of traditional healers and birth attendants, who are trained and supervised by the staff of the formal health facility nearest to the community. It will therefore be necessary to gear formal health services to support the primary level, including the reorientation of training curricula and of already trained health workers.

The establishment of systems of primary health workers in villages may be expected to bring a number of other benefits in addition to the greater and more equitable access to health services. A considerable number of jobs will be created, and a substantial contribution made towards community motivation, involvement and participation.

Housing, water supply and environmental sanitation are critical to people's well-being and make up a substantial proportion of the total infrastructure, especially in urban areas. Their provision offers considerable scope for the use of labour-intensive techniques, thereby not only increasing employment in the informal sector but also reducing costs. In Tanzania, for instance, the informal construction sector can produce a six-room improved traditional house for less than half the cost of a much smaller house constructed on a housing corporation estate.

Main urban water-supply systems probably offer the least potential for technological innovation, although the ditch-digging and pipe-laying phases could use more labour and less equipment than is typically the case. There is more potential for labour-intensive techniques in the construction of water-distribution systems. Pipe-laying and the provision of communal water taps and washing and toilet facilities can not only be carried out by labour-intensive methods but also cost substantially less than alternative systems which in urban areas entail piped connections to and plumbing in individual houses. Large-scale waterborne sewage systems are so expensive as to make studies of alternative hygienically effective systems a priority area for research. Systems requiring periodic emptying may be compatible with the processing of waste into a form suitable for transport to adjacent agricultural areas, where it can be used to supplement chemical fertilisers, thus offsetting part of the operating costs of the sanitation system and simultaneously easing balance-of-payments difficulties.

It would not be appropriate to discuss in this report the still controversial issue of population policies in any detail. However, they must be briefly referred to in relation to the type of development strategy that is under consideration here. On the one hand, the rate of population growth is obviously the main determinant of the number of people whose basic needs have to be met. Rapid population growth necessitates a substantial concentration of resources on the meeting of basic needs, through increased food production and the provision of education and health services. It has also led to heavy pressure on scarce land resources in many countries. If population grew at the low instead of the medium variant of the United Nations projections, the total of 1,000 million additional productive jobs required by the end of the century could still be somewhat reduced. On the other hand, the growth of the population and labour force, if only it could be more fully utilised, is a potent factor in meeting the rapid increase in basic needs.

There appears to be still considerable controversy as to the correlation between rates of population growth and of economic development. Although there is undoubtedly a population problem at the world level, based mainly in the finite nature of a number of essential resources, some at present sparsely populated countries still see it as in their own interest to promote rapid population growth. Most countries, however, including those that contain the great majority of the world's population, have adopted policies aimed at reducing population growth.

In addition to reaffirming national sovereignty over population matters, the World Population Conference, in its World Population Plan of Action, specifically recognised the place of population policies in over-all policies for economic and social development. Population policies are, however, seen as being far wider than simply family-planning programmes.

In the long run economic and social development will itself lead to reduced population growth, as has already occurred in the developed countries. Nevertheless there is widespread agreement, as witnessed by the policies of a large number of developing countries, that intensified and more appropriate family-planning programmes are required to reinforce this process. The World Population Conference affirmed the right of all couples to the necessary information and facilities to plan the number and spacing of their families in a responsible way. Indeed, many people would wish to see this right included among basic needs.

The factors that influence people's attitudes to family size are extremely complex. The various components of economic and social development influence these attitudes in opposite ways and with different time-lags. Much further research is needed to determine the over-all net effect of different patterns of development. There is already some evidence, however, that development strategies aimed at reducing social inequalities and at the rapid and widespread satisfaction of basic needs and the consequent raising of aspirations may be very effective in changing attitudes to family size, especially if backed up by the availability of the necessary information and facilities for family planning.[1]

Finally, it is necessary to refer to policies affecting women. Even though the United Nations declared 1975 International Women's Year, the role of women in contributing to meeting basic needs in society as a whole, as well as their own basic needs, is still far from being recognised. Even more than men, the great majority of women in developing countries are engaged in activities of a traditional nature, mainly in rural areas. Their contribution to the satisfaction of the basic needs of the household is as great as, if not greater than, that of men. Rural women in particular share with men, and often (especially in some African countries) take the major responsibility for, the task of growing food crops for the family either in the family field or on their own patches, although usually this is barely recognised in the statistics of the agricultural labour force. Their household activities are completely ignored in the statistics of national product. Yet they prepare food, fetch and carry water and wood (sometimes over long distances), make, or at least wash and mend, the family's clothes, look after and educate children, and maintain minimum standards of health and cleanliness in the home. These tasks are vital, time-consuming and physically arduous.

---

[1] Eva Mueller: *Effects of different patterns of rural development on demographic change* (Rome, FAO, 1975; mimeographed).

There are thus two facets to a basic-needs strategy for women in developing countries. One is to enable them to contribute more effectively to the satisfaction of their families' basic needs, within the framework of their traditional responsibilities. The other, which is a fundamental need of the women themselves, is to ease their work burden while furthering their economic independence and their more equitable integration into the community, beyond the narrow circle of the family.

Especially in rural areas, most women in developing countries are overworked rather than underemployed, and a more appropriate technology for the tasks they perform implies labour saving, in order to improve the quality of their employment, rather than employment creation. Much emphasis is often placed on the relief of drudgery in agricultural work by mechanisation, but this unfortunately would in many cases reduce employment opportunities at the same time. There is much scope, however, for relieving the drudgery of women's household work by the provision of accessible water points, rural electrification, and simple technological improvements in the processing and preparation of food in the home.

Government extension and other services are not only almost entirely staffed by men but are almost entirely directed to them. Where women are approached by such services, it is mainly to help them to be better wives and mothers rather than to be better food producers and fuller members of society. In many countries girls are grossly under-represented in the educational system. Even where they have access to education, what is provided is rarely appropriate for their needs.

SECTORAL IMPLICATIONS

In most developing countries the proposed new strategy would imply more emphasis on the expansion of the traditional rural and informal urban sectors than has typically been the case. The direct impact of increasing employment in these sectors will be multiplied several-fold, because most of the increased income will be directed to basic goods. This does not mean, however, that the modern urban sector or the large-scale commercial farm sector should be ignored. But the new approach would imply that these sectors should be evaluated in terms of the contribution they make to overcoming acute poverty. The more developed a country, the more options it has in implementing such a strategy and the less restraints are likely to be necessary on the patterns of growth of the modern sector.

As regards the rural sector, it was suggested earlier that in many countries the implementation of the new strategy is likely to have to begin with agrarian reform. Improved access to land, water and complementary inputs will often be found to be essential for the increased employment and income-earning opportunities for the rural poor that are necessary for a subsequent redistribution of income from growth. Where large holdings are typically underutilised, agrarian reform may also be necessary to provide for the increase in food production required to meet basic needs. Small farmers are likely to utilise land more fully than large farmers and to adopt labour-intensive technologies using implements that can be manufactured domestically. Output per hectare tends to rise as the size of operational holding falls. Agrarian reform is thus likely both to increase the supply of basic food and to ensure that it is distributed to some of those in greatest need. Agrarian reform may also be necessary to enable large masses of people to participate more fully in society. It is significant that in most of the World Employment Programme comprehensive employment strategy mission reports, notably those for Colombia, Kenya, the Philippines and Sri Lanka, agrarian reform was a principal policy recommendation.

In some densely populated countries the extremely unfavourable and worsening land-man ratio may make it impossible to distribute individual holdings large enough to permit efficient farming and fully employ family labour. Thus, quite apart from political considerations, it may be necessary in some cases to organise some form of communal land use. In any case, the redistribution of land into small holdings or co-operative farms will have to be complemented by an improvement in the flow of credit, inputs, extension, marketing and other services. The institutions and input distribution methods that have hitherto been biased largely towards serving a small number of wealthy landlords and large farmers are unlikely to be appropriate for broader groups of small farmers or co-operative or collective units. Extension services and credit, for example, may need to be provided on a group basis, especially in view of the shortage of finance and trained manpower.

Agrarian reforms have not always been successful in the past. Sometimes political will has been sufficient to pass the necessary legislation but not to avoid the successful evasion of its provisions. Where there has been sufficient political will, agrarian reform has sometimes been carried out too hastily, with insufficient attention to the need to provide the necessary supporting services for the new farm operators. It is particularly important to foresee the consequences of agrarian reform, such as a possible temporary fall in the marketed output of food, and to plan to meet them through commercial imports, food aid or even the introduction of rationing for a short period.

Agrarian reforms will need to be supplemented by price changes which encourage cultivators to economise on capital and other scarce resources and use labour more intensively. Water charges should generally reflect the true cost of providing irrigation facilities, and interest rates the real scarcity of capital. The prices of farm machinery should not in general be subsidised, and those of fertilisers only when this is clearly necessary to promote their use in the early stages of their introduction.

In many cases the development and introduction of new technology will be of high priority. If appropriate incentives are provided by the price system, this will clearly help. But direct support of national research institutes by the government is also essential, as well as the establishment of close working arrangements with appropriate international research institutes.

Non-agricultural rural activities have also tended to be neglected in most countries. The expansion and improvement of small-scale processing and manufacturing and greater investment in roads, storage facilities and rural housing are central to an integrated rural development strategy and to meeting the basic needs of the poorer rural strata, as well as to providing increased employment opportunities on a full-time or part-time basis. The development of decentralised rural towns can contribute both to increasing rural employment opportunities in non-agricultural activities and to relieving the congestion of the existing large towns. The improvement of local building materials and construction techniques would make an important contribution to satisfying the basic needs of the rural population.

The introduction or expansion of labour-intensive rural public works schemes is an important policy ingredient for the rural areas. In some countries this may be the only or the most efficient way of increasing quickly the incomes of landless labourers and very small land-holders. More generally, such schemes are important for three reasons. They can meet some basic needs directly (e.g. rural infrastructure and housing), and some indirectly through higher investment. They can use labour time which could not be used in agricultural production, thereby raising average annual productivity. They can also augment rural cash incomes.

It will also be necessary to ensure massive improvements in the availability of social services and amenities in rural areas and in the general quality of rural life, if rural-urban migration is to be slowed down to a pace that does not increase urban unemployment.

Urban strategy is more complex, because initial redistribution is less simple and because the case for large-scale, capital-intensive production is stronger. However, the situations where more labour-intensive methods are unlikely to have a positive impact on the availability of basic goods and services are concentrated in certain branches of manufacturing and in transport. Construction, public services and some branches of manufacturing (for example, garments and furniture) can usually use labour-intensive methods efficiently.

With many products, such as bicycles, a majority of components are suitable for small-scale, labour-intensive production. However, certain components, final assembly, design and marketing are better organised on a large scale, so that direct control can be maintained over technology and skilled personnel. Complex subcontracting relationships of this type characterised the Japanese economy during its early industrial development. They are much less typical of most developing countries today. In part this is a result of importing complete " up-to-date " technology from industrial economies, and in part it is because of the interest of multinational enterprises in concentrating production in their own units rather than dispersing it among independent subcontractors. Tariff protection is also important, however, as is the low level of the relevant technical and organisational skills in the informal sector in many developing countries. It is necessary first to identify potential areas for subcontracting, then to require large enterprises to take up these opportunities (by regulations, incentive payments, or fiscal penalties), and to provide (or encourage large firms to provide) training and technical services to the small-scale subcontractors.

In capital-intensive industries producing basic goods there is scope in some countries for the introduction of multiple shifts, in order simultaneously to increase the supply of such goods, expand employment opportunities and make fuller use of scarce capital.

ASPECTS OF IMPLEMENTATION

As already emphasised, an effective development strategy requires coherence. Various aspects of policy have been discussed in largely piecemeal fashion above, but it must be stressed again that all the individual elements of a strategy must be evaluated in terms of their interaction and over-all impact and not simply as isolated items. A piecemeal approach is likely to be marked by inconsistency and inefficiency. For example, raising the income of the urban informal sector by subsidising the creation of jobs is likely both to reduce the funds available for basic services and to cause an absolute increase in urban unemployment by encouraging rural-urban migration. Indeed, the meaning of many individual measures cannot be evaluated outside a package and a specific country context. An example is wage controls. These can be used as part of an income equalisation and employment promotion strategy, as part of a price stabilisation policy not primarily directed to increasing employment or output, or as a means of increasing profits.

A weakness of many formulations of national development policy is that they are divorced from political reality. They tend to assume the existence of an autonomous State which pursues a generalised national interest as articulated by its technicians, independent of political constraints. At best such an approach can outline the institutional and technical means for a strategy, the level and distribution of its costs and benefits, and alternative technically practicable sequences and combinations of measures. Left at that point, however, a strategy is not capable of being implemented. In order to put a plan into action account must be taken of the size and organisation of the interest groups and regional coalitions which would benefit or lose from the proposed policies and the consequential changes in social status and political influence. The political and administrative implications of some of the policies recommended by the ILO employment mission to Kenya have been examined in this light, and the likely supporters and opponents of a wide variety of policies identified.[1]

Some general points can be made about certain political implications of the proposed new approach to development. In most developing countries a substantial majority of the population would benefit from a needs-oriented strategy. The potential beneficiaries are, however, seldom organised in such a way as to be able to exert sustained pressure on their own behalf. They also lack sufficient education, status and wealth to contribute effectively to political and administrative processes. The proposed new policy would also entail costs for at least some upper-income groups, and these, while small in numbers, are usually well organised and able to exert sustained pressure on officials and politicians.

Because of the divergences among interest groups and within classes, governments often have some degree of flexibility in initiating policy and strategy changes. Their ability to implement them, however, is clearly related to their ability to promote consensus, weaken groups likely to lose from them and organise support from those who would benefit. In this connection, the active participation of trade unions and peasant organisations is an important factor. Labour administrations have a particularly important role to play in government machinery in view of their over-all concern with social policies. In many countries, however, their main weakness is that they have little or no contact with the large poverty groups in the rural areas and the urban informal sector. Some broadening of the role of labour administrations in such countries seems necessary.

In some circumstances a national commitment might help to overcome the opposition of some groups. Their allegiance to national development may, under favourable conditions, override their immediate material interests. Given organised mass support, such groups may not be a threat to the viability of the proposed approach, but their lack of commitment to it may reduce the efficiency of its implementation. This will be especially true if a significant portion of highly trained manpower joins the " brain drain " as a result of the introduction of the new approach.

---

[1] Warren Ilchman and Norman Uphoff: " Beyond the economics of labor-intensive development: politics and administration ", in *Public Policy*, 22 (2) (Harvard University Press, Spring, 1974).

The main prerequisite for the effective implementation of this approach would thus appear to be an effective, decentralised and democratic administrative structure to translate policies into decisions and action, and mass participation in the development process by the poverty groups. Non-conventional administrative procedures and career patterns are also called for, because the new system requires much greater discipline and commitment on the part of civil servants.

As expressed in the Director-General's Report to the Asian Regional Conference, " for the policies to be adopted and to be implemented persistently it is no doubt necessary to give the poverty groups a political weight which is much more commensurate with their number than it is where mass poverty is widespread; organisation of these groups is a major means of bringing this about ".[1] Organising the unorganised poverty groups is accordingly a priority requirement.

Action will be necessary to make the problems of poverty better known to the more prosperous sections of the society, to sensitise public opinion to them, and to mobilise support for policy measures for the alleviation of poverty. At the same time, the poor themselves should be helped to organise, through education and the development of an appropriate institutional framework.

This could be supported by educating the leaders of various groups (for example trade unionists, co-operative movement leaders and community development workers) who might be able to assist in the organisation of the poor, or could indirectly represent them or defend their interests. Mass functional education programmes could be developed to give the poor and underprivileged basic knowledge in the field of organisation. Alternative forms of co-operative organisations might be studied, or new types of community development programmes specially designed for the poorest sections of society. Local government structures might also be looked at from the angle of the degree of popular participation they afford.

It is rarely possible to mount balanced assaults on all goals at the same time. Institutional, financial, political and administrative constraints necessitate the adoption of a selective approach in using policy instruments and careful attention to the timing of new initiatives and programmes. The criteria for choosing priority tasks at any given time would generally be that a target is of critical importance, that its attainment is possible, and that the means used will help resolve subsequent priority problems or at least not aggravate them. For each criterion, political and administrative as well as economic considera-

---

[1] ILO: *The poor in Asian development: an ILO programme*, Report of the Director-General, Eighth Asian Regional Conference, Colombo, Sep.-Oct. 1975 (Geneva, 1975), p. 76. Also Rural Workers' Organisation Recommendation, 1975 (No. 149), adopted by the International Labour Conference at its 60th Session (1975).

tions are important. For example, agrarian reform is practicable only if political forces with more strength than those of the landlords can be mobilised.

While basic long-term targets and the means for reaching them can be planned well in advance, interim strategies need to retain a significant degree of flexibility.

The length and complexity of the transitional phase in implementing a basic-needs approach depends on many factors, including particularly the extent of any initial redistributive measures that would be required.

One virtually inevitable transitional problem is an initial rise in the demand for basic goods ahead of the increase in supply. The greater the speed and effectiveness with which income and wealth are redistributed, the more rapid will be the increase in the demand for basic household goods. Similarly, the broader and faster is the spread of mass organisation and mass participation, the stronger will be the pressure for a rapid extension of public services. These increases in the effective demand for specific goods and services constitute evidence of the initial success of the approach, not of its failure. But unless there is considerable excess capacity, or a high supply elasticity, or abundant foreign exchange with which to purchase imports, the introduction of the proposed approach is likely to be accompanied initially by a shortage of basic goods. Unless these are anticipated and remedial measures introduced, such shortages could undermine public support for the entire programme.

The initial phase of implementation may also cause a temporary fall in production. The specific reasons for this vary widely from one country to another and seem to depend mainly on the social structure and on the composition of output. Anticipation of the impact of specific measures, based on detailed case-by-case studies, should allow governments to plan how to minimise the output losses arising from each policy change and to identify the sequence of institutional and redistributive measures which keeps total losses to a manageable order of magnitude.

It is unlikely that transitional problems of excess demand for basic goods or losses of production can be avoided entirely. To avoid the first would imply failure to increase the effective demand of the poor; to prevent the latter would require the absence of any major redistribution policy. The probable growth in demand for essential goods and services and probable interim losses in supply can be projected, with a view to allocating resources to reconcile them. It should be possible in the short run to increase the supply of basic goods by changing the composition of imports or increasing their volume, possibly financed by exporting goods previously consumed by upper-income groups. Food aid could also be particularly appropriate for this purpose. If the necessary increase in imports is not feasible, a temporary rationing system may be the best way to avoid a rise in prices. In the longer run, however, production will have to be increased, by expanding employment and raising the productivity of labour.

Because of uncertainty and the consequent need for flexibility, even a well articulated and fully established basic-needs approach will always be in a state of transition. As the minimum targets approach attainment, new, higher and more challenging targets will be set. Because development is a process in which targets, however realistic, have to be modified in the light of both failures and successes, transition is not a brief phase but an integral part of the quest for a more prosperous and equitable society.

It may be useful, before drawing conclusions from this general presentation, to recapitulate the main ingredients of the proposed new approach to development:

1. It requires raising the volume and productivity of employment, and hence the incomes, of the poverty groups, whose basic needs are manifestly not being met.

2. For this purpose, it calls for increased investment in the " traditional " agricultural and " informal " urban sectors and the removal of obstacles to their development, especially by reducing inequalities of access to production services and assets.

3. It requires provision of basic consumer services to the entire population, financed from progressive taxation.

4. It entails reduced inequality of household consumption of goods and services for meeting basic needs.

5. It uses trade expansion—and other measures for improved international economic relations agreed upon at the Seventh Special Session of the United Nations General Assembly—as instruments to meet import requirements without excessive or permanent dependence on foreign aid.

6. It calls for the setting up of institutions which facilitate popular participation in the development process through trade unions and similar organisations, in order to ensure a continuing national commitment to a basic-needs approach.

As was emphasised earlier in this report, each country will have to decide for itself the most suitable policy options with a view to launching and implementing such a strategy. Generalisations would be risky and perhaps meaningless in a world which is characterised by so much diversity. A few concluding remarks may however be in order.

First, it is believed that a " package " approach, which combines different but inter-related elements and calls for their introduction jointly, is likely to lead to the successful implementation of the strategy.

Second, meeting the minimum basic needs of the poor within the space of a single generation is bound to involve structural changes and major policy reorientations. The time span needed for the attainment of basic-needs targets through conventional strategies is believed to be much longer. While this period could be shortened by combining growth with an explicit policy of redistribution, a shift in the pattern of growth itself would also be essential.

Third, although the details would vary from country to country, a basic minimum of components of such a strategy include greater access of poverty groups to resources such as land, education and other social services, appropriate fiscal and other policies for resource mobilisation and the redistribution of income, and the institutional reforms necessary to translate these policies into action.

Fourth, irrespective of the weight attached to the different components of the strategy, its implementation requires a political commitment and appropriate administrative capacity and structure.

Fifth, participation of the poverty groups in the policy-making process is a priority requirement to ensure that their interests are taken care of. The organisation of these groups, which are at present largely unorganised, is a means of giving them a weight commensurate with their numbers.

Although the approach proposed here is characterised by a higher degree of self-reliance, the minimum basic needs of the poor in developing countries will be met more quickly to the extent that the international environment is favourable and international assistance available. These aspects are discussed in more detail in later chapters.

The ILO itself may be able to assist in a number of ways. If the proposed approach to development strategy is found useful, it may be desirable to hold one or more expert meetings to examine its implications in more detail and compare national experiences. Assistance could be provided to governments or workers' organisations on request in the establishment of national basic-needs targets and minimum living standards, in the promotion of organisations for the poverty groups, and in the formulation and implementation of appropriate national strategies and policies. Research under the World Employment Programme might be directed to some of the problems outlined in the previous pages.

Moreover, while it has been stressed in this chapter and in Chapter 2 that the basic-needs targets will have to vary from one country to another, the Conference may wish to consider whether it would not be desirable to establish a universal level of minimum basic needs as targets to be achieved within a generation and to which all countries would be committed. Should the Conference so decide, it could envisage various ways in which a set of such minimum targets could be proposed to, and adopted by, the ILO member States and the world community. It could, for instance, recommend that such target setting be included in the revision of the International Development Strategy for the Second United Nations Development Decade and in the preparation of international policies for the Decade beginning in 1980. It could propose that international agreements and/or instruments be adopted by the international agencies concerned. It could also examine the extent to which existing ILO standards—for example the 1964 instruments on employment policy—might be revised or new instruments adopted. The objective would be to commit all nations to working together to achieve the targets thus set—both for their own populations and for the populations of other countries.

EUROPEAN SOCIALIST COUNTRIES

4

On the whole the USSR and other European socialist countries have achieved rapid rates of growth of net material product in recent years while avoiding major cyclical fluctuations.[1] This does not imply that employment problems have been absent. There remain difficulties associated with longer-term manpower planning and the provision of high-productivity employment which, in some respects, are similar to those encountered by the industrialised market economies in their pursuit of structural change and development.

These socialist countries have also attained a stage of development such that the material basic needs of their populations have largely been met. Basic needs in these countries are therefore more of a qualitative nature.

THE PURSUIT OF FULL EMPLOYMENT

Although specific policies differ from one socialist country to another, employment problems are now viewed in all of them as part of the more general problem of improving productivity and efficiency both at the level of the firm and in the economy as a whole. While their labour problems do not therefore include those of unemployment and surplus labour, it was not always so.

In the early years of Soviet planning the authorities had to grapple with a serious problem of urban unemployment and extremely low-productivity employment in rural areas. The strategy adopted was to link employment policy to a programme of rapid industrialisation. That is, the attainment of full employment became a by-product of the priority accorded to industry. This

---

[1] Net material product includes the following economic activities: agriculture, forestry, fishing, hunting, mining, manufacturing, construction, transport and communications, trade and catering. It differs from the concept of net national product used in other countries in excluding public administration, defence, personal and professional services and similar activities.

was a distinctive feature of employment policy not only in the USSR but in the other socialist countries as well.

Rapid accumulation, industrialisation, reorganisation of agriculture and manpower planning thus formed a package only partly designed to solve the employment problem. To achieve full employment these national policies were supplemented by more local programmes and policies, often of an ad hoc and temporary nature. Labour-intensive public works schemes were introduced; multiple shift working was increased; work squads of the unemployed were formed; training and retraining programmes were established; and when all else failed, cash benefits were distributed to the unemployed.

Careful attention was paid to the choice of technology, particularly in the early stages when unemployment was a significant problem. In general, enterprises used capital-intensive techniques in the new branches of industry, where this was dictated by the character of the production process, but it was decided to use labour-intensive, capital-saving methods of production in those industries in which there was the possibility of choice, and in which the use of low-mechanised technology was justified from the point of view of the maximum utilisation of all available resources, including manpower. Labour-intensive methods were especially important in the ancillary operations in industry, not only in the USSR but also in Poland and Hungary.

Similarly, small-scale industry played an important role in the early stages of development in the USSR. Most of these industries were located in rural areas and thus were able to take advantage of the availability of enormous numbers of seasonally unemployed workers and provide for them a supplement to their income from farming. These small-scale industries had many additional advantages: they required little capital investment; they used local rather than scarce imported resources and technology; by being close to the market, they saved on transport; and in the case of some products—carpets, furs, lace and embroidery—they even earned foreign exchange. As the degree of industrialisation and the relative abundance of capital increased, these industries gradually disappeared.

RECENT EMPLOYMENT EXPERIENCE AND EMERGING PROBLEMS

According to official statistics, in all socialist countries, except in Yugoslavia, open unemployment was virtually eliminated by the 1950s. In subsequent years a combination of a shift of labour out of agriculture, increasing female participation in the paid labour force and the coming of age of children born in the postwar baby boom ensured that labour bottlenecks did not arise until recently. In future, however, labour scarcity is likely to become an increasing problem.

Table 8. Average rate of increase of output per worker, 1961-74
(per cent per annum)

Country	1961-70	1971-74
Bulgaria	7.6	n.a.
Czechoslovakia	3.5	4.6
German Democratic Republic	4.5	5.5
Hungary	4.7	6.5
Poland	4.4	7.9
Romania	6.6	6.2
USSR	5.8	4.8

n.a. = not available.
Source: Statistical data supplied by United Nations, Economic Commission for Europe; for Romania, Statistical Yearbook of the Socialist Republic of Romania (Bucharest, 1975).

The able-bodied population is increasing by less than 1 per cent a year in several socialist countries. In fact, total employment increased very slowly throughout the 1960s. It grew most rapidly in Poland (1.6 per cent a year), showed no change in Romania and Bulgaria and actually declined fractionally in the German Democratic Republic. These tendencies are unlikely to alter in the coming years.

In such circumstances it is evident that sustained rapid growth of output depends on a rapid increase in the productivity of labour. Indeed, as table 8 indicates, productivity rose very quickly during the 1960s in all the European socialist countries (as it did in all the developed countries). Only in the USSR does the rate of increase in productivity appear to be slowing down at all, although this may now be happening in Czechoslovakia also. In Poland, Hungary and the German Democratic Republic productivity growth is still accelerating.

Nevertheless, the high rates of growth of output have been accompanied by emerging new problems in the employment sphere: labour scarcity, problems of adjustment to a rapidly changing sectoral composition, high rates of turnover and an increasing unwillingness of workers to engage in arduous, dirty, dangerous or otherwise unpleasant tasks. The socialist economies, like the industrialised market economies, thus face the challenge of improving both the efficiency of manpower utilisation and the quality of the work environment.

The recent rapid growth in output and productivity has been accompanied by a high degree of apparent price stability. In all of the socialist countries consumer prices are determined by government and can, therefore, be kept virtually stable. Thus in Czechoslovakia the prices of basic consumer goods have not changed in 20 years, although prices have risen slightly for non-essential goods. In Hungary the rate of inflation has recently increased to about 3 per cent a year.

Price policies have been complemented by wage and income policies. The wage structure in the European socialist countries is characterised by low differentials. In Bulgaria, for example, the minimum wage is about two-thirds the average salary of all enterprises.

In addition, a considerable part of the national income in socialist countries is distributed in kind to the population in the form of collective or public consumption. Health and educational services, for example, are free, as is the use of many cultural, recreational and sporting facilities.

As a consequence of these policies the socialist countries have created a society in which the distribution of income is relatively egalitarian. The World Bank publication mentioned earlier in this report, for instance, contains data on five European socialist countries, namely Bulgaria, Hungary, Poland, Czechoslovakia and Yugoslavia, which were classified as countries with " low inequality ". In all but one the share of income received by the poorest 40 per cent of the population was at least 23 per cent, the exception being Yugoslavia where, in 1968, the share was 18.5 per cent. Czechoslovakia (in 1964) was the most egalitarian of the five countries, the share of the lower 40 per cent of its population being the highest of the 66 countries covered in the study, viz. 27.6 per cent.

STRUCTURAL CHANGE IN THE EUROPEAN SOCIALIST ECONOMIES

The trends in growth, productivity, prices and income distribution which have been described occurred during a period of swift structural change. The proportion of the labour force engaged in industry and construction rose rapidly in all countries: by 1973 the proportion varied from 36.3 per cent in Romania to 49.9 per cent in the German Democratic Republic.

The expansion of industrial output and employment has been associated with a steady fall in the proportion of the labour force engaged in agriculture and forestry. As can be seen in table 9 the proportion is still rather high in all the countries except Czechoslovakia and the German Democratic Republic, and much higher than in most industrialised market economies, but the occupational composition of the labour force continues to shift rapidly.

As in the industrialised market economies, increasing proportions of the labour force are also being absorbed in the services sector. Indeed in Czechoslovakia and the German Democratic Republic more people are already engaged in supplying educational, cultural and health services than are employed in agriculture, and the proportions are approaching equality in the USSR. Additional numbers, of course, are being employed in trade and related

Table 9. Proportion of the labour force engaged in agriculture and forestry, 1960 and 1973 (percentages)

Country	1960	1973
Bulgaria	55.5	31.5
Czechoslovakia	25.9	15.9
German Democratic Republic	17.3	11.6
Hungary	38.9	24.4
Poland	44.2	32.2
Romania	65.6	42.1
USSR	38.7	25.2
Yugoslavia	57.0	44.0

Source: *Statistical Yearbook of the CMEA 1974* (Moscow, 1975). For Yugoslavia, ILO: *Yearbook of Labour Statistics*, 1966 and 1975.

activities, and this proportion is likely to increase at a rising rate if priorities continue to shift in favour of consumer goods.

Again, as in the industrialised market economies, efficient development can be achieved through the reallocation of labour from low productivity to higher productivity activities. The need for such improvement in labour utilisation is particularly evident in the socialist economies where labour shortages are already making an appearance and there is little prospect of relief from population growth or increased labour force participation rates.

It is anticipated that by 1981-85 the able-bodied population will fall in Bulgaria and Hungary, remain roughly constant in Czechoslovakia and rise only about 0.7 per cent a year in Romania. The current labour shortage in Poland is likely to persist for some years as a consequence of the fall in the population growth rate and the high rate of economic growth. In the USSR there will be continued shortage of manpower in big cities, on new construction sites, and especially in regions with a low population density such as Siberia or the Far East, where enormous mineral and energy reserves are located.

Moreover, the rapid growth of education and training is certain to result in a fall in the proportion of the able-bodied population engaged in productive occupations. Nor is there any possibility of increasing substantially the participation rate of women since they already constitute a large proportion of the paid labour force. At present, of the total number of women of working age, 75 per cent are in paid employment in Bulgaria, Hungary and Romania, 85 per cent in Czechoslovakia, 80 per cent in the German Democratic Republic, over 70 per cent in Poland and over 80 per cent in the USSR. There is also a problem of high rates of labour turnover, particularly among young workers engaged in arduous jobs in remote areas.

The most productive utilisation of labour and the possibilities of overcoming labour shortages depend upon the sectoral allocation of labour, which is itself related to the extent and nature of these economies' participation in international trade, and on the speed of technical progress. Of particular concern in the European socialist economies is the allocation of labour between agriculture and industry. In the past, it is generally agreed, agriculture has received inadequate attention in most European socialist countries. This is now being remedied to some extent, but past neglect has resulted in rather large differences in productivity between the agricultural and the industrial sectors. The need to increase the availability of a wide range of foodstuffs as well as to make additional labour available to the expanding industrial and service sectors both point to the desirability of further increases in investment and efficiency in the agricultural sector. Faster technical progress in agriculture can, by making additional labour available to other sectors, make a further important contribution to over-all efficiency and growth.

The organisation of the agricultural sector varies considerably from one socialist country to another. At one extreme is Poland, where the degree of collectivisation is low. State farms, co-operatives and agricultural groups account for only 23 per cent of the arable land, the rest being under private holdings, typically in farms of 5-10 hectares. At the other extreme is Bulgaria, where virtually all land is collectivised, and where the average size of the co-operative farms has increased from 2,000 to 4,000 hectares in the 1950s to 20,000 to 30,000 hectares today. In between is Romania: about 9 per cent of the land is owned by individual farmers, about 30 per cent comes under the state sector and 60 per cent under co-operatives.

The agricultural sector of the USSR is, of course, much larger than that of the other socialist countries and its performance strongly affects the average of the group as a whole. Co-operative farms predominate, although there are many state farms as well; output from private plots now accounts for about 15 per cent of marketable farm output.

In the past 15 years considerable effort has been devoted to increasing output and productivity in the agricultural sector in the USSR. Investment in farming has increased faster than in industry and its share of the total has almost doubled, from 14 per cent in 1960 to 27 per cent in 1974. Agricultural incentives have been improved: the prices received by farmers have been raised and a special bonus for surpluses has been introduced. Production has responded to these measures, but continues to fluctuate, partly because of changes in climatic conditions.

During the 1960s agricultural output in the USSR increased at an annual rate of 3.1 per cent. In the first four years of the present decade, however, the rate of growth fell to 2.1 per cent a year, partly as a result of the poor weather and consequent bad harvests of 1972 and 1974. The harvest in 1975 also was bad. The key problem arises from the fact that the growth of income per head has led to a rapid increase in the demand for meat, which in turn has implied an equally rapid growth in the demand for feed grains. Hitherto, large numbers of livestock were slaughtered in years of bad harvests, but with the new policy of increasing and maintaining meat consumption there were instead very large grain imports in 1972 and 1975.

Parallel to the need for faster progress in agriculture, there is an increasingly recognised need to shift more resources to the production of manufactured consumer goods. Any shift of emphasis from the production of intermediate and capital goods industries to that of consumer goods and services would probably, however, intensify labour shortages. In the first place, the latter on the whole tend to be more labour-intensive than the former. Secondly, such a shift implies a reduction in resources allocated to investment which in turn may slow down productivity increases. Exploitation of the opportunities offered by international trade, on the other hand, could enable socialist countries to move quickly toward higher levels of consumption through exchange of intermediate and capital goods for labour-intensive manufactured and agricultural products imported from developing countries. That is, it should be possible for the developed socialist countries to achieve some of their consumption objectives by altering the pattern of trade rather than the pattern of production. This would enable them to use the labour force more efficiently. Since the developing countries are steadily increasing their ability to produce and export manufactured goods, it would seem that both requirements of domestic policy and the needs of the poor countries point to the desirability of more intensive participation of the socialist countries in trade relations with them.

The development of the socialist economies has reached a stage where there must be simultaneously a change in the composition of output, and hence in the sectoral composition of investment, and in the rate of labour-saving technical change. In the past, because of the abundance of labour, it was possible to raise average productivity through a process of capital widening. In future, because of the achievement of full employment and the reduced rate of labour force growth, additional effort will have to be concentrated on efficient allocation, capital deepening and an acceleration in the rate of technical progress.

There is not much scope for increasing the rate of growth of employment. First, action on the birth rate, even if desirable and successful, will be effective in increasing the labour supply only in the long run. Second, there are only limited possibilities for increasing labour force participation rates or the number of hours worked. On the contrary, higher living standards and longer periods of education are, as in other developed countries, likely to result in demands for more leisure and a postponement of the age of entry into the labour force. Finally, schemes to enable students, housewives and pensioners to work on a part-time basis, while highly desirable on social grounds, are unlikely to have much effect on total labour input.

One of the possible answers to the labour problem lies in a better national and international division of labour combined with a further increase in investment in agriculture, and continued acceleration of technological progress. As has been seen, the frequently recommended sectoral shift toward the production of consumer goods may make some labour problems more difficult, because of the more labour-intensive nature of these activities. Technological progress, particularly in agriculture, is one answer, by setting people free to move to other sectors. The importation of more consumer goods from developing countries is another. This would assist in solving some of the employment and basic-needs problems in both the socialist and developing countries.

All this implies that people may have to move more and be trained or retrained more. The introduction and generalisation of incentives is likely to be an essential ingredient in facilitating this process and at the same time would help to raise the effectiveness of the decision-making process.

It is in this context that the economic reforms now under way acquire their significance. The reform movement started in the 1960s, e.g. in Hungary and the USSR, but related policies have been introduced only recently in some countries. The purpose of the economic reforms is to increase productivity by decentralising decision making and placing greater responsibility for economic performance at the branch and enterprise level. These reforms necessarily entail a shift in emphasis from administrative methods of planning to planning through the use of financial incentives and signals akin to those of market prices. The number of directives to enterprises has been reduced and the central planning authorities have tended to concentrate more on national economic management and the setting of aggregative targets. Evidently many issues are yet to be resolved. The most urgent requirement is to find a way of reconciling the independence of enterprises with national planning. The solution to the economic problems of the socialist countries requires both a reallocation of national resources among sectors and a more efficient use of resources by enterprises.

Another urgent requirement will be to satisfy the more qualitative basic needs of the citizens of socialist countries. As in other industrially advanced societies, the satisfaction of basic material needs through rising living standards and higher levels of education leads to demands for an improved quality of life; greater participation in decisions affecting management of enterprises; and an improved working environment, including greater safety, health and satisfaction at work.

The economic reforms at present under way in socialist countries, and the general loosening of central controls, should greatly facilitate the attainment of these objectives. The system of workers' self-management in Yugoslavia is one of the furthest-reaching experiments in participation in the world, and several important steps have been taken in other socialist countries to give workers greater participation in many management issues—e.g. the personnel structure and the utilisation of funds for remuneration.

The quality of the working environment, including safety and health at work and job satisfaction, is likely to have to be high on the agenda of social needs in the coming years. The socialist countries have, in this respect, a certain amount of experience, but also many problems which they share with other industrialised countries. A fuller exchange of experience with countries facing similar problems might be of mutual benefit.

INDUSTRIALISED MARKET-ECONOMY COUNTRIES

5

The industrialised market economies achieved a rapid sustained growth of output during the 1960s and early 1970s. The real GNP of OECD member States rose by 5.4 per cent per annum between 1960 and 1972. In Western Europe and Japan the rates were even higher, averaging well over 6 per cent per annum. Employment levels rose faster than population, due to an increased inflow of migrant workers and a growing proportion of women entering the labour force. There were also changes in income distribution, with the share of national income accruing to labour tending to rise, and the attainment in several countries of high standards of living.

During this period cyclical fluctuations occurred, but of a much smaller magnitude than those experienced in the boom of 1972-73 and the subsequent downturn.

Recorded unemployment rates are now at high levels in the majority of the industrialised market economies. While the definitions vary somewhat from country to country, unemployment amounted, on average, to over 5 per cent of the total labour force of these countries in September 1975 (see table 10 for a summary of the relevant data). The total number of unemployed persons, 17 million in September 1975, is considerably higher than at any time in the past 40 years. In analysing the causes of this unemployment and the related labour market problems, and possible policies for dealing with them, it is essential to distinguish between their short-run cyclical aspects and those which are related to longer-term structural changes.

SHORT-RUN CYCLICAL PROBLEMS

The present high unemployment rates indicated in table 10 are associated with an over-all recession of unusual severity in the industrialised market economies. This is reflected in stagnation or decline in real gross national product, industrial production and the volume of world trade. In some

Table 10. Unemployment rates in developed market economies
(percentage of total labour force)

Country	1965	1970	1973	1975 (September)
North America:				
Canada	3.9	5.9	5.6	8.1
United States	4.5	4.9	4.9	8.1
Asia:				
Japan	0.8	1.2	1.3	1.9
Europe:				
Austria	2.7	2.4	1.6	1.5
Belgium	2.4	2.9	3.6	6.6 (August)
Denmark	2.0	2.9	2.4	10.2 [1]
Finland	1.4	1.9	2.3	2.1
France	n.a.	n.a.	n.a.	4.1 [2]
Germany (Fed. Rep.)	0.6	0.7	1.2	4.4
Ireland	5.6	7.2	7.2	12.0 (July)
Italy	3.7	3.2	3.5	3.3 (July)
Norway	0.9	0.8	0.8	2.7 (third quarter)
Netherlands	0.7	1.1	2.7	4.8
Sweden	1.2	1.5	2.5	1.8
United Kingdom	1.5	2.6	2.7	5.4
Oceania:				
Australia	1.3	1.4	1.9	3.9 (August)

n.a. = not available.

[1] These data refer only to the insured labour force (some 40 per cent of the total). However, the means of estimating unemployment has remained the same over the whole period. The comparable figure with other countries would be around 5 per cent for 1975. [2] Unofficial estimate.

Source: ILO: *Bulletin of Labour Statistics*.

countries low open unemployment rates disguise a substantial increase in short-time working. Labour force participation rates and average hours worked also declined. This recession, which began in late 1973 and gathered force throughout 1974, has been unusual in its length, its depth and its widespread incidence. It followed an equally unprecedented boom which, particularly in its later stages, was itself associated with an unusually rapid rate of inflation. The carry-over from that boom-induced inflation, together with the increase in petroleum prices in October 1973, generated the " new " phenomenon of a severe recession accompanied by continuing rapid inflation. While the recession undoubtedly moderated this inflation somewhat, it continued at rates greater than are usually tolerated in the industrialised countries and thus inhibited governments in their application of the traditional monetary and fiscal instruments of anti-cyclical policy. The inability or reluctance of governments to introduce strong macro-economic anti-recession measures, for fear of fuelling the inflation, has undoubtedly prolonged the recession. At the same time, continued inflation has contributed to further business and household uncertainty, thus dampening investment plans, heightening the tendency to save, and exacerbating the lag in recovery.

It is anticipated that growth in industrial production and GNP will gradually be resumed in the industrialised market economies. The experience of the 1974-76 recession, however, suggests that traditional national anti-cyclical policies may be inadequate for the future management of cyclical fluctuations. In the first place, the increased interdependence of the major national market economies (notably the United States, the European Communities and Japan) reflected in the nearly perfect synchronisation of their recent cyclical experience requires that there be much closer co-ordination of domestic macro-economic and exchange rate policies than in the past. This need has already been recognised in principle. Secondly, the emergence of " stagflation " has renewed interest in incomes policies not only as a means of dampening cost-push inflationary pressures but also to tackle the problem of income relativities which may be a major cause of job dissatisfaction. Thirdly, structural changes in the developed market economies, which are discussed below, require the development of new policy instruments and new approaches for the handling of specific unemployment and labour market problems. These new policy thrusts must be able more accurately to pinpoint and remedy the sources of difficulty so that traditional macro-economic policies need not be constrained from performing their still essential over-all role.

STRUCTURAL CHANGE AND PROGRESS

Structural changes, which are accomplished over longer periods of time, regardless of temporary cyclical fluctuations in the level of economic activity, are inherent in the process of economic development, indeed in all of human progress. Such changes are not new to the industrialised market-economy countries. Since the Industrial Revolution at least, real incomes in these countries have grown not merely because of rapid rates of capital accumulation but also because labour shifted from low-productivity to higher-productivity, higher-income earning activities, because constantly improving technology was adopted, and because of the seizing of opportunities to benefit from international exchange. In the past 25 years these countries have substantially transformed their economies and achieved remarkable over-all income gains through their continuing capacities for response to changing technologies, tastes and trading opportunities. Economic policies which generally encourage innovation, stimulate competition, assist in the transition processes and, through appropriate social and manpower policies, ensure an equitable sharing of the resulting gains are those most likely to generate the economic and social dynamism which permits harmonious development and structural change.

Structural change takes a variety of forms. The easiest to accommodate is that which arises from shifts among or within similar industries and results in over-all expansion of production as new goods or services are produced to meet additional demands generated by increasing productivity and incomes. The development of the electronics industries, for example, had these characteristics. Employment and management, technical and manual skills expanded with the growth of the electronics industries, creating new opportunities for workers in lower-productivity occupations and new entrants into the workforce.

The growth of trade among the industrialised market-economy countries led to shifts of industry but, because much of it was intra-industry trade, firms and workers found it relatively easy to accommodate to the increasing degrees of specialisation involved by marginal increases of investment and skills over time. Internal industry shifts, such as those to the production of smaller motor cars now taking place within the motor vehicle industry and the incorporation of environmental safeguards in many others, are also relatively easy to accomplish, particularly in well managed economies that penalise inefficiency and reward productivity increases. There is, however, a concern that the new emphasis on environmental protection, by making production more costly, may retard the rate of growth in the long run. This is of course an option that an affluent society might prefer. But its potential impact on employment levels in both industrialised and developing economies should not be ignored. It is, however, worthy of note that environmental protection in itself generally creates employment.

The expanded imports of manufactures from developing countries by the developed market countries raise certain special problems. The characteristics of the developed-country industries involved in exporting to developing countries are totally different from and typically unrelated to the characteristics of those most affected by the recent rapid growth in manufactured imports from much lower-cost countries. The prospects for increased intra-industry trade in both directions such as has typified trade expansion within the European Communities are rather remote. The adjustment of affected firms and workers to this particular type of trade may therefore be correspondingly more difficult. That is not to say, of course, that these potential difficulties are at all insurmountable. Chapter 7 is devoted to the policy issues surrounding the expansion of that trade with developing countries.

In the 1950s and 1960s considerable shifts of labour from declining to expanding industries did in fact take place. Whilst employment in the labour-intensive industries of Belgium, the German Federal Republic, Sweden and the

United Kingdom declined by some 700,000 in the 1960s, *total* industrial employment in these countries increased by 600,000. Again, the European Coal and Steel Community, for example, has been able, through its social policies, to help in the redeployment of large numbers of miners displaced by imports of oil and by natural-gas discoveries. Indeed, this has been cited as one of the most striking examples of rapid structural change, facilitated by progressive adjustment policies, to take advantage of a new international division of labour. However, as a result of the substantial shift in energy prices and the security risks incurred by a heavy dependence on imports, a reappraisal of energy policies has taken place in the developed market economies. This may lead to greater self-sufficiency. This case illustrates the importance of finding a balance of advantage in trading relations so that the gains are fairly distributed between the trading partners.

It is generally more difficult to bring about structural change when the effects are highly localised (particularly when the new jobs are available only in other parts of the country), when particular groups are disproportionately affected (e.g. women) or if the industry is regarded as " traditional " or " natural " or " socially important ". For instance, agriculture is often regarded as " a way of life " as well as an industry, and " traditional values " are supposedly buttressed by its support. A variety of arguments are elicited to justify an industry's special qualification for protection. They may have validity and substantial appeal to those directly concerned, particularly during times of recession. But the industrialised countries have achieved their economic pre-eminence through constant adjustment to technology, markets and tastes. The need for change in a society which desires to satisfy its citizens should not be in dispute; what must, above all, be sought is the most socially acceptable and economically efficient method of effecting the change.

STRUCTURAL CHANGE IN THE INDUSTRIALISED MARKET-ECONOMY COUNTRIES

The industrialised market-economy countries represent a wide spectrum ranging from those, such as the United Kingdom, which have recently experienced lagging rates of growth and capital accumulation as well as structural problems to those, such as Japan, some of the Scandinavian countries and the Netherlands, which have recently grown more rapidly. They have combined efficiency and equity in such a way that the bulk of their population has been able to enjoy unprecedented levels of private consumption together with a high degree of access to public goods and services. These countries are also the ones which have been able to handle the present recession with relative ease. There is no necessary correlation, however, between the severity of a country's structural problems and the level of unemployment at any particular moment. The United Kingdom, for example, has certain recognised structural problems yet has managed to have a low rate of unemployment until very recently.

International comparisons must, in any case, be made with considerable caution because of the differences that exist from country to country in the measurement of unemployment, and because of their varying circumstances.

One must be wary, then, of over-generalisation about the structural characteristics of the industrialised market economies. There are nevertheless some common features in their recent experience. Measured unemployment rates, for instance, are typically higher today, even in boom periods, than they were 25 years ago. Moreover, within each national labour force the incidence of unemployment varies enormously among constituent groups. The aggregated unemployment data are therefore in some respects misleading. In particular, unemployment rates are noticeably higher for females, the young and certain minority groups. In the United States, for example, while the national unemployment rate in May 1975 was 9.2 per cent, that for adult males was 7.3 per cent, that for adult females 8.6 per cent, that for teenagers 22 per cent and that for black teenagers 40 per cent.[1] They are also highly variable among areas of the same country. In the United Kingdom, while the national ratio of registered unemployed to notified unfilled vacancies in mid-1975 was 6.1, that in Wales was 14.0 and that in the north-west was 15.0.[2]

As far as the structure of production is concerned, there is under way a general shift from industrial activities to the service sectors. Some of these expanding service activities are quite labour-intensive and the occupations within them relatively poorly remunerated. Others are " social " activities, such as nursing services for the aged and the handicapped. The demand for such services is likely to grow as the average span of life is extended. These are basic-needs services which an affluent society should be able to afford. However, productivity growth, as best we can measure it, in these parts of the service sector typically lags behind that in the manufacturing sector. Thus implicit in some of these shifts may be a slow-down in aggregate economic growth as conventionally measured. Some expanding service activities are, however, highly intensive in the use of knowledge and skill and are likely to generate high returns from improved productive technologies either for domestic use or for sale to other countries. Nevertheless, since social welfare is clearly increased by these intersectoral shifts, alternatives to the conventional growth accounting seem deserving of exploration.

---

[1] OECD: *Economic Outlook*, July 1975, p. 30.
[2] *Barclays Review*, Nov. 1975, pp. 77 and 90.

At least as important as this broad intersectoral shift is that within the industrial and agricultural sectors toward more skill-intensive and capital-intensive activities resulting from labour-saving technical changes. The labour thus released is the major source of the increased labour for the expanding service sectors mentioned above. To some extent, this shift is associated with the expansion of labour-intensive imports from poorer countries.

Whatever the specific intra-industry or inter-industry shifts which have been taking place in any particular country, the increasing average unemployment levels suggest growing difficulties in maintaining the " match " between the composition of demand and that of supply in the labour markets of developed countries. To some extent this may result from the very pace of the change in the composition of demand; labour force characteristics are lagging behind the shift to more skill-intensive industries, with, as has been seen, particularly unfortunate effects for women, the unskilled and the disadvantaged.

Women form an unduly large proportion of the workers affected by competitive imports and other structural changes. The relatively shorter education of girls is one reason, but the lack of opportunities open to women in highly skilled, productive and well remunerated trades such as engineering and electrical trades is a more important one. Although women account for a substantial proportion of the workforce in industrialised market economies, they still tend to be clustered in unskilled, labour-intensive industries and in traditionally " women's " occupations which have correspondingly low remuneration. The lack of employment opportunities is underlined by inadequate child-care and other supporting social services, so that they are often forced into narrow, part-time, broken-shift segments of the service sectors where remuneration is particularly low, and they are consequently the first to be laid off in case of difficulties.

By no means all of the structural changes taking place in the developed market economies are the product of exogenous technological change, inter-industry shifts in production or alterations in the international division of labour. Underlying the shift to service activities, for example, is a significant general alteration in societal attitudes to work, leisure and the quality of life. This change of attitudes, in addition to influencing the over-all composition of demand and hence the output mix (since most of these services are not tradeable), also influences the supply side of the labour market.

Attitudes towards work in the wealthier countries are changing in a number of ways. In the first place, there is now far more public concern with income distribution than merely with the right to employment. Incomes policies designed to ensure an equitable distribution of income and wealth, or at least of additions thereto, have everywhere become matters for public discussion and, already in some instances, implementation. A right to a minimum-needs income, commensurate with the productive capacity of the whole society, has become a major issue. In some countries such income guarantees have by and large been achieved by the combination of constructive structural change with social policies which ensure the transfer of funds to the disadvantaged groups in society. In others " negative income tax " proposals, aiming at similar objectives, are under active consideration.

In virtually all the industrialised market economies there have been vast improvements in systems for the provision of benefits for unemployed workers. In the 1930s workers were simply laid off despite inadequate and often non-existent unemployment relief. During the past 25 years the industrialised market-economy countries have all built up systems of unemployment compensation rather than mere relief. These again differ from country to country, but in general they provide at least a temporary " floor " so that a family or individual income earner affected by unemployment does not fall below some basic level. In countries with high standards of unemployment compensation, including such relatively high-unemployment countries as Canada and the United States, average unemployment benefits do not fall far short of the wages normally received by unskilled workers. Many countries have also recently extended the periods for which unemployment compensation is available. These various social security schemes could now be said to constitute a " basic-needs " policy in the developed country context. The Conference may wish to consider how they may be strengthened in order to meet the evolving " basic-needs " or poverty standards in industrialised countries.

Secondly, workers in the developed countries are increasingly concerned with the conditions of their workplaces. They now seek " better " jobs rather than merely more jobs and therefore resist unnecessarily authoritarian organisational structures; and they are less and less tolerant of routine, dirty, unsafe or otherwise unpleasant occupations. Pressures for greater worker participation in management decision making are part of this new attitude towards employment. These questions were thoroughly discussed at the 1974 International Labour Conference which gave the mandate for expanded ILO activities in the field of working conditions. In response, the ILO recently launched an International Programme for the Improvement of Working Conditions and Environment. This should provide valuable assistance to governments, trade unions, and employers' organisations in meeting these aspirations in the years to come.

Thirdly, another dimension of this altered set of workers' preferences is their more frequent objective, and even expectation, of upward mobility during their working lives in terms both of skill and of responsibility. Such objectives contrast with attitudes more often characteristic of societies in which workers typically value the right to a specific job rather than the opportunity for movement to more interesting and skilled jobs. Expectations of upward mobility imply considerable demands on a country's educational and social policies. They presuppose a strong and effective education system in which all children, regardless of social background, have access to high-quality education. Such a system cannot be confined to secondary and tertiary education but must provide opportunities for continuing education and training throughout a worker's life.

Increased workforce mobility also requires that all the social benefits to which a worker is entitled—medical benefits, unemployment insurance, leave and pension rights—are vestible, that is, that the workers can take them with them as they move to more challenging opportunities. While this vestibility is generally found in Europe, benefits in Japan and the United States are more frequently tied to a firm or sometimes to an industry, limiting the ability of workers to respond to opportunities created by structural change.

Lastly, the trade-off between leisure and additional consumption of goods and services is also becoming an increasingly important issue as standards of living rise. There are of course national differences in this respect. United States and Canadian wage contracts tend to emphasise hourly earnings, while European trade unions have traditionally been relatively more concerned with paid holidays and pensions. Australian unions have won three months' long-service leave after ten years' work. A minimum of four weeks' annual leave has been generalised in France. But the value of leisure is rising generally with the rise in earnings, so that pressure is developing for a shorter working week and higher premiums for overtime, shift and weekend work. Educational leave, " sabbaticals " and more flexible retirement options are also frequently on the agenda for labour market bargaining and planning, in line with the provisions of the Paid Educational Leave Convention (No. 140) and Recommendation (No. 148) of 1974.

All of these alterations in tastes and employment structures by now make it necessary to consider redefining the very concept of " full employment ". Undoubtedly part of the higher recorded rate of unemployment is attributable to the longer periods spent by workers in searching for more attractive work opportunities or in individually arranged " sabbaticals ", both of which are rendered more attractive by higher over-all wages and improved unemployment benefits. Another element in this unemployment is that of highly educated individuals who have acquired sophisticated skills which do not happen to correspond to the composition of the effective demand for labour. In such circumstances, such graduates may be forced to view their education simply as a consumer good which carries its own reward and resign themselves to greater flexibility in their job aspirations. Where such unemployment is the product of the " voluntary " choice of workers who are looking for " better " jobs or expressing a preference for leisure and are able to afford it, it should not be given the same policy attention as that imposed upon workers from minority groups or depressed areas who would readily seize upon any job opportunities which arose.

SHORT-TERM EMPLOYMENT POLICIES

The macro-economic policy instruments available to the governments of industrialised market-economy countries for the purpose of dampening cyclical fluctuations through the manipulation of aggregate demand and the money supply are well known. As has been seen, structural changes in these economies may be rendering it more difficult to engage successfully in this type of aggregate " fine tuning " and may even be calling some of the traditional policy targets into question. Many of the micro-level policy instruments which can be deployed against the specific victims of cyclical unemployment may also be used for pinpointed attacks upon the roots of structural and longer-term problem groups and areas. Without wishing to de-emphasise in the slightest the importance of suitable monetary and fiscal policies for effective macro-management of the developed countries' economies, the discussion here will concentrate upon the increasingly important micro-economic policy weapons.

Government expenditures on specific projects

Government expenditures upon particular socially desirable projects—particularly in the light of changing preferences in such fields as urban housing or construction, environmental protection and land reclamation—can be timed so as to alleviate cyclical unemployment. Public works programmes have long been recognised as potentially useful anti-unemployment measures. They now acquire new importance because of the ease with which they can be directed at the particular target groups and areas which are increasingly the object of social concern and because of the increased public valuation of their " output ".

Some national governments, in addition to developing their own programmes, have encouraged local government authorities to prepare contingency construction plans which can be activated in a recession. In Sweden, for example, the central Government subsidises the cost of preparing such plans and makes special funds available in a recession to finance building and other municipal investments. Norway also encourages municipalities to keep an inventory of planned public works which can be implemented at short notice.

Government assistance to specific industries

Some industries are highly prone to cyclical fluctuations, and governments have therefore focused demand upon them in periods of recession as a quick means of creating employment. Housing construction is the prime example for it is labour-intensive, provides linkages to building materials industries and, by improving the living environment, also encourages other expenditures. Italy and the Netherlands have recently expanded government house-building programmes, France has provided financial assistance for construction, the United States has eased restrictions on housing finance, and the Italian Social Housing Institute has guaranteed to purchase unsold dwellings to stimulate private building construction.

Government assistance to specific firms

Direct assistance to particular firms to prevent dismissals and stimulate employment is a relatively new development. Sweden, where firms are encouraged to initiate new investment in periods of low labour demand by tax allowances and access to previously accumulated special funds, has probably the most sophisticated set of such measures. Swedish firms hiring additional workers from the public lists of the unemployed to undertake anti-pollution investment also receive special subsidies.

In a number of countries (including Italy, Japan, Norway and the United States) firms have at times been persuaded to retain workers by direct or indirect government subsidies in spite of a temporary lack of orders. This means that the workers do not have to bear the social or economic costs of dislocation and that the firms are able to retain a skilled workforce that is interested in the viability of an enterprise. This may be particularly important when workers already enjoy some form of participation in the running of a firm. The short-term government budget costs are also generally lower than in any alternative methods of job creation. However, it does involve the considerable danger of inhibiting structural change within the firm and the economy. Careful and detailed use of government intervention is thus required if such policies are not to conflict with the need for long-term structural change.

Government assistance to workers

As has been noted above, unemployment benefits are now everywhere provided for workers who are the victims of cyclical employment fluctuations. However, new entrants to the labour force (and sometimes females or other disadvantaged groups) are not always covered by these schemes. Moreover, in particularly severe recessions such as the present one, the maximum length of time during which compensation to the unemployed can be paid under existing legislation has proven insufficient. Extension of the coverage and liberalisation of the terms of its benefits are therefore called for in most industrialised market economies.

Work-sharing programmes

The relatively high levels of remuneration prevailing in the early 1970s in the industrialised market-economy countries have made work-sharing in times of temporary difficulty much more practicable and acceptable than it would have been in earlier days. Employers and managers who wish to retain their skilled and experienced workforce without paying the full costs of maintaining it naturally favour such arrangements, but they also benefit the workers for the same reason as subsidies to firms. As has been seen, the resulting shorter working hours and longer vacations may also frequently accord with their emerging preferences.

In the United States this approach has been combined with the insurance which provides supplementary payments for workers temporarily laid off so that the combination of their unemployment compensation and earnings add up to the equivalent of full employment pay. Work-sharing arrangements there have been written into contracts in a number of industries, including textiles, clothing, rubber and plastics, transportation equipment and communications. In the Federal Republic of Germany local employment offices have actively encouraged firms to devise short-term working plans in preference to displacing workers; the Federal Ministry of Labour also extended the period of payments of short-time work benefits by area or by sector to 24 months. Many Japanese firms have traditionally guaranteed job security until retirement at 60 years to " permanent " though not to temporary employees. In times of recession the firms use the workers for activities which are not immediately productive and reduce working hours.

POLICIES FOR STRUCTURAL CHANGE

All of the policies considered for the alleviation of short-term employment problems are also usable for the purpose of overcoming some of the employment problems generated by longer-term structural factors. The latter, however, involve certain specific difficulties, requiring the elaboration of further policies which at the same time support both equitable and efficient long-term development. Trade unions, employers and governments should co-operate in the development of such policies which are in their joint interest. Those relating particularly to the expansion of trade with developing countries are reserved for further discussion in Chapter 7.

Labour market policies

As has been seen, unemployment benefit programmes now provide a basic income " floor " for workers who are laid off and fail immediately to find another job. Where structural problems rather than cyclical fluctuations are responsible for unemployment the temporary character of these benefits may be inadequate to maintain incomes for the often necessarily longer period of job search. In addition to extending their general coverage, as suggested above, special benefit programmes may have to be constructed for the workers in areas or industries which are particularly hard hit by structural changes.

Such special benefits may range well beyond mere income maintenance. It may be necessary to provide subsidised training for more productive jobs when on-the-job training is either not available or inadequate. Many countries now provide such training, encouraging workers to undertake it by relatively high maintenance payments. The returns both to the worker and to society on such investment are probably high.

Workers and their families may have to move to take advantage of more productive employment opportunities. In large countries particularly, this may require further assistance with the search for jobs, and in all countries workers may require assistance with actual removal expenses. The costs of moving from a depressed area where the value of houses is declining to a dynamic area where the costs of housing are high are likely to be unusually great. Since lack of housing is a frequent reason for failure to move to more productive jobs, such subsidies are again socially well worth while. Swedish adjustment-assistance measures include provision for government purchase of the houses of workers who are forced to relocate.

The frequent regional concentration of industries that have to be phased out makes for further adjustment complications. If " senile " industries are relatively labour-intensive and " footloose ", this may be because they were originally placed in rural communities to provide supplementary incomes to low-productivity agriculture. Others, developed in particular areas for reasons of a historic nature, may no longer be appropriate. If such regional problems are not solved as they arise but, in the absence of positive policies, are allowed to accumulate, the poverty of the lagging areas can adversely affect the whole economy. Adequate alternative local opportunities do not usually exist. Improving agricultural productivity is likely to reduce employment further. In some cases it may be efficient to bring in new industries but often this will not be the case. Balanced national development, giving adequate weight to the preservation of regional natural characteristics as well as to productive efficiency, is thus likely to require assistance to whole families to move to areas where productivity may be more easily increased.

In countries in which social benefits cannot be transferred from one job to another, special measures will also have to be taken to ensure that the workers do not lose their pension and other benefits. Early retirement provisions, provided they are liberal enough to provide a real inducement, are often the best solution for older workers.

Adjustment assistance for firms

Assistance with adjustment may be offered to firms (or to farmers) as well as to workers. By offering them compensation for abandoned or devalued assets and assisting them to shift their activities into areas with brighter long-term market prospects, their pressure for trade barriers and their resistance to the required structural changes may be reduced. Care has to be exercised, however, to ensure that such assistance does not become yet another example of disguised protection and subvention. It is normally to be expected that firms will have taken into consideration their long-term prospects when they entered their chosen field of activity and that therefore any necessary costs of transfer have already been allowed for in the firm's normal budgeting operations.

Some countries have taken the further step of nationalising firms affected by temporary or structural difficulties to prevent the dismissal of workers. A great deal depends on how such a policy is carried out. If it leads to greater efficiency it is clearly desirable. If it inhibits internal and external structural changes, as it quite possibly may, it probably is not. A country that accumulates marginal enterprises in its public sector will almost certainly find the management and political problems of handling such a sector increasingly difficult.

Large internationally oriented firms are generally better able to adjust themselves to changed market conditions than small domestic firms. In some instances they will be able themselves to invest in production or to purchase in a low-income country. Such investments are becoming increasingly common even in smaller firms. However, many of these smaller firms may require technical assistance in finding or developing new, more suitable products and producing them competitively. They may also require loans to undertake new production and, in some cases, to move to a new location.

Firms which adjust successfully can often continue to employ their workers. Large firms are especially likely often to find employment in expanding branches for workers from declining branches. Efforts to provide such automatic " adjustment assistance " to their own workers should obviously be encouraged.

Perhaps, in the long run, efforts by firms to improve the quality of the working environment will have a more important impact upon the " development " (broadly defined) of the industrialised market economies than any measures relating to the mere provision of jobs of whatever character. Firms should be encouraged to seek such qualitative improvements through experiments with new forms of work organisation, altered work patterns and generally better work environments. Such experimentation, which should be encouraged at least as vigorously as more " productive " innovation if the new emphasis upon the quality of life is taken seriously, may sometimes prove privately profitable. More frequently it seems likely to involve extra costs, or at least increased risks, to the experimenting firms. In addition to supporting firms structurally readjusting themselves, governments should therefore consider support for firms engaging in such quality-improving experiments.

These are just some of the ways in which social and economic policies may be harmonised to meet the changing needs and aspirations of the inhabitants of the developed market economies. The focus has been on domestic, national issues. But almost by definition these countries are participating very actively in the much wider world markets. National policies inevitably have international repercussions. Developed countries have both a responsibility and a self-interest to try to ensure that the instruments devised to further their own development goals do not have an adverse impact on their trading partners, particularly the developing countries. Greater efforts are required to reconcile conflicting interests and to strengthen complementarities so that international relationships will yield mutual benefits. This will be the theme of Part Three of this report.

PART THREE

INTERNATIONAL STRATEGIES

THE INTERNATIONAL SETTING

6

The responsibility for the provision of basic needs to the population of any independent country, in the final analysis, rests with the government of that country. Nevertheless, this should not be interpreted to mean that developing countries are being asked to fend for themselves alone. International trade between developing and developed countries, and among developing countries themselves, has a significant role to play in the proposed new approach, as capital flows and aid in the form of grants can have.

International reforms which could support development have been the subject of extensive discussion in a variety of forums for a number of years, e.g. in meetings of GATT, FAO, UNCTAD, UNIDO, IMF and the World Bank, and the recent world conferences on population, food and the environment. At the Seventh Special Session of the General Assembly of the United Nations in September 1975, Resolution 3362, already mentioned in this report, calls for a number of measures which span a very wide range of issues including the stabilisation of developing countries' earnings from primary product exports; higher prices for these exports; expanded access for manufactured exports to the markets of the rich countries and other support for Third World industrialisation; the transfer of additional resources to the developing countries and mitigation of their debt burden; a reform of the international monetary system designed to link aid with the expansion of special drawing rights; the development of scientific and technological capacity in the developing countries, and the transfer of technology to them at better terms; the control of restrictive business practices adversely affecting developing countries' trade; improved world food policies; economic co-operation among developing countries; and the restructuring of the United Nations system. The operational details of these various reforms remain to be negotiated in further and more specialised international meetings such as the Fourth Session of UNCTAD to be held in Nairobi in May 1976. Clearly, it is not for the ILO to duplicate these efforts. But this Conference can play an important role in the elaboration and search for agreement on those elements of the proposed international economic reforms which are best considered in the tripartite mode of the ILO's deliberations.

Changes at the international level have important implications for the possibility of success of basic-needs programmes (as well as for less poverty-oriented national development programmes). It may be worth considering the relative importance of the various elements of the international environment which have an impact upon the developing countries, and in particular upon their efforts to provide basic needs to their peoples.

Table 11 shows the principal means through which developing countries acquire foreign exchange, viz. through exporting and through imports of capital. While the particular proportion varies from one developing country to another, it is quite evident that exporting is a far more important source of foreign exchange than flows of private and official foreign capital. Exports from the developing countries to the industrial market economies in 1974 were over five times as great as total net capital flows from them. Even excluding the exports of the members of OPEC, remaining exports were twice as large as total capital flows. Of course, exporting entails an immediate resource cost which capital flows do not (although they may entail other political and economic costs). However, in the context of a basic-needs strategy, how the foreign exchange, obtained either through exports or through capital inflows, is used becomes all the more important. It is desirable that the foreign exchange should be geared to the consumption needs of the poorest and to the investment requirements for the production of goods and services essential for the fulfilment of basic-needs targets.

Trade between the developing and socialist countries is very small, although it is expanding rapidly. Exports to the socialist countries in 1974 were over six times as large as capital imports from them.

Changes in the terms of trade are more important than changes in the terms of aid. Long-run trends in relative world prices are difficult to detect, but there is no doubt that the terms of trade of the non-petroleum-exporting developing countries have recently fallen sharply. The combination of world recession and an oil crisis has been so severe that, despite a continued increase in the volume of exports, the import purchasing power of their exports fell markedly. The poorest developing countries were hit especially hard in 1974-75. As a result, their imports had to be cut to levels below those of the beginning of the decade.

Only a small proportion of the trade of developing countries is with each other. As can be seen in table 11, about 20 per cent of Third World trade is between members of the group (that is, US$47,000 million as a proportion of US$233,000 million), although the proportion rises to above a quarter if the

Table 11. Developing countries' exports and capital imports, by source, 1974
(thousand millions of US dollars)

Exports	To industrial market economies	To socialist economies	To developing countries	World total [1]
1. *Total exports*	172	8	47	233
Petroleum exporters	110	2	21	135
Non-petroleum exporters	63	6	26 [2]	97

Capital imports	From industrial market economies	From socialist economies	From OPEC countries	Total
2. *Capital flows : net*				
Official development assistance [3]	11.3	1.3	3.4	21.7
Other official	2.1		3.6	
Private voluntary agencies	1.2	—	—	1.2
Direct investment	7.2	—	—	7.2
Portfolio	2.4	—	—	2.4
Export credits	2.5	—	—	2.5
Eurodollar loans	5.0 [4]	—	—	5.0
Total	31.7	1.3	7.0	40.0

[1] Totals include some countries not included in the other three columns.   [2] Of which US$4,000 million represents exports to OPEC countries.   [3] Includes capital flows in which there is a grant element of 25 per cent or more, using a discount rate of 10 per cent.   [4] Many of these resources originated with OPEC countries.

Sources: GATT: *International trade, 1974/75* (Geneva, 1975), pp. 142-143; OECD: *Resources for developing countries, 1974*; UNCTAD: *Financial co-operation among developing countries: financial co-operation between OPEC and other developing countries*, (Geneva, doc. TD/B/AC.19/R.8, 29 Oct. 1975; mimeographed).

petroleum exporters are excluded. Various attempts have been made to stimulate more Third World trade, notably trade liberalisation agreements and schemes for regional integration, but with limited success so far. More active policies with regard to credit, transport and communications, particularly when combined with joint industrial planning, may result in greater success in future. Indeed, the unexploited trade potential, if realised, could lead to gains in income as well as facilitating collective self-reliance.

Conventional balance-of-payments accounts record international flows of capital but not those of labour. This is essentially because it is difficult, though not impossible, to place a monetary value on flows of labour. Migration of labour—both skilled and unskilled—is thus not included in the above table. Nevertheless, it is an important element in economic relations between rich nations and poor and is discussed at greater length in Chapter 8.

THE ROLE OF INTERNATIONAL TRADE

Between 1960 and 1974 the volume of world trade increased at about the same pace as world industrial production. Throughout almost the entire period of this unprecedented expansion, however, the share of the non-petroleum-exporting developing countries continued to fall. In 1960 their share of the value of total world trade was about 14 per cent. By 1974 it had fallen to a little under 12 per cent. Of course, if one counts the OPEC countries the share of the developing countries recently leaped to nearly 30 per cent. Even so, in comparison with previous decades Third World trade grew rapidly until the current world recession.

International trade is an instrument for raising national income beyond the level which could be attained in autarky. Trade expansion is thus not an end in itself but is desirable to the extent that it enables a country to achieve its income and growth objectives. In small countries, where economies of scale limit the range of products which can be produced efficiently for small local markets, international trade is more important than in large countries which enjoy more options. Thus while the average export share of gross national product in developing countries is about 20 per cent, it is only 3.5 per cent in India and 5.5 per cent in Bangladesh. It follows that international policies designed to affect export prices and earnings are likely to have a greater impact in the smaller, more trade-dependent economies than in the larger, less trade-dependent ones.

Emphasis on basic needs rather than on aggregate output implies a concern with the distribution of the gains from trade. Naturally, one is concerned with the division of the gains between the developing countries, on the one hand, and the developed countries and multinational enterprises, on the other. In addition, one is concerned with the distribution of benefits between developing countries and among members of a particular developing country's population. If basic needs are to be emphasised, while the search for measures which will raise aggregate incomes for developing countries is continued, special priority will need to be given to international policies which channel the gains from trade (and capital flows) to the poorest developing countries and the poorest people in developing countries.

As regards the distribution of benefits among countries, the trade policies of developed countries aimed at the fulfilment of basic needs must attempt to raise and stabilise real prices and earnings of the primary commodities sold by the poorest countries. Such measures might include special preferences for the poorest countries in wider-ranging commodity schemes, such as are found in the Lomé Convention. Greater access to developed-country markets, particularly for those semi-processed and processed commodities originating in the poorest countries, would also be of great use. This could be achieved by eliminating the escalation in tariff rates which generally accompanies higher levels of processing; by stimulating more competition among multinational processing and marketing enterprises in world markets for these same products; and by improving the generalised system of preferences with reference to products of greatest interest to the poorest countries.

Such reforms of trade policies in support of basic-needs strategies are bound to have a limited impact because of the unfortunate fact that large numbers of extremely poor people live in countries such as India and Bangladesh where a relatively small part of total income enters into international trade. This merely underlines yet again the proposition that national development policies must play the major role in reducing world poverty.

Moreover, even in those countries where the ratio of exports to gross national product is high, and consequently where international reforms can have a significant effect on aggregate income, the direct beneficiaries of such reforms will often not be persons in the traditional rural sector or informal urban sector. The very poverty of the poor, and their lack of resources, insulates them from most of the benefits flowing from the faster currents of world commerce. One must not exaggerate the point, and obviously the implementation of a basic-needs strategy would help; but a rearrangement of international trading relationships of the type discussed is unlikely to have a significant and immediate impact on mass poverty and inequality.

Improved trade policies in developing countries are complementary to other national policies designed to raise the living standards of the poor. Indeed, it was argued in Chapter 3 that a shift in the incentive structure was an essential component of a basic-needs strategy and that this new set of incentives had important implications for trade. For example, the new set of incentives proposed in that chapter would greatly encourage the use of more appropriate products and technologies. Since these products and technologies are of interest primarily to the developing countries, there is likely to be an expansion of technological development and eventually of trade in these items among the developing countries themselves. Correspondingly, there would be a diminished reliance upon less suitable imports from the rich countries. Thus a potential exists for the emergence of a new international division of labour within the developing world, with different countries specialising in different appropriate consumer and capital goods, each produced with technologies appropriate to the local resource endowment. Already 25 per cent of the manufactured exports and 40 per cent of the capital goods exports of developing countries go to other developing countries. A basic-needs strategy would greatly intensify this pattern of trade. In this way the strategy would be supportive of developing country objectives of self-reliance.

At the same time, as far as developed country trade relations are concerned, there are likely to be substantially increased incentives to engage in labour-intensive manufacturing for export to them, rather than manufacturing which substitutes for imports from them. To some extent, new incentives and the activities of multinational enterprises have already generated significant alterations in the structure of developing country exports. Manufactured products (excluding non-ferrous metals) rose from only 9 per cent of total exports from developing countries in 1960 to 16 per cent in 1974.

The opportunities to expand exports of manufactured goods are not confined to the markets of the advanced market economies in which private firms can be expected to respond to improved market incentives. On the contrary, the relatively small amount of trade conducted between the developing countries and the European socialist economies (see table 11) suggests that there is substantial potential for expansion of this mutually beneficial trade. The same pattern is evident in developing countries' trade with the socialist countries as in that with the industrialised market economies: between 1960 and 1973 the share of manufactured goods in total developing country exports to socialist countries rose from 11 per cent to 27 per cent.

Since export marketing is a skill- and capital-intensive activity in which there are significant economies of scale, there is a danger of encouraging the development of large-scale, unnecessarily capital-intensive exporting establishments, perhaps even foreign owned and probably using imported technology, rather than the expansion of the smaller, more labour-intensive domestic establishments which, though efficient, lack the capacity to market. Both higher income and greater equality could be attained by the creation of co-operative or publicly owned marketing agencies or trading houses to perform the specialised and relatively capital-intensive purchasing, bulking and export marketing function. As in the case of agricultural export marketing boards which have long existed in many developing countries, such institutions would permit the growth of small-scale production which is, in any case, frequently more socially efficient.

The expansion of exports which could be expected from a restructuring of incentives within the developing countries and the liberalisation of world trading arrangements would not be confined to labour-intensive products. Developing countries already supply many products (for example in the electrical equipment and resource-processing sectors) which cannot be so described. To conceive of the developing countries' expanded trading opportunities in these terms is to adopt too static a view of their potential comparative advantage in international exchange. It is true that, other things being equal, the poorest countries are likely to be relatively more efficient in the production of the most labour-intensive products. But the particular countries which are the poorest at any given time change. The very income gains that expanded trade, among other influences, makes possible will alter the structure of international competitive advantage. It is the object of each individual country to upgrade its technical capacity and skill, and not to remain bound to any particular type of exporting which may have been advantageous for the purpose of raising income or employment in the short run. Developing countries planning to employ the instrument of international trade in pursuit of their development strategies, whether geared to basic needs or not, should therefore think in terms of their longer-run dynamic comparative advantage as influenced by the structure of growth and the technology which will emerge in consequence of the strategies and policies which are pursued in the meantime. Those Eastern European socialist economies which are at present engaged in the export of highly labour-intensive products in the textiles, clothing, footwear and electronics sectors to the market economies, for example, would only remain in this type of production for as long as it happens to be convenient in their pursuit of longer-run objectives.

THE ROLE OF DEVELOPMENT ASSISTANCE

Collective self-reliance is a distinctive feature of basic-needs strategies. This does not, however, rule out the use of external resources in the service of such strategies. It is true that external capital flows have in the past often given encouragement to large-scale projects using imported technologies and expertise, with all the other effects associated with them. However, once the commitment to pursue a basic-needs strategy has been firmly established and the necessary structural changes set in motion, the inflows of external capital under appropriate forms and conditions can materially assist in the acceleration of the attainment of basic-needs targets.

Means of increasing the volume and the effectiveness of such financial flows have long been the subject of debate in other international forums. In the context of the present report, with its stress on basic needs, special attention must be focused upon the role of the capital flows which take place under governmental auspices on concessional terms. As can be seen in table 11, official development assistance and other official flows from all sources (including the socialist countries and OPEC members) accounted for a little over half of the total capital flows to developing countries in 1974. Excluding OPEC sources, these official flows made up roughly 8 per cent of the developing countries' total exports to the developed market and socialist economies (that is, US$14,700 million as a proportion of US$180,000 million) and 21 per cent of their non-petroleum exports (that is, US$14,700 million as a proportion of US$69,000 million).

Table 12. Net Official Development Assistance (ODA) from OECD Development Assistance Committee (DAC) countries and multilateral agencies, 1964-74

Year	ODA in current prices (US$ millions)	ODA as % of GNP of DAC countries	Price index (1964 = 100)	ODA in constant 1964 prices (US$ millions)	Index
1964	5 952	0.48	100	5 952	100
1965	5 895	0.44	100	5 895	99.0
1966	5 995	0.41	103.6	5 787	97.2
1967	6 552	0.42	105.1	6 234	104.7
1968	6 320	0.37	106.8	5 918	99.4
1969	6 632	0.36	109.1	6 079	102.1
1970	6 811	0.34	113.4	6 006	100.9
1971	7 691	0.35	121.5	6 330	106.4
1972	8 538	0.33	133.6	6 391	107.4
1973	9 376	0.30	169.8	5 522	92.8
1974	11 262	0.33	190.2	5 921	99.5

Sources: ODA in current prices: 1964-1969 OECD/DAC: *Development co-operation: 1974 Review*, pp. 201, 202; and ODA as % of GNP: 1970-1974 OECD/DAC: *Draft press communiqué on 1974 flows* (Paris, OECD, 12 June 1975). Price index: calculated from OECD/DAC: *Development co-operation: 1974 Review*, op. cit., p. 209 for the years 1964-73. For 1974 the GNP average price level increase for the DAC of 12 per cent on 1973, as given in OECD/DAC: *Draft press communiqué on 1974 flows*, op. cit., p. 13 was used.[1]

[1] If the index for the prices of exports from industrialised countries is used—and it is a concept similar to this which underlies the OECD 1964-73 index—then the 1974 index number would become 212.6 instead of 190.2 since the increase in export prices between 1973 and 1974 was 25.2 per cent. In this case the real value of ODA, in terms of 1964 prices, would have been US$5,297 million, i.e. only 89 per cent of the 1964 level.

Under the terms of the International Development Strategy for the Second United Nations Development Decade, the developed countries accepted, with some reservations, 0.7 per cent of gross national product as the target for the annual amount of official development assistance to be provided to the developing countries by the middle of the 1970s. By 1974 only Sweden had reached this target; several smaller countries had attained levels of over 0.5 per cent, but the largest contributors had fallen further away from the target. In 1974 the OECD average remained at only 0.33 per cent of gross national product. In the previously mentioned Resolution 3362 the deadline was extended to the end of the decade. Table 12 shows the stagnation in the real value of official development assistance over the past decade, during which time incomes per head in the industrialised countries climbed by about 50 per cent. Receipts per head of official development assistance have clearly been falling steadily over the past decade. Moreover, the real value of these capital flows is considerably smaller than these figures suggest. Because of the well known cost of procurement tying, the real value of these transfers is reduced by perhaps as much as 30 per cent. There is thus need for improvement in both the quantitative and the qualitative aspects of development assistance.

In order to assist in the provision of basic needs, official development assistance would have to be directed to the poorest countries and to poverty groups in other developing countries. It should be made available for such purposes and in such forms as to be usable for these purposes. Most bilateral contributors to official development assistance have now announced their intention of shifting aid towards the poor people and poorer countries. In the face of the drastic deterioration in the poorest countries' terms of trade during 1974, the World Bank, the IMF and the United Nations General Assembly put together special loan facilities and an emergency relief and development assistance programme to assist them. But development assistance receipts per head in the majority of these countries remain only marginally higher than the developing country average; and their real value has continued to fall.

Restructuring the country allocation of official development assistance in favour of the poorest countries is, by itself, not enough to ensure its usefulness for a programme geared to basic needs. Nor is it enough for donors to announce their intention to support more rural and poverty-oriented projects as well. Basic-needs programmes involve projects of smaller scale, less bankability and a higher proportion of local and recurrent costs. Where development assistance continues to favour large-scale projects demonstrating solid conventional benefit-cost ratios, and to require procurement in the supplying country, it simply cannot be used for the pursuit of basic-needs strategies except indirectly by freeing resources for alternative uses from the projects which continue to be eligible for conventional assistance. This implies important reforms in present official development assistance policies (particularly as they are applied to the poorest countries) in the direction of greater flexibility, less project orientation, more untying or at least support of local and recurrent costs, a higher proportion of grants, easier credit terms and longer-term commitments. To the extent that a project approach is retained, new means of assessing social benefits and costs should be applied so as to attach proper weight to distributional effects; these will automatically generate greater support for projects which assist the rural and the informal sectors.

Some reforms have recently been introduced with respect to OECD members' aid-tying practices. In a memorandum of understanding coming into force in 1975 most of the industrialised market-economy countries agreed to permit procurement on official development assistance loans in other developing countries. Some individual donors have also unilaterally eased their tying requirements by extending the range of products eligible for purchase, permitting increased local cost financing and, in a few instances, even permitting purchases to be made wherever supplies can most cheaply be obtained. However welcome such measures may be, they are no substitute for a general agreement to untie both grants and loans offered to developing countries, discussions of which were abandoned late in 1971. It is suggested that these discussions should now be resumed, paying particular attention to the possibility of untying development assistance to the poorest developing countries for whom an untying agreement could achieve the greatest effect towards the satisfaction of basic needs Generalised untying would facilitate the direction of external assistance to the poorest people in wealthier developing countries as well.

Development assistance for the agricultural sector, especially that provided through the World Bank, has increased substantially in recent years, although it is still far from sufficient. Estimates presented to the World Food Conference indicate that the acceleration of the average annual increase in production in the developing countries from 2.6 per cent to 3.6 per cent requires an increase in development assistance for agriculture from the current level of about US$1,500 million to at least US$5,000 million a year by 1980. The World Food Conference proposed the establishment of an International Fund for Agricultural Development, which it is hoped may be set up during the course of 1976. The establishment of this new source of finance may provide an opportunity for more development assistance to be channelled to basic-needs programmes and projects.

Food aid is of special interest to a basic-needs strategy. In the initial phases of the implementation of such strategies the redistribution of purchasing power to the poverty groups is likely to lead to sharp increases in demand for foodstuffs. In situations where food production cannot be quickly increased, food aid may provide a cushion at a critical transitional phase. It also has an important role to play in relieving hunger in emergency situations and in providing wage goods needed in the implementation of labour-intensive rural public works. But care needs to be taken to ensure that it does not blunt the drive in the long run for self-sufficiency in national food production. The United Nations/FAO World Food Programme has displayed many features of a food aid policy which can reinforce the over-all thrust of a basic-needs strategy. Over a period of 12 years, food aid projects have supported jobs for over 6 million persons. The World Food Conference adopted a quantitative minimum target for food aid of 10 million tons of cereals a year, and recommended the expansion of the scope of the World Food Programme. The International Undertaking on World Food Security, calling for an internationally co-ordinated system of nationally held cereal stocks, is also highly relevant to the meeting of basic needs on a sustained basis, and involves assistance to developing countries especially for the initial building-up of stocks to safe levels.

INTERNATIONAL ISSUES OF SPECIAL CONCERN TO THE ILO

There are numerous dimensions to the international framework within which developing countries must create and implement development policies. It is not possible for this Conference to concern itself with them all. Nor would it, in any case, be appropriate for the ILO to duplicate the efforts to arrive at improved international trading and financial arrangements which are under way in other forums such as the United Nations, GATT, UNCTAD and the IMF, however crucial they may be to the achievement of the basic-needs targets which have been stressed in this report. Rather, it can best focus upon those issues which lend themselves to resolution through a tripartite form of discussion, and which fit into the ILO's general responsibilities for labour.

Among such issues are those surrounding the emergence of a " new international division of labour " in which increasing shares of growth in world industrial production are expected to accrue to the developing countries. The Second General Conference of UNIDO called for up to 25 per cent of world industry to be located in developing countries by the year 2000, as against the present 7 per cent. If a structural change of this magnitude is carried out over the next quarter of a century, this will have major implications for employment shifts and structure in both the developed and the developing countries. In particular sectors there has already been such a major restructuring of the geography of industry.

The redeployment of industries has generated considerable conflict and concern over the distribution of the resulting gains and the fate of the possible losers from this process. Yet there is widespread agreement that such structural changes in the world economy are, ultimately, in the best interests both of the developing and of the developed countries. In this respect these issues are quite different from most of the other elements in the debate over the possible shape of a new international economic order. Needless to say, a new international division of labour has important implications for the achievement of basic-needs targets in both the short and longer run. As has been seen, labour-intensive manufacturing for export is likely to be stimulated immediately by the incentive structures which are part and parcel of a basic-needs strategy. In the longer run the attainment of basic-needs targets will remain crucially dependent upon the achievement of a more balanced distribution of world production and income, which in turn is dependent upon the maintenance of opportunities to take advantage of the possibilities for specialisation and exchange in an expanding world economy.

The following four chapters accordingly deal at greater length with the inter-related questions of adjustment assistance, labour migration, technology, and multinational enterprises. These, while important issues in themselves, are all associated with the phenomenon of a restructured world economy and a new international division of labour.

While the present high unemployment rates in the industrialised market economies, and even the non-cyclical components thereof, have many causes, as has been seen, the structural difficulties which may be associated with an expansion of their imports from the developing countries are deserving of special attention in a discussion of global development problems and the fulfilment of basic needs. Trade adjustment assistance programmes have a very important role to play in the developed countries' adjustment process.

Labour migration is no doubt related to the rate at which labour-intensive industrial production has been relocated from the industrialised countries to the developing countries. The cheap labour which immigrants from developing countries provided in Western Europe may in some cases have reduced the incentive for European-based enterprises to buy or invest abroad in the product categories in which the developing countries were already demonstrating their competitiveness. With present restrictions upon further immigration, more structural change will become necessary, provided that pressures for protection against imports are resisted.

In this context, multinational enterprises deserve special attention since they are an important vehicle for bringing about the restructuring of world industrial production. They are both major buyers and sellers of the relevant goods, they possess intimate knowledge and sometimes control of the relevant markets and they are important suppliers of the necessary technologies and of capital for this and other purposes.

The role of technology for the achievement of a new international division of labour is self-evident; but its wider importance in the pursuit of basic-needs strategies of development requires that the subject of its adaptation and development in the developing countries receives even more extensive attention.

TRADE-ADJUSTMENT ASSISTANCE

7

The total volume of exports from developing countries grew at a rate of 7.7 per cent per annum during the opening three years of the Second Development Decade after averaging 6.8 per cent during the First Development Decade. In 1973 over three-quarters of those exports went to developed market countries compared with 5 per cent to socialist countries and nearly 20 per cent accounted for by trade among the developing countries themselves.

Manufactured exports from developing countries rose even more impressively, at an annual rate of nearly 15 per cent. They represented 24 per cent of their total exports in 1973, but, because of the rise in oil prices, only 16 per cent in 1974. Again the bulk went to developed market economies (65.6 per cent) and 4.1 per cent to socialist countries.[1]

Since this trade expansion was associated with an unprecedented period of expansion in world industrial production and trade, fears as to its possible effects upon employment in the developed countries were muted. However, the world depression, discussed in Chapter 5, brought these and other emerging employment problems into sharper relief. Altered trading patterns could now be seen by workers, firms and governments to be an important element in the on-going process of structural change and development in the developed countries. The ease with which the process of adjustment to this particular element of structural change is achieved is of fundamental importance to the export prospects of the developing countries. Failure to achieve smooth adjustment may inhibit efforts to reduce trade barriers and indeed generate pressures for increased protection in the developed countries. While effects on employment have attracted most attention in the manufacturing sector, the importance of achieving a smooth process of adjustment to trade-induced structural change is equally great in the agricultural sector where there exist

---

[1] United Nations: *World Economic Survey, 1974* (New York, 1975).

significant trade barriers against sugar, beef, vegetable oils and various temperate foodstuffs. The obstacles to increased agricultural exports from the developing countries are mainly food subsidies and support prices for the domestic farmers in the developed market economies, and (particularly in socialist countries) high taxes on certain products based upon imported raw materials which keep consumption levels low.

As was stressed in earlier chapters, it is very much in the interest of the developed countries themselves constantly to transfer labour and other resources from lower-productivity to higher-productivity activities. Apart from the immediate over-all national income gains realised, most notably by consumers, countries which fail to take timely action to phase out inefficient industries or to discontinue socially unprofitable lines of production make the ultimately necessary adjustment still more difficult. Many of the most active firms and workers will by that time already have left the weakest industries on their own initiative, leaving a hard core of the relatively disadvantaged resisting the inevitable changes with even greater vigour. Adjustment policies geared to the needs of these workers—typically older workers, women and members of minority groups, including the disabled—and to the least efficient managers and firms are then likely to be considerably more difficult and costly to implement.

The encouragement of international trade between developed and developing countries, by improving the international division of labour and thus raising productivity all round, should be attractive to both. The altered incentive structures within the developing countries which are recommended in Chapter 3 will encourage increases in their supplies of exports to the developed countries; indeed, their partial adoption in some developing countries is one of the major explanations for the rapid growth in their manufactured exports which has already been achieved. Yet these exports face substantial tariff and non-tariff barriers in developed-country markets. Particular efforts should therefore be made to develop special adjustment-assistance policies in these countries which would encourage trade liberalisation and reduce the risk that these additional exports would run into further trade barriers there. Such policies would support developing-country development efforts, whether oriented to basic needs or not. They are, at the same time, an important component of the over-all package of national and international policies recommended in this report for the achievement of basic-needs targets.

DIMENSIONS OF THE TRADE-ADJUSTMENT PROBLEM

The over-all effect on employment in developed countries of improved market access for developing countries' exports is difficult to estimate. In order to make such an estimate one must employ crude assumptions about the extent of possible trade liberalisation, the likely consequent reduction in production volumes in the most affected industries (which can be expected to vary from industry to industry), the production and employment generated in developed countries' exporting industries as an indirect consequence of the expansion of imports, and the length of time over which all of these adjustments will take place. Something can, nevertheless, be said about the rough orders of magnitude likely to be involved.

International adjustment in the agricultural sector has been studied for some years by the FAO. Based on a specific set of gradual adjustments that appear feasible, it is estimated that additional employment opportunities might be created in the developing countries amounting to 4 to 5 million man-years in the primary production of agriculture, fishing and forestry products. The corresponding reduction in employment in the production of competing commodities in the developed countries is estimated as only about half-a-million jobs during the whole decade of the 1970s. Not only is this not very significant in relation to the annual reduction of about 2 million that is already occurring in the agricultural labour force of the developed countries but it is also likely to be at least partly offset by the gains in agricultural exports that would accrue to these countries themselves as a result of the over-all trade expansion envisaged as part of a process of international agricultural adjustment. Nevertheless, although the total magnitude is likely to be small, a number of country case studies indicate that significant adjustment measures may be required in individual cases.

An UNCTAD study, based largely upon the results of a research report of the ILO, generated some rough estimates of the gross number of jobs which might be lost in the fairly short run in the major developed market countries in consequence of the elimination of non-tariff barriers and a 50 per cent reduction in tariffs vis-à-vis their trading partners, affecting mostly manufactures.[1] Only a small proportion of the resulting job losses, it was found, could be attributed to increased exports from developing countries. (The bulk was associated with increased trade among the developed countries.) Their total absolute number amounted to less than 100,000 for the aggregate of the six original member States of the European Communities, the United States, the United Kingdom and Japan together; this amounts to a tiny fraction (about one-twentieth of 1 per cent) of the total labour force of these countries. It is true that these job " displacements " would be concentrated in particular

---

[1] UNCTAD: *Impact on employment of international policy measures in the field of trade and development* (Geneva, 1975; mimeographed). The estimates were based in part on data in H. F. Lydall: *Trade and employment* (Geneva, ILO, 1975). It is noteworthy that the trade barrier reduction of the model would also result in 480,000 additional jobs in the developing countries.

industries and areas. An earlier UNCTAD study demonstrated, however, that even in the most sensitive industries (footwear, clothing, leather and leather products, electrical machinery and basic metal products) gross job displacement from expanded imports from developing countries would be unlikely to reach as much as 2 per cent of their total workforce [1]; in all but five of the 60 industries reviewed in this study such job losses were less than those normally experienced in consequence of productivity gains. While the number of jobs lost in particular communities could conceivably amount to more significant proportions of local labour forces, one cannot escape the conclusion that the effects of the liberalisation of trade with developing countries—let alone of a simple standstill on further trade barriers against them—upon employment in the developed countries would be of slight aggregative importance.

Moreover, these estimates do not allow for the inevitable expansion of jobs which would follow from the export growth associated with an expansion of trade. Estimates of the effects of unilateral trade-barrier reductions in the United States suggest that over-all employment would actually rise in consequence.[2]

It should be noted also that these figures are based upon what are probably substantial overestimates of the short-term capacity of developing countries to supply the products in question. In actual fact, changes in trade patterns take time to accomplish. At present only a small number of developing countries would be able to take full advantage of increased market access. In the past some of the developing countries have not even been able to fill their agreed quotas for exports of clothing and textiles to high-income countries or to take advantage of the generalised system of preferences. Many developing countries have not as yet reoriented their production strategies and incentive systems in such a manner as to encourage much investment in export industries. Further improvements in credit arrangements, transport and marketing networks might also be needed before a significant response would be noted. Even a major move toward trade liberalisation would therefore require a considerable transitional period before the full effects would be realised—more than enough time to permit the necessary adjustment to be worked through in the affected industries of the developed countries.

---

[1] The results of this and other related studies, together with the relevant references, may be found in ILO: *Adjustment assistance, the problem and its magnitude* (Geneva, 1975; document for limited distribution). See also C. Hsieh: " Measuring the effects of trade expansion on employment: a review of some research ", in *International Labour Review* (Geneva, ILO), Jan. 1973, pp. 1-29.

[2] P. Magee: " The welfare effects of restrictions on U.S. trade ", in *Brookings Papers on Economic Activity* (No. 3, 1972), table 7, p. 682.

The relative insignificance of these employment effects could even be used in support of an argument to the effect that no *special* adjustment measures need to be implemented in industrialised countries to cope with increased imports from developing countries. Ideally, as has been seen, what is required is that suitable over-all labour market policies exist which can be activated whatever the cause of structural change. It may not only be simpler, administratively, to institute and operate such a generalised labour market policy but its existence would also help to remove opposition to the whole range of desirable changes which must be made in any dynamic economy. Indeed, since trade effects cannot always be isolated from other stimuli for structural change, a country's over-all response to trade-caused problems is likely to be only as good as its over-all economic policies, and in particular its manpower policies. However, trade among countries at different levels of development, in that it less frequently creates the potential for expanded intra-industry trade, also causes some specific problems which require particular action.

THE CONTEXT FOR TRADE-ADJUSTMENT ASSISTANCE

Without economic and social dynamism, specific adjustment assistance objectives for trade-affected firms and workers become very difficult to achieve and this is why adjustment programmes have failed in so many countries in the past. As was argued in Chapter 5, a set of economic policies that encourages innovative and competitive production, enabling firms to anticipate and handle adjustment changes with relative ease, is one cornerstone of such policies. Japanese " industrial structure policy " has been unusually forward-looking with respect to the prospects of future imports of manufactures from developing countries. The Netherlands, too, is proposing to introduce an " anticipatory restructuring policy " especially to assist industries which are adversely affected by imports from developing countries.[1] Education and social and active manpower policies which create an upwardly mobile workforce, however, are equally essential. Most of the adjustment policies so far introduced which have been specifically related to trade problems have tended to provide too little assistance too late.[2] A new approach to adjustment assistance for

---

[1] *Memorandum on the restructuring of the Netherlands economy and development co-operation*, Memorandum presented to the States General of the Netherlands, 9 Dec. 1974, p. 10. The Memorandum explicitly places adjustment assistance within the context of general change by saying: " The restructuring process currently taking place in the Dutch economy is not a new phenomenon in itself. On the contrary, changes in the structure of production have been taking place almost constantly for many decades now. One of the biggest factors has been changes in the international division of labour; other factors include technological advancement " (p. 4).

[2] It is still too early to draw firm conclusions from the new United States trade-adjustment assistance programme, as expanded in the 1974 Trade Act. However, some 30,000 workers were assisted under the Act during the first few months after it had been passed by Congress and budgetary outlays had reached an annual rate of US$350 million.

workers and firms affected by trade with developing countries appears to be needed.

There can be little doubt that past failures to implement satisfactory adjustment measures have created resistance to change. Workers' organisations, anxious to protect the gains made in the past, have expressed a legitimate fear that wage rates might be undermined by the import of cheap goods from abroad. The owners of capital have also wished to preserve the threatened value of their investment. When industries subjected to increased competition from abroad experience downward pressures on relative wages and the return on capital, these pressures can be interpreted as "warning signals" that structural changes are occurring. Attempts to eliminate these pressures through tariffs, quantitative import restrictions, " voluntary " export restraints or other non-tariff barriers will harm not only the countries potentially able to supply competitive products but also, as has been seen, the protecting countries themselves.

A more appropriate response would have two elements. First, a stimulus (e.g. by accelerated depreciation allowances and sponsored research and development) would be given to technological progress in those sectors which can readily adapt to changing comparative advantages (i.e. by becoming more capital- and skill-intensive). Secondly, dynamic adjustment policies would ease the transfer of resources from those sectors which cannot easily make this transition to more dynamic, competitive activities. It is necessary to distinguish between these two complementary paths to avoid grossly oversimplified classifications of whole industries into inherently labour-intensive (to be phased out) and capital- and skill-intensive (to be encouraged) categories. The industrial structure is much more complex and heterogeneous and the scope for change varies enormously from one segment to another.

Nevertheless, the reasons for the fear of change are not hard to find. The developed-country manufacturing industries so far most affected by the increased imports from developing countries are those in which large segments make intensive use of unskilled and semi-skilled labour, e.g. textiles, clothing, footwear and electronics. There is usually relatively low mobility among low-skill, labour-intensive occupations, and some of the workers displaced by imports are likely to put additional supply pressure on the labour market in those industries. Other industries employing similar types of labour are also likely to experience relative wage rate declines, through the operation of the relevant labour markets. The distribution of income in the developed country will thus tend to move against low-paid workers if governments do not actively pursue income maintenance or redistribution policies to forestall such an outcome.

Moreover, the affected industries are often geographically concentrated in the more depressed areas of the developed countries. In some instances they have been kept going only by injections of public funds intended to prevent regional increases in unemployment. The problems of the industry are transmitted, through linkage and multiplier effects, to the areas in which they are located. In such cases whole communities may be in decline, sometimes with effects for a second and even third generation; age-structure and dependency problems are created as the most active people leave, and an over-all decline takes place in earnings and the value of assets, including those, like houses, owned by workers.

To the affected workers, firms and communities, the benefits of an improved international division of labour and of structural changes at best appear to be distant and often seem totally out of reach. The future only threatens them with declining incomes and asset values. It is not surprising that they are often strongly protectionist. Protectionist pressures can be expected to be particularly vigorous and effective if there is little indication that the consumers of the nation are deriving any of the promised benefits from structural change, or if there is suspicion that the most needy groups within developing countries are not receiving many of them either. When multinational enterprises move their plant from a developed country to a developing one, at least in those instances in which there is limited competition in the relevant industry, there may be legitimate concern as to the distribution of the resulting gains. They can, after all, be largely absorbed in the increased profits of large (quite possibly foreign-owned) producing, importing or retailing firms. A credible policy of structural change and adjustment assistance must therefore be coupled with vigorous measures to ensure the maintenance of competitive practices in the relevant sectors, and, more generally, must retain a broad concern for the income distribution implications of change.

THE ELEMENTS OF TRADE-ADJUSTMENT ASSISTANCE POLICIES

It should continually be stressed that appropriate macro- and microeconomic policy on the part of the government can materially ease the transfer of resources, and thereby ensure that desirable structural change takes place. Appropriate policies can, in contrast to past experience, facilitate the transfer of the workers and firms affected to more productive jobs and industries, and ensure that a fair share of the costs for those unable to take advantage of such moves because of age, infirmity, family responsibilities or other handicaps, are borne by the rest of society.

What then should be the major elements of a trade adjustment policy? Above all, its principles ought to be drawn up in advance by interested groups—unions, employers, consumers and governments—and its details set out clearly.

In the past, where governments have offered adjustment assistance rather than increased protection in response to import pressures, they have tended to concentrate on making inefficient import-competing industries more competitive by further investment. When applied indiscriminately, this has rarely been successful. Many of the firms continue instead to be struggling, low-wage enterprises. In contrast, where there has been a clear determination to assist firms and workers to abandon certain lines of production and concentrate on others, or to move out of an uncompetitive type of product to more competitive activities, as in the Japanese textile industry, the adjustment process has been much faster, smoother and more beneficial.

It should be possible to anticipate those structural changes which will be called for in consequence of increased competition from developing countries. Inability or reluctance to forecast has meant that adjustment assistance policies have generally come into operation only when severe difficulties have already been encountered by the industry—difficulties which have led to personal hardship. Of course, such forecasts will not be possible in all cases. Yet it is easier to anticipate which industries or lines of production will be affected by competition from low-income countries than it is to forecast other forms of structural change. While it is impossible to predict changes in tastes or in technology with much confidence, it is known that there is a strong likelihood of unskilled labour-intensive sectors in the industrialised countries becoming uncompetitive in the fairly near future.

There are indicators which might be employed to warn of impending troubles in particular industries. Expanding imports indicate declining comparative advantage, providing of course that they have not been subsidised by the exporting country. The careful analysis of trade trends in relation to branches and sub-branches of industries, and at times even to the components of individual products, can result in the identification of weak industries well before trade-adjustment problems become acute. Another obvious sign is that certain groups of products are being produced under cover of high tariffs or other protection. The quantitative restrictions on the imports of garments, textiles, footwear and cutlery indicate that some types of products within these categories, particularly those aimed at the lower quality and price segments of the market, are not competitive in high-income countries.

Attention should be paid to finding an acceptable rate of adaptation to new trade patterns. Although in a time of full employment and booming economic conditions some of the firms in declining industries may be reluctant to move out because their particular markets may not be declining and some workers in these circumstances still feel entitled to their particular jobs and are also reluctant to move, in general it is clear that full employment and vigorous growth conditions make adjustment easier. Such a time is the optimal time for adjustment to be undertaken. The rate of growth of exports of manufactures from developing countries to high-income market economies accelerated, for example, from an average of some 15 per cent per annum in the 1960s to more than 20 per cent per annum in the boom of 1972-73, without any noticeable impact upon adjustment problems. But even if these changes are promoted in the most favourable economic and social climates, as they should be, it is essential to establish a proper calendar with a reasonable rate of change agreed upon by the social partners.

In contrast, experience suggests that trade adjustment for firms and workers is difficult in sluggish, slowly moving economies which cannot handle other forms of structural change, that it is more difficult in times of unemployment, and that it is particularly difficult in times of high unemployment. Firms cannot move because their incomes decline and potential markets shrink. Once unemployment appears, workers fear that leaving an existing job will mean a prolonged if not permanent period of unemployment, or the need to take a lower-paid job. Their fears have been justified in the past when employment, retraining and similar agencies have been swamped in periods of unemployment and thus were not able to handle adjustment problems even when special funds were available. It is for this reason, among many others, that it is to be hoped that the economies of the industrialised nations will be rapidly restimulated and that full employment conditions will soon return.

As was seen in Chapter 5, developed countries frequently pursue " regional policies " out of a political or social desire to maintain levels of income in relatively depressed areas. Such policies are not, of course, regarded as part of a trade-adjustment assistance programme, but they may have an equivalent effect if they assist workers and firms to move out of relatively unproductive activities into more productive ones. On the other hand, regional policies sometimes run at cross purposes with trade-adjustment policies by encouraging, through special subsidies, the very industries which it would be most advantageous to phase out. Since depressed regions are typically those areas of the developed countries most closely resembling the developing countries in labour characteristics and costs, the manufacturing activities attracted there by neutral incentives will, other things being equal, be those most likely eventually to attract developing country competition. Government facilities, service industries, research activities and tourism may therefore be more suitable for such regional policy efforts than the encouragement of many kinds of relatively labour-intensive manufactures. Regional policies and planning need to be co-ordinated with broader efforts to plan for structural changes engendered by new trading and other patterns.

THE COST OF TRADE-ADJUSTMENT ASSISTANCE

Effective trade-adjustment assistance, while beneficial to the country, may not be cheap in terms of government budget implications. Data from the United States, where relatively good estimates of adjustment costs are available [1], illustrate the orders of magnitude involved. Retraining alone is likely to cost more than US$1,000 per worker. The costs of relocating workers have been estimated as being from US$1,000 to US$2,000 if undertaken by a firm, and as much as US$5,000 if financed by government. Workers spend on average some 36 weeks in transition to a new job, and they would have to be supported at a level commensurate with their past average earnings during this period. Assuming even a low US$100-a-week level of support, this would mean another US$3,600 a worker. The cost of adjustment per worker would thus be between zero for the few fortunate ones who find another job immediately, and almost US$10,000 for the worker who has an " average " adjustment problem of the kind which would require government action. A government programme in the United States capable of absorbing the full adjustment costs for 40,000 of such " average " dislocated workers annually—surely an overestimate of fiscal requirements in the light of the employment estimates above, and the fact that many displaced workers will not need assistance—would therefore cost about US$400 million per year (exclusive of administrative costs). This estimate of the possible fiscal costs of a generous trade programme for workers, while it may sound expensive in absolute terms, amounts to only about 0.1 per cent of the total Federal Government budget of the United States and, of course, a far smaller percentage of its gross national product. There is no reason to believe that the fiscal costs of adequate trade-adjustment programmes would be any greater, relative to government budgets, in other countries, and there is some reason to believe that they might be less. The prospective benefits, from greater efficiency, higher productivity and wages per worker, cheaper products for the consumer and the growth of incomes and employment in the supplying countries, should exceed them.

Most of the facts and analyses in this chapter have been drawn from the experience of developed market economies. This reflects their predominance in world trade and the nature of their economic systems which exposes their industries and labour force to greater competition from abroad. But it could also be argued that the economies of socialist countries and of developing countries themselves could benefit from greater external stimulus to change and efficiency. As was stated in Chapter 6, several socialist countries have

---

[1] The data used are from R. Baldwin and J. H. Mutti: " Policy issues in adjustment assistance: the United States ", in H. Hughes (ed.): *Prospects of partnership* (Johns Hopkins University Press, 1973).

reached a situation of an over-all manpower shortage and are concerned by low productivity in some sectors and the need to raise quality. The transfer of labour into higher-productivity sectors could be accelerated by a greater reliance on imports from the developing world with a consequential widening of consumer choice. Changes in the turnover tax structure and increased foreign currency allocations would facilitate this adjustment. A rise in the per head consumption of labour-intensive imports from the developing world would be an important contribution to their welfare. The scope is considerable. The 1973 levels of total imports from the Third World were US$12 per inhabitant in the USSR and US$18 in other Eastern European socialist countries. In non-competing tropical products like coffee and cocoa, per head consumption levels in 1972-73 were 0.15 kilogram and 0.51 kilogram respectively in the USSR compared with 5.04 and 1.90 kilograms in the six original countries of the European Economic Community.[1]

INTERNATIONAL POLICIES

International action is required to link the alleviation of trade-adjustment problems to reductions of the relevant trade barriers. Individual countries will always, of course, reserve the right to conduct trade policies in whatever manner seems in their own national interest. This right might, however, be subject to some degree of international acceptability or even control. At the present time, Article 19 of the General Agreement on Tariffs and Trade (GATT) permits " emergency action " on certain imports on condition that: *(a)* there is actual or threatened injury to domestic industries, due to " unforeseen developments ", *(b)* the countries concerned consult each other first, and *(c)* the import restraints are imposed in a non-discriminatory manner. These conditions are at the same time too lax, in that they authorise import restrictions without corresponding obligations to readjust the protected industry and eliminate the restrictions; and too strict, in that the requirement of non-discrimination has made it difficult to pinpoint protectionist measures with respect to the source of the " injury ".[2] This strictness has led to widespread evasion of Article 19 through the use of " voluntary " export quotas extracted from exporting developing countries by threats of unilateral imposition of trade barriers which would be even more harmful to the exporting countries in their effect. Article 19 might therefore be amended so as to permit greater flexibility for the developed countries in protecting their

---

[1] United Nations: *World Economic Survey, 1974*, op. cit., Ch. 3.

[2] Jan Tumlir: " A revised safeguard clause for GATT? ", in *Journal of World Trade Law* (Vincent Press, Twickenham, Middlesex), July/August 1973, p. 405. See also idem: *Proposals for emergency protection against sharp increases in imports* (London, Trade Policy Research Centre, 1973).

industries against disruptive surges of competitive imports, and greater assurance to the developing countries that, over the longer run, uncompetitive industries in the rich countries will not continue to receive " escape clause " protection. As in the case of the 1974 international textile agreement, agreed limits to the use of such import restrictions against developing countries and international surveillance of these restrictions and related adjustment performance should also be established.

An interesting idea which has been advanced by the International Metalworkers' Federation is the proposal to insert a " social clause " in the GATT treaty. This would support the creation of maximum new job opportunities in developing countries and the elimination of subsidies which would hinder the readaptation of economic sectors and distort world trade. In return it would provide employment and income guarantees for the workers affected and support anticipatory structural adjustment measures.

To the extent that all industrialised countries, whether market-economy or socialist, participate in a determined effort to open their borders (or at least impose a standstill on further trade barriers) to imports from the developing world, the burden of adjustment for any one country is thereby lessened. Each country has an interest in ensuring that trade access is made easier everywhere. It would seem that all would benefit from regularised consultation and joint surveillance not only of import barriers but also of national adjustment programmes and policies as they relate to the exports of the developing countries. Fiscal constraints and political opposition could also be eased by the creation of an international reconversion fund for the purpose of assisting in the financing of trade-adjustment assistance programmes.[1] Initial national contributions to the fund might be related not only to the usual criteria like national income and national income per head but also, inversely, to the share of developing countries in national markets for manufactured products. The latter criterion would provide a built-in incentive to liberalise trade with developing countries. Such a fund would best be administered on a tripartite basis and its managers might well take on the responsibility for the general monitoring and consultation functions recommended above.

Some international agreements on trade adjustment have already been reached. In the European Communities where market access for developing countries is, with the exception of the United Kingdom, generally still relatively low, a Social Fund has been established for adjustment assistance. Further recent initiatives within the Communities include a Directive on Collective Dismissals which contains minimum standards on collective redun-

---

[1] This was suggested at the Eleventh Congress of the International Confederation of Free Trade Unions (ICFTU), Agenda Item 8: " Economic security and social justice ", *ICFTU Policies 1975-78* (Mexico City, Oct. 1975), p. 21.

dancies which must be complied with by member States within two years of its adoption. In most Western European countries the objective is to reach agreement on a " social plan " setting out the phasing and procedure of the labour force reduction, the criteria of selection of workers discharged, the financial provisions and the help to be given in retraining or finding another job.

In the agricultural field the 1975 FAO Conference adopted a Strategy of International Agricultural Adjustment, embodying eleven guidelines as a global policy framework. It requested the FAO to monitor and assess progress towards the achievement of the agreed objectives and policies of international agricultural adjustment. The guidelines include a provision that international assistance for investment in the agriculture of the developing countries should be raised to at least US$5,000 million a year in 1975-80, to enable them to respond effectively to the opportunities created by adjustment policies.

Difficulties of international collaboration need not imply postponing an individual country-by-country approach to import liberalisation and trade-adjustment assistance. It remains in each country's interest to avail itself of the full potential benefits from comparative advantage in the international division of labour. Provided that sufficient time is allowed for the transitional period, liberalisation can, even at the national level, be achieved equitably as well as efficiently.

In many respects the problems of such " middle-level " countries as Ireland, Yugoslavia, Spain and Portugal resemble those of the more depressed areas of the developed countries. Many of their manufactured exports resemble those of the developing countries: indeed they already frequently compete with them for access to richer markets. While all of the general analysis and recommendations with respect to structural change and adjustment assistance apply to them as well, the particular industries affected by their own trade liberalisation may differ from those so affected in the richer developed countries. Indeed their own exports may be among the major beneficiaries of trade liberalisation in richer countries. Special arrangements would therefore have to be made to handle their rather different problems, possibilities and obligations.

How could the ILO help to promote a harmonious adjustment process? It would seem that ILO experience and instruments would be relevant in the following areas.

First, more needs to be known about the nature and magnitude of the problem. Research in vulnerable sectors might seek to identify more precisely the social characteristics of the occupational groups most likely to be affected by trade-induced structural change. This information would be helpful in assessing the mobility of the labour force and the precise form of the adjustment assistance, including retraining, most required.

Second, the ILO's recent work in the field of technological choice (see Chapter 9) could provide valuable guidance for the difficult evaluation of the policy options between social and economic measures to encourage resource transfers on the one hand and those to promote technological change and productivity growth on the other.

Third, an examination could be made of how national social security schemes could be geared to provide adequate coverage and maintenance of the basic needs of those concerned, who tend to be among the lowest income groups.

Fourth, the ILO's tripartite structure would facilitate the dialogue between the interested parties which must precede any negotiated, commonly agreed guidelines and practices to be adopted in the field of trade-adjustment assistance. Tripartite expert meetings could be held to consider these issues prior to their review by ILO Industrial Committees.

Fifth, these Committees might, on the basis of more detailed studies of the technological, design and other options available, provide tripartite advice on the structural problems which might best be tackled by adjustment assistance policies encouraging transfer of labour and capital resources to other sectors, and those which could be handled by greater product specialisation or technological change. Their advice could be a significant input in the sectoral consultations called for by the Seventh Session of the United Nations General Assembly.

Sixth, the ILO's training expertise could be tapped in various ways. The Turin Centre has built up a network of major enterprises in several European countries which co-operate with its fellowship programme. Colloquia could be arranged between representatives of these industries and delegates from Third World countries to consider the training and retraining requirements of selected industries in which new patterns of international specialisation are likely to emerge. ILO management and vocational training centres in developing countries could focus more of their programmes (stressing export marketing techniques, product design and quality control) on specific sectors with good export prospects to ensure that they will be in a good position to take advantage of the new opportunities created by a reduction in trade barriers. Particular attention would be paid to skill formation activities in the small-scale, traditional sectors so that there can be a direct link between international trade-adjustment measures and national basic-needs policies within developing countries.

This list is not exhaustive but it does indicate some of the key areas where the ILO can contribute to the development of international trading relations yielding both social and economic benefits to all parties.

INTERNATIONAL MANPOWER MOVEMENTS 8

International migration in search of employment and better income-earning opportunities has been an important feature of world economic relations in the past two decades. Such migration has taken place in most regions of the world. Vast numbers of people move among the developing countries themselves, though relatively little hard data are available on this. Migrations between and to socialist countries are small in scale and may therefore be treated as a form of co-operation in the field of manpower utilisation and training. Movements of labour from one developed market economy to another are numerous, varied and in some instances quite substantial.

Most voluminous, however, are the migrations from developing countries to industrialised market-economy countries. The magnitude of these migrations and the issues they raise for migrants and for sending and receiving countries are at the heart of this chapter. A conservative estimate of the number of Third World migrants working in the industrialised market-economy countries and in the high-income OPEC members in the Middle East might be around 12 million. While the overwhelming majority of these workers would be classified as unskilled and semi-skilled, in recent years there has also been a marked acceleration in the emigration of highly trained and professional persons from developing countries.

MIGRANT WORKERS

The largest number of migrant workers can be found in Northern America, almost all of them in the United States. The overwhelming proportion are immigrants without valid papers and most of these are Mexicans. The United States Immigration and Naturalisation Service (INS) " has officially estimated that in the 1970s upwards of 4 million aliens who enter the United States illegally each year remain undetected. . . . In total, the INS estimates that there are between 7 and 12 million illegal immigrants currently residing in the United States.[1] This greatly exceeds the 400,000 or so immigrants admitted annually for permanent residence, among them many professionals and related workers. Some 1.5 million people from developing countries are permanent resident aliens. The United States further admits each year an average of 115,000 non-immigrant workers, one-third of whom are semi- or unskilled labourers.

Canada recently introduced a system of temporary employment visas designed to admit " non-immigrants " as workers for a period up to 12 months. Between 80,000 and 90,000 visas are issued each year, with a little under half going to farm work, hotel and catering and other relatively unskilled jobs that are usually taken up by people from developing countries, especially the Caribbean area.

The Caribbean area and particularly the members of CARICOM provide a very important contingent of migrants to the United States and Canada. However, the important flow which existed in the 1950s towards the United Kingdom has diminished.

Even though no movements of similar magnitude take place in Central and South America, they have been remarkably intensified in the past decade. In this connection the migration of Bolivian and Paraguayan workers to Argentina and to a certain extent of Colombians to Venezuela should be mentioned.

Western Europe has been at the forefront of the discussion concerning migrant workers, even though it accommodates only about half as many Third World workers [2] as Northern America. Table 13 shows the number of officially registered migrant workers. It is possible that a further 10 per cent of the total, most of them from poor countries, may be present illegally. There are about 1.4 million " coloured " workers in the United Kingdom (not included in table 13), the great majority of whom are British subjects.

The main countries of immigration are France and the Federal Republic of Germany, which together account for about 70 per cent of the 6 million or so foreign workers. Switzerland has the highest proportion of foreign workers in its labour force (24 per cent). Luxembourg, not included in the table, has a similarly high proportion, followed by France and the Federal Republic of Germany (9), Austria and Belgium (7), Sweden (6) and the Netherlands (5). Ten or 15 years ago Italy, Spain and Greece were the chief migrant-sending countries. More recently, Yugoslavia, Turkey, Portugal and the Maghreb countries have become the main suppliers of labour. Proportions of the

---

[1] Vernon M. Briggs, Jr.: " Mexican workers in the United States labor market: a contemporary dilemma ", in *International Labour Review* (Geneva, ILO), Nov. 1975, pp. 351-352.

[2] That is, apart from Italians, Spaniards, and " others " in table 13.

Table 13. Migrant workers in selected countries of Western Europe, 1974 (thousands)

Country of employment	Southern Europe						North Africa			Other	Citizen immigrants	Total	Migrant workers as percentage of economically active population
	Greek	Italian	Portuguese	Spanish	Turkish	Yugoslav	Algerian	Moroccan	Tunisian				
Austria	—	—	—	—	30	166	—	—	—	23	—	218	7
Belgium[1]	9	90	3	28	7	—	2	16	1	101	—	257	7
France	5	220	385	260	33	58	450	145	85	189	125	1 955	9
Germany, Fed. Rep. of	225	370	85	165	590	470	2	15	11	417	—	2 350	9
Netherlands	2	10	4	20	33	9	—	24	1	61	50	215	5
Sweden	10	4	—	—	—	24	—	—	—	184	—	222	6
Switzerland	6	338	4	83	17	28	—	—	—	234	—	711	24
Total	257	1 032	481	556	710	755	454	200	98	1 209	175	5 928	9
Migrant workers as percentage of economically active population	8	6	14	5	5	9	12	5	7	—	—	—	—

— = Figures not available, magnitude negligible, or category not applicable.
[1] 1971.
Source: National statistics.

economically active population working in industrialised countries of Western Europe range from 5 per cent in Turkey and Morocco to 12-14 per cent for Portugal and Algeria.

Migrants tend to occupy jobs which are unpleasant and have low status, and which are consequently shunned by national workers. In both France and the Federal Republic of Germany the proportion of all jobs occupied by migrants is highest in construction, followed in France by mining and quarrying and agriculture, and in the Federal Republic of Germany by manufacturing and agriculture, in that order. The services sector is least dependent on migrants except for a few branches such as hotels, catering and domestic help.

A distinctive feature of this migration in Western Europe is considered to be its temporary character. Major immigration as well as emigration countries did not want inflows and outflows to be permanent. Many, but by no means all, migrants shared this intention. However, the demand for migrant workers turned out to be structural; the unemployment situation in the countries of origin did not improve substantially, with the notable exceptions of Greece, Italy and Spain; and a great number of migrants found the material attractions abroad irresistible despite the continuing insecurity surrounding their status as non-nationals. With the onset of the recession in 1974, more severe restrictions on migration from developing countries were introduced in most West European countries; whether this is only a temporary measure or not remains to be seen. Since these controls were tightened, return flows have been smaller than previously, although the unemployment rate of foreign workers has tended to exceed that of nationals. Fears of difficulty of re-entry appear to be responsible for the reduced return flows.

Several of the high-income OPEC countries of the Middle East region are heavily dependent upon foreign workers. Three-quarters of Kuwait's labour force are migrant workers as are one-third of both Saudi Arabia's and Bahrain's. Foreigners are employed in a wide range of occupations.

In addition to the 400,000 in Saudi Arabia alone, there are 600,000 other foreigners employed in this region. Their numbers are certain to rise, at least in the short term. Extra foreign manpower requirements in Saudi Arabia have been estimated at 300,000-500,000 for the 1976-80 plan. The requirements of Iran were initially put at 700,000 by 1978 but appear to have been revised downwards since the fall in demand for oil.

More than 400,000 foreign-born Africans were employed in the Republic of South Africa in 1974.[1] This total includes 75 per cent of the 365,000 Africans

---

[1] Excluding Namibia, where some 40 per cent of the contract labour force comes from Angola.

employed in mines affiliated to the Chamber of Mines. Five out of six Lesotho citizens holding wage-earning jobs are in South Africa. Even for rapidly developing Botswana the proportion of citizens abroad is still more than one in four. Malawi suspended recruitment by South Africa following an aircraft crash in April 1974 which killed 72 Malawian miners.

The deplorable living conditions and the withholding of basic human rights of these temporary migrant workers have already been documented in Special Reports of the Director-General on the Application of the Declaration concerning the Policy of Apartheid of the Republic of South Africa.[1]

BRAIN DRAIN

During the decade 1962-72 over 170,000 highly skilled and professional persons migrated from developing countries to the United States, Canada and the United Kingdom alone (see table 14). If the industrialised countries of continental Western Europe and Australia are added, the total number of such migrants is probably at least a quarter of a million. There are also considerable flows of skilled personnel from one developing country to another. The high-income OPEC countries, in particular, have drawn heavily on the skills available in other developing countries.

The changes from the earlier system of immigration based on quotas by nationality in some countries such as the United States and Australia, and the preference given to professionals over other categories of immigrants in virtually all developed countries, are primarily responsible for the sharp increase in the brain drain in the 1960s and early 1970s.

About 75,000 of these migrants went to the United States, a relatively large proportion of them in the early 1970s. Indian scientists and engineers (13,000) and scientists, engineers and physicians from the Philippines (11,000) together accounted for one-third of the United States intake. About half of the 38,000 migrants to Canada from developing countries came from Asia (especially the Philippines and India), and about half of the 50,000 United Kingdom immigrants came from India and Pakistan. Immigrants from developing countries provided between 25 and 50 per cent of the annual United States increase in physicians and surgeons, 15 to 25 per cent of the annual increase in engineers, and about 10 per cent of the annual increase in scientists.

For some developing countries, the outflows of trained people have been quite significant in relative as well as absolute terms. For example, gross emigration from the Philippines in 1970 amounted to half of annual graduations for nurses, and to even higher proportions for physicians, surgeons and dentists.

---

[1] The *Tenth Special Report* contains a section on " Foreign African migrants in South Africa ", International Labour Conference, 59th Session, Geneva, 1974, pp. 44-46.

Table 14. Migration of professional, technical and related workers from developing countries to the United States, Canada and the United Kingdom, 1962-72

Region	Scientists and engineers			Physicians and surgeons			Teachers			Total		
	United States 1962-72[1]	Canada 1963-72	United Kingdom 1964-72	United States 1962-72[1]	Canada[2] 1963-72	United Kingdom[3] 1964-72	United States 1962-72[1]	Canada 1963-72	United Kingdom 1964-72	United States 1962-72[1]	Canada 1963-72	United Kingdom 1964-72
Asia	35 708	6 132	3 239	16 239	8 792	11 628	n.a.	5 055	8 818	51 947	19 979	23 685
Africa	2 334	523	1 035	912	302	3 845	n.a.	501	5 296	3 246	1 326	10 176
Latin America	6 974	207	1 402	5 704	199	495	n.a.	159	496	12 678	565	2 393
Europe (Greece)	279	610	n.a.	128	420	n.a.	n.a.	282	n.a.	407	1 312	n.a.
All other developing countries	2 947	3 174	2 708	2 059	6 202	13 499	n.a.	5 095	7 967	5 006	14 471	24 174
Total, developing countries	48 242	10 646	8 384	25 042	15 915	29 467	n.a.	11 092	22 577	73 284	37 653	60 428

n.a. = Not available.
[1] Excluding 1970. [2] Includes dentists, graduate nurses, medical and dental technicians. [3] Doctors, dentists and nurses.
Sources: United States: J. Bhagwati and W. Dellalfar: "The brain drain and income taxation", in World Development, 1973, table 1, p. 98 for 1962-69; National Science Foundation: Highlights, Immigrant scientists and engineers, 1973, p. 2 for 1971-72;
Canada: D. Devoretz and M. Maki: The brain drain and income taxation: some Canadian estimates, table 1;
United Kingdom: P. Balacs and A. Gordon: "The brain drain and income taxation: a UK case study", table 6. Both these papers appear in J. Bhagwati (ed.): The brain drain and taxation: theoretical and empirical estimates (North Holland Publishing Co, Amsterdam, 1976).

EFFECTS OF MIGRATION

In the vast majority of cases there seems little doubt that the workers who migrate benefit materially, although there may be social and other personal disadvantages, particularly those arising from family separation. Millions of people who were poor, unemployed or underemployed have found work yielding an income larger than would have been open to them otherwise. They have acquired some training or industrial or other experience; they have been exposed to new ideas and ways of life. Sometimes they have migrated as single individuals and sent money home for the support of dependants. In other cases they have been accompanied, or later joined, by dependants. In these cases, too, they may have sent some money home for the support of parents or other relatives remaining behind. In either case dependants, in a material sense at least, have also benefited.

Migration also has wider effects both on the countries from which the migrants come and the ones to which they go. It is, therefore, necessary to look at these effects from the point of view of these two groups of countries.

Sending countries

Temporary emigrants, and in most cases the members of their family who have been authorised to accompany or join them, are still citizens of the migrant-sending countries of origin. Hence improvement in the welfare of the migrants themselves and their dependants may be regarded as a key benefit to those countries. Apart from this important point, two further potentially significant short-term benefits accrue to countries of origin from unskilled migration for employment—reduction of unemployment and underemployment and of income inequality (which implies improvement in the job-finding and income-earning prospects of those who remain), and improvement in the balance of payments. The extent to which these two benefits are in fact attained depends on a number of factors.

A key factor is whether the emigrants are easily replaceable or not. If the migrants are unskilled persons who would otherwise have been unemployed or heavily underemployed, the gains to those remaining and the improvement in the home country income distribution are clear. If they are skilled or professional persons, their absence potentially harms the country of origin, which had to bear the costs of educating and training them, by intensifying shortages of skilled labour resources. Moreover, the temporary employment of migrant workers in jobs which are below their level of skill and qualifications leads to wastage of human resources. Furthermore, in the present circumstances, only a minority of such migrant workers are acquiring skills and work experience which facilitate their reintegration into the national production process. On the other hand, migrants may send home substantial remittances, which can make a valuable contribution to the home country's balance of payments. In 1974, for instance, the Mediterranean countries received at least US$7,000 million in remittances from migrants working in Western Europe. If saved and invested, these sums may also increase the country's rate of economic growth and level of income per head. At the same time, some migrants may acquire new skills and work experience, which could be utilised on their return home.

However, in actual practice these benefits are not always realised. Often it is not the poorest people who are able to migrate. In certain Mediterranean countries, migration has had the effect of intensifying shortages of skilled manual labour. Large-scale migration from the countryside, especially if it is confined largely to younger and better educated sections of the population, as in the countries of southern Africa, may contribute to rural stagnation. While these considerations do not offset the short-term advantages of migration noted above, they point to the need for improving the situation.

Receiving countries

The ability to import labour temporarily as required means that a country has, in effect, a reserve supply of labour. This increases the flexibility of the economy's response to shifts in the level and structure of demand. In times of recession migrants tend to be dismissed first and are often sent home, providing an anti-cyclical cushion against unemployment for national workers. In the expansionary phase, access to foreign labour dampens inflationary pressures, thereby contributing to stable growth.

For employers in industrialised receiving countries the migratory labour system seems to offer a clear balance of advantages. For workers and trade unions the case is less clear. On the one hand, migrants tend to do the socially undesirable jobs, and their spending raises the demand for all jobs, including those done by nationals. On the other hand, unskilled and semi-skilled migrants tend to be concentrated in the lowest-paying jobs. Their presence may prevent wages from rising and may cause nationals who cannot leave such jobs to suffer. This has been reported in the case of illegal immigration into the United States and for the Republic of South Africa, although in the latter case other factors are far more important. It is, however, doubtful whether this analysis can be generalised to all situations. Much depends on the impact of migration on over-all economic growth. To the extent that migration leads to faster growth, as it seems to have done in the European countries most dependent on foreign labour, the absolute level of wages for less skilled groups would be higher than in the absence of migration.

Whatever the economics of the matter, it seems clear that social problems and tensions mount when the foreign population of a country grows too rapidly. These problems include pressure on housing, transport, schools, hospitals and other social services, and racial and ethnic discrimination. Much of this pressure results from the inability or unwillingness of receiving countries to supply migrants and their dependants with the public services that are due to them. Almost everywhere migrant workers pay exactly the same direct and indirect taxes as local workers and have social security contributions deducted, yet they receive disproportionately little in return. The latter is partly due to the fact that because migrants typically are young, healthy and often single, their demands on the social services are proportionately smaller than those of the local population.

With regard to the brain drain, highly skilled and professionally trained migrants help to supplement the supply of persons with their particular skills in receiving countries. In general, they are better able to integrate themselves into the host society than unskilled and semi-skilled temporary migrants, and social problems tend to be less severe.

An important long-term issue in this area concerns the impact of migrations of unskilled persons on the output structure in the industrialised countries and hence on the international division of labour. This is a complex subject and not enough is known to warrant firm conclusions. This is one area which calls for further study and research. It has been argued by some that migrations of unskilled persons depress relative wages for unskilled and semi-skilled occupations in the receiving industrialised countries. This in turn enables the latter to continue producing labour-intensive manufactures which might otherwise be produced in and exported from developing countries.

This may be true, but in a dynamic context the situation is far more complex. The presence of migrant workers may enable labour-short economies to achieve higher rates of economic growth, thereby stimulating capital accumulation and technological progress and generating larger imports from developing countries. Whatever the ultimate impact of migration may be in a particular situation, it seems clear that there would continue to be a demand for migrant workers in certain categories of jobs even if the developing countries steadily increase their share of the world production of the more labour-intensive manufactures.

POLICY IMPLICATIONS

The preceding analysis shows that in the short-term benefits of migration to the sending and to the receiving countries as well as to the migrants are clear. The possible long-term economic and social costs are more difficult to evaluate. However, in the case of loss of professional or highly trained persons the costs of migration outweigh the benefits from the sending countries' point of view.

Some of the social costs are, however, more readily apparent and call for remedial action.

The aim of national and international policies should be threefold: (1) to reduce the hardships and inconveniences incurred by migrants and their families without blocking their opportunities to gain net benefits in this way; (2) to provide more attractive alternatives to migration so that bilateral and multilateral co-operation between countries where such migrations exist leads to reducing to a minimum migrations arising from unemployment and poverty; and (3) to ensure that the welfare of other citizens in the sending or receiving countries is not adversely affected by migration or its alternatives and that the over-all gains are shared in a manner each society deems appropriate.

National measures: sending countries

From the point of view of the strategy proposed in this report, the sending country may wish the poorest segments of its population to benefit most from migration and to limit the brain drain. Selection and control by administrative procedures infringe basic human rights, tend to be inefficient and anomalous, risk encouraging corruption, and may also be unacceptable to the receiving country. Economic incentives and disincentives need to be created so that the same results are achieved directly or indirectly. There is a great deal of practical action which governments, employers and trade unions can take to give effect to these principles.

Highly skilled and semi-skilled workers coming from industries or occupations with an actual or potential shortage of labour might be excluded from any publicly assisted migration schemes. Every effort could be made by the employment services to find domestic vacancies for prospective migrants at levels appropriate to their skills. Effective education and information campaigns could be undertaken to make clear the full implications of the emigration policy to the population and to warn prospective migrants of the false inducements offered by dubious middlemen. Trade unions could discourage their skilled members from emigrating and take action to disseminate recruitment offers among unemployed and unskilled workers.

Second, schemes might be established (savings societies, co-operatives, agro-industrial projects) to encourage the productive use of remittances. For example, the employment creating effects of remittances might be mobilised along the lines adopted in Yugoslavia in recent years. Migrants originating from the same region could pool their savings to buy relatively cheap and labour-intensive machinery, especially if the materials to be processed could be bought from a local producer in the home country. Assured of supply, the machinery could be worked in the home villages of migrants; priority of employment might be given to members of the migrants' families. Training and supervisory needs would be comparatively small; returning migrants might be able to put some of their skills to use as instructors and supervisors.

Third, suitably skilled workers residing abroad might be given incentives (housing, job security) to return home and make productive use of their skills for the benefit of their countries.

National measures: receiving countries

Governments, employers and trade unions should ensure that migrants are protected against exploitation, and are accorded equality of opportunity and treatment. These principles and the means of applying them are spelt out in some detail in the Migrant Workers (Supplementary Provisions) Convention, 1975 (No. 143), and the accompanying Migrant Workers Recommendation, 1975 (No. 151). It is to be hoped that special efforts will be made to ratify the Convention and to give effect to the provisions of the Recommendation.

Receiving countries could also do much to facilitate the return of migrants to their home countries. Since one of the critical factors in the return of needed manpower is the lack of housing, the provision of adequate accommodation is essential to achieve any return movement. Two possibilities are open. First, industrialised countries could make a special allocation of foreign aid for the provision of accommodation for return migrants. Second, a key group of foremen, gang leaders and skilled craftsmen in the construction industry could be chosen from identified migrant workers willing to return; this target group would be given training for the purpose of setting up construction co-operatives; and with the help of appropriate government assistance, plus the injection of part of the migrants' savings, it would be given the opportunity to erect housing both for its own members and for other potential return migrants in the areas where they are needed. Three important goals could thus be achieved simultaneously: (i) the home countries would regain scarce building workers; (ii) co-operative attitudes would be fostered; and (iii) one of the dimensions of basic needs—lack of shelter—would be tackled directly. Once the initial targets of accommodation for the building workers themselves and for a certain number of skilled return migrants had been met, the expansion of the area would ensure subsequent employment for the members of the co-operative.

International measures

Recruitment of substantial numbers of migrant workers in one country for employment in another country should be governed by agreements between the countries concerned, after consultation with employers' and workers' organisations. One of the principal aims of such agreements should be to prevent migrations in abusive conditions.[1] Another major goal would be to bring about steady rather than fluctuating flows of emigrants, return migrants and remittances and to make them predictable, continuous and assured so as to facilitate the implementation of long-term programmes for economic and social development. Receiving countries could help by providing semi-annual notifications of the magnitude and broad categories of expected demand for manpower six months ahead of impending return movements. This would naturally have an indicative rather than a binding character and would leave employers free to make their dispositions. It would facilitate the planning process of sending countries, in particular as regards information for, pre-selection and possible training of candidates for emigration.

The collaboration on pre-migration training begun in the Mediterranean area should be intensified and extended to other areas. This would be necessary and appropriate to effect the fullest participation of the unemployed, under-privileged and socially most needy persons, while ensuring that employers obtain the skills they ask for. As a rule, migrant-sending countries could bear the costs of equipment and migrant-receiving countries could defray the personnel costs with or without reimbursement from employers.

When migrants return to their home country their entitlement to short-term and long-term social security benefits may be in question and should be resolved in a spirit of international co-operation and maintenance of migrants' rights. Where migrants who are in receipt of short-term benefits such as unemployment payments return, they should either be paid the remaining entitlement in the form of a lump sum, or the lump sum should be transferred to the competent authority of the home country with a view to providing the returned migrant with local unemployment benefits for the maximum permissible time. Where migrants or their dependants return while under medical treatment, the competent body of the previous country of employment should be held responsible for expenses until the end of the treatment. Here and below, " return " is meant to exclude extended holidays.

The main long-term benefits are old-age pensions. When migrant workers and their dependants return two types of situation arise. First, the laws or regulations of the former country of employment, or international social security agreements, may entitle them to the receipt of pension according to the *pro-rata-temporis* principle on reaching pensionable age. Second, employment abroad may not give rise to social security rights under the laws or regulations of migrant-receiving countries or international arrangements, as is often the case for seasonal or temporary workers. In either situation, new forms of

---

[1] See the Migrant Workers (Supplementary Provisions) Convention, 1975 (No. 143), Part I.

bilateral or multilateral co-operation should be established to protect the rights of workers and dependants as well as to ensure an equitable distribution of the responsibilities and of the gains from migration. Efforts could, for instance, be directed towards paying over the amounts in question to the competent social security authorities of the migrant's country of origin, which should then disburse them at local rates or establish social action funds in the fields of social security. These proposals should not be incompatible with the insurance or fiscal principles prevailing in certain migrant-receiving countries.

Rich countries have acquired a certain responsibility towards not only the migrants but also the countries from whence they come. Poor countries owe it to their citizens to pursue development strategies which would enable them to be productively employed at home. One way of reconciling these obligations would be to institutionalise bilateral or multilateral co-operation for taking practical steps to increase the flow of capital and know-how to migrant-sending countries with a view to establishing a new and mutually more beneficial division of labour, particularly with respect to import-competing labour-intensive lines of production. A complementary step in this direction could be the implementation in developed countries of active trade adjustment assistance policies, as discussed in Chapter 7.

Supporting ILO activities

Various international labour Conventions and Recommendations referred to earlier in this chapter provide a framework for the protection of migrant workers and their families. In addition the ILO has already provided its technical support to most multilateral regional social security agreements in Africa, Central and South America and Western Europe. This type of action is being developed as regards other regions. The ILO might also give assistance in the establishment of a system designed to improve information on the availability of jobs for migrants and the potential demand for them. This would involve collection of information on working and living conditions, immigration laws and regulations, and manpower needs in the receiving countries and on the number and type of workers interested in emigration in the sending countries. Such information could be pooled and made available for the benefit of all countries interested in receiving or supplying migrant workers as well as for the benefit of present and future migrants themselves. Workers' and employers' organisations could play an important role in the establishment of a clearing-house for information of this type. Such a clearing-house function might be arranged on a regional basis in the first instance. For example, given the growing manpower requirements of the OPEC members in the Middle East and the ready availability of such manpower in several Asian countries, such a system could play a potentially useful role there. This suggestion is in line with the idea of a regional skilled manpower pool outlined by the Prime Minister of Sri Lanka at the 60th Session (1975) of the International Labour Conference and endorsed by the Eighth Asian Regional Conference (Colombo, 1975). The Conference may, therefore, wish to recommend the establishment of an ad hoc group to study the objectives, functions and organisation of a clearing-house system along the lines set out above.

Policy implications : brain drain

Some of the principles and proposals outlined earlier are also relevant to measures that might be considered in the context of brain drain. This is an area where the primary responsibility rests with the developing countries suffering from loss of trained manpower. However, the developed countries can assist in at least two respects. First, as noted earlier, their immigration laws generally favour professional and other highly qualified migrants. Consideration might be given through bilateral, regional or multilateral agreements among the affected countries to minimising such preferences. Second, several developed countries have been unable to train adequate manpower in certain fields such as medicine and engineering to meet their national needs and have relied on migrants from developing countries to make up the shortfall. Increased output of personnel in those fields through expansion of the necessary training facilities will go some way in slowing the brain drain.

National or multinational schemes may be introduced to encourage nationals currently residing abroad to return home. The selective migration programme conducted by the Intergovernmental Committee for European Migrations (ICEM) in Latin America is an interesting experiment in this regard. Under this programme, ICEM contacts potential immigrants living in industrialised countries (both nationals currently living abroad and others), and helps them to find suitable jobs in Latin America. It also provides them with a range of services to ease the transition process, including liaison on salary and job conditions, partial payment of moving expenses, provision of initial medical insurance and settling-in allowances, reunification of families, and so on. Programmes of this type provide a potentially significant means of combating, or at least offsetting, the brain drain. Consideration might be given to the extension of such type of programmes to other regions where the brain drain is an important problem.

In developing countries, consideration might be given to requiring students to serve a certain number of years in the home country before emigrating; if they wished to emigrate without serving, they would have to repay the government the subsidy element in their education. Such schemes operate more or less successfully in a number of countries. Reforms in education and training systems called for under the strategy proposed in this report may contribute to a reduction in the brain drain. The role of foreign training, which is an important factor in the present brain drain, might also be expected to decline under the suggested new approach.

TECHNOLOGICAL CHOICE AND INNOVATION FOR DEVELOPING COUNTRIES

9

Technology has long been recognised as an important factor in development. Historical studies have demonstrated the substantial contribution of technological progress to the long-term rise in labour productivity and output in the industrialised economies, and its impact on the level and structure of employment and incomes.

Discussion of technology's role within the developing world has been subject to considerable controversy, however. The issues and the interrelationships involved are certainly complex. But the task of the policy maker has not been made easier by the tendency for the advice rendered to him on this topic to be polarised into two, widely divergent schools of thought.

On the one hand, the protagonists of the latest, advanced technology have argued that:

— modern techniques are the most efficient; their adoption will allow the development gap to be closed more quickly;

— modern technology provides economies of scale which result in capital saving (i.e. lower capital/output coefficients) and larger surpluses at the enterprise level; if invested, these surpluses will increase the future rate of growth of output;

— modern technology is necessary to achieve high quality standards, particularly for international markets;

— modern technology often economises on scarce managerial and technical skills and reduces material wastage;

— in most sectors there is little practical choice available; the so-called technological spectrum between traditional and modern techniques is really a vacuum;

— reliance on obsolete, labour-intensive technologies would condemn the developing countries to technological backwardness and stagnation;

— any employment problems that might ensue from concentration on modern technology are best handled by income transfers (social security, subsidies, free services) to those affected or by special employment-creating programmes in one or two selected sectors where greater technological flexibility is said to exist (e.g. public works).

On the other hand, the advocates of labour-intensive technologies claim that:

— a technology's characteristics cannot be separate from the socio-economic environment in which it has to operate; technical efficiency should not be confused with economic efficiency;

— most modern technology originates in the highly industrialised economies whose needs and circumstances are currently very different from those prevailing in developing countries in terms of factor (land, labour, capital, entrepreneurship) endowment, size of markets and enterprises, consumer incomes and tastes, skill levels, structure of distribution, transport facilities, etc;

— the most desirable technologies for developing countries are therefore those which require little capital per worker (i.e. labour-intensive), can be used efficiently on a small scale, are easily serviced and repaired, do not require high levels of education or training to operate and utilise locally available materials;

— a much wider range of technologies with these characteristics exists than is believed by the central planners; they are not readily available because price distortions and other biases encourage the suppliers of technology (research institutions, machinery manufacturers, multinationals) to concentrate on the initially easier transfer of current, " off-the-shelf " technology designed for the major markets of the industrialised countries;

— where the requisite labour-intensive, capital-saving technologies do not exist, it would be worth while to devote increased resources to the development and adaptation of suitable indigenous technologies; given appropriate incentives and institutional arrangements, the benefits ought to outweigh greatly the costs (economic, social and political) of the present dependence upon alien technologies;

— technology should be treated as a strategic variable in development strategy in which the policy maker guides the investor's choice between alternatives (new or existing), either directly by central planning decisions or indirectly through policy instruments affecting the " price signals " faced by private entrepreneurs; otherwise, there is little prospect of combining growth with equity;

— the high and increasing capital intensity of advanced technology, plus the severe constraints on the investment funds available, would mean that only a very small proportion of the labour force would benefit from this kind of technological progress; the majority would be condemned indefinitely to stagnation, underemployment and reliance on " trickle-down " or charity for any future growth in their incomes.

Confronted with these conflicting views, and in the absence of incontro-vertible evidence either way, it is not surprising that the policy makers in the developing world have tended to adopt what they considered to be a " neutral " position on this controversy. But of course the existing constellation of forces affecting technological policy and investment decisions is not neutral. For a variety of reasons it is generally leaning heavily in favour of the transfer of unadapted capital-intensive technology, at least in those large-scale public sector projects included in development plans or sponsored by foreign aid programmes, in private investment by multinationals and activities supported by major financial institutions.

The situation remained like this during the early years of independence and the first few development plans. But as part of the reappraisal process leading up to the mid-term review of the Second Development Decade and the Seventh Special Session of the United Nations General Assembly, an increasing number of analysts and policy makers have questioned the wisdom of prevailing technological policies.

As a contribution to this evaluation the ILO World Employment Pro-gramme has sought to provide the planners, policy makers and investors with objective, factual data upon which to make an independent assessment. It has undertaken a series of studies in several economic sectors and groups of products and services.[1] The investigations have been carried out in the main within developing countries, often with the collaboration of local economists, engineers and technologists and their institutions. Particular emphasis has been placed on estimates of the employment and income distribution effects of alternative technologies in actual operating conditions, without neglecting the aspect of economic efficiency.

The ILO has by no means been alone in this work. Similar investigations in complementary fields have been pursued by several other agencies within the United Nations family. The Food and Agriculture Organisation has sponsored several studies on the effects of farm mechanisation on production and

---

[1] ILO: *Technology and employment in industry: a case study approach,* edited by A. S. Bhalla (Geneva, 1975); idem: *Roads and redistribution: social costs and benefits of labour-intensive road construction in Iran,* by G. W. Irvin *et al.* (Geneva, 1975); idem: *Second-hand equipment in a developing country: a study of jute processing in Kenya,* by C. Cooper and R. Kaplinsky in collaboration with R. Turner (Geneva, 1974); and idem: *Mechanisation and employment in agriculture: case studies from four continents* (Geneva, 1973).

employment. The United Nations Industrial Development Organisation has been the executing agency responsible for industrial research institutions set up at the national and regional levels under United Nations Development Programme auspices. The World Bank has put substantial effort into a study of alternative road construction techniques. The United Nations Conference on Trade and Development and the World Intellectual Property Organisation have been particularly concerned with the search for faster and cheaper ways of diffusing patented technology more widely to potential users in developing countries.

Outside the UN system, various aspects of the problem are being explored by, for example, Yale University, the Massachusetts Institute of Technology and the Georgia Technological Institute in the United States, by the Intermediate Technology Development Group, Strathclyde University and the Tropical Products Institute in the United Kingdom, and by the Aachen Technological University in the Federal Republic of Germany. Within developing countries, some significant findings have already emerged from institutions in India, Ghana, Tanzania and the Republic of Korea.

In the private sector the pioneering work of Philips in its Utrecht pilot plant and the considerable resources invested by General Motors and Ford to develop a low-cost versatile vehicle and power source may be noted.

These are just a few examples of the burgeoning efforts being made across the world to provide reliable information and concrete solutions to assist the policy maker in framing his technological policies. Many questions remain. And of course this expanded activity still represents only a tiny fraction of the resources devoted to the technological problems of the developed countries. But it has provided a substantial body of evidence to guide policy decisions.

What conclusions can be drawn at this stage?

First, the range of technologies available and in use throughout the world is much wider than may have been thought. This is true for agricultural cultivation and harvesting techniques, the majority of industrial products (particularly those with a technological life of more than 20 years), excavation, earth-moving and some road and building construction techniques, means of transport and a variety of service activities.

Second, there are indeed several products and processes (e.g. fertilisers, some chemicals, steel) where current advanced technologies represent the most appropriate solution in circumstances where the optimum may be unattainable in the short run. In certain circumstances (e.g. availability of good quality raw materials and cheap energy) the economic advantages of the capital-intensive plants required will outweigh any social disadvantages. But in order to ensure that this kind of technology is confined to uses where it is clearly superior on balance to alternatives (including importation of the finished product), more rigorous application of social benefit-cost analysis needs to be made by planning authorities. Possible " backwash " effects on the traditional sectors should be considered. As far as possible these technologies should be restricted to the exploitation of export markets where strong comparative advantages exist or to the satisfaction of domestic basic needs in least-cost ways where there are few indigenous substitutes.

Third, if this kind of screening process is applied, further steps need to be taken to ensure that those capital-intensive techniques passing through the screen really do maximise total resource utilisation (and not just labour productivity) in actual operations. Training of managers and skilled workers is critical in this. ILO-assisted training institutes and the Turin Centre already play important roles in this respect. But some reorientation of training curricula and case study material seems to be desirable. Greater emphasis should be placed on raising the productivity of capital, through, inter alia, the organisation of shift work, activity analysis, preventive maintenance, and performance incentives linked to machine utilisation rates. Managers need to be taught to scrutinise all processes (e.g. material transport) which might be as effectively performed by manpower, aided by simple equipment, rather than by automatic devices.

TECHNOLOGICAL PROGRESS IN THE TRADITIONAL SECTOR

The adoption of such measures would free substantial investment resources which could then be directed to raising the technological levels of the bulk of the labour force in the small-scale, traditional sectors, with a long-term objective of eliminating technological and economic dualism. This corresponds closely to the pattern of development which has taken place in Japan.

The lesson from Japanese experience which has special relevance to developing countries is subcontracting, which gave small-scale enterprises access to improved technical know-how and finance while relieving them of some of the management and marketing functions better performed on a large scale. Also important is the applied technological research carried out in Prefectural Research Institutes (with specialisation according to locational advantages) and the emphasis on technical training and extension services reaching out to the small producer. As a result, over the past 20 years, the rate of technological change has been greater in small establishments than in large ones, leading to a convergence in productivity and wage levels which had previously been widely different.

An additional factor to note in Japanese experience in closing the technological and income gap between the traditional and modern sectors has been the strength of the cultural identity of the average consumer with traditional Japanese designs and materials in clothing, footwear, processed foodstuffs and beverages and housing materials and decorations. This allowed the traditional producers considerable time to adjust to the competition of imports after the Meiji restoration. In many developing countries this cultural identity with indigenous products has been severely weakened. It needs to be revived through advertising, the demonstration effect of the élite, governmental purchasing policy and perhaps fiscal incentives. Expanding domestic market opportunities for the products of the small-scale producers will thus provide the incentives and funds for progressive technological change in the sector. The developing countries with the most vigorous small-scale producers tend indeed to be those which have retained national characteristics in consumer taste.

A corollary is the presence of an indigenous engineering industry capable of meeting the needs of the producers for low-cost, intermediate or appropriate technology. Prominent examples are India, Pakistan and Egypt. Their engineering workshops show remarkable vitality and skill in using what some observers might regard as obsolete machine tools to fabricate machinery and implements covering a substantial part of the technological spectrum.

The contribution of the indigenous engineering industry to an appropriate pattern of technological progress could be further enhanced if a number of handicaps were removed. These include difficulties in obtaining imported raw materials at competitive prices due to the licensing system; inadequate access to credit; unfair competition from foreign engineering firms resulting from a combination of duty-free machinery imports, over-valued exchange rates and tied aid programmes; the provision of subsidised capital and other scarce inputs to large-scale projects with technological specifications outside the reach of the indigenous engineering units; government training programmes tending to concentrate unduly on long-term courses and the latest techniques rather than on improvements which can be realistically applied in the circumstances; and the absence of special programmes to provide these engineering firms with blueprints, specifications or even sample models of proven engineering designs from abroad despite the great ingenuity in copying and eventually adapting such designs which they have demonstrated.

The total effect of these constraints has been to retard unduly the growth of the engineering industries in many developing countries. Yet very few enterprises are so self-sufficient in technology that they can invent new processing machinery as well as develop new product designs. Experience in developed countries has demonstrated that a close relationship between engineering firms and their product clients provides the feedback between research, practical application and market requirements which is so vital to harmonious technological change.

The extent to which the technological needs of the smaller, largely agrarian developing countries can be satisfied by a domestic engineering industry is of course severely limited initially, except in such fields as animal-drawn vehicles and agricultural implements, building and hand tools generally.

However, they would have much to gain from strengthening their technological links with other developing countries (including especially India, Pakistan and Egypt) whose engineering experience and capacity are probably more relevant to their needs than the current preoccupations of the engineers and technologists in the highly industrialised countries.

This form of collective self-reliance among developing countries would seem appropriate, particularly when comparative advantage would allow for a rational division of labour and exchange between them (e.g. between the land-abundant countries of Africa and the overcrowded industrial centres of South Asia).

In all developing countries there is ample scope for training programmes to develop the requisite engineering and design skills. The ILO is already heavily involved with institutions, training machinists, fitters, welders, electricians, mechanics, woodworkers, bricklayers, pattern makers and foundry operatives. Industrial engineering techniques feature prominently in management curricula. In the main, the focus is on techniques required in the modern, large-scale sector, although valuable programmes have been devised for the informal sectors in some small-industry institutes, crafts training centres, co-operative common facility workshops, etc. Their impact on a basic-needs strategy could be increased in various ways, e.g. by providing day-release and night school courses for upgrading the skills of those already employed; establishing mobile demonstration workshops to introduce geographically scattered small entrepreneurs to improved technologies; recruiting experts for internationally assisted projects with practical experience of small-scale engineering in developing countries; and by training draughtsmen and design engineers for specialised appropriate technology institutions with the objective of making blueprints and models embodying low-cost technology more widely available to small engineering workshops.

THE RELATIVE EFFICIENCY OF SMALL-SCALE APPROPRIATE TECHNOLOGY

The performance of small units employing a combination of traditional and intermediate technology generally compares favourably with large-scale units on the efficiency indicators of particular relevance—capital/output, capital/surplus coefficients, yields per acre of land, and personal propensities to save and invest. Several explanations have been given for these findings. Their product/technology/skill mix is better adapted to the environment. Prices of the production factors available to the small-scale entrepreneur reflect relative scarcities and opportunity costs more accurately, so they are provided with greater inducements to get the most out of their land, capital and imported inputs and to make more intensive use of cheap, abundant labour.

Their large-scale counterparts are too often subsidised and over-protected and have unmotivated, inexperienced managers. Some studies have shown that the comparison between the small and large-scale enterprises revealed by the census data may even underestimate the relative efficiency of the former. For example, recalculation of the cost of inputs and value of output in the large-scale enterprise sector in Ghana and Pakistan in the 1960s, using competitive international prices rather than distorted domestic prices, has shown that their efficiency has been grossly overstated in the published data. Conversely, unduly conservative estimates of the value of output in the unenumerated informal sector have sometimes been included in the national accounts.

This evidence of course does not imply that small units have intrinsic advantages across the board. But it does suggest that, in the particular circumstances of developing countries, technologies with the most appropriate scale and factor proportions will be encouraged by ensuring that prices accurately reflect relative scarcities. The indications are that, compared with the present structure, this would tend to raise capital-intensity levels somewhat in the small-scale sector while increasing labour absorption in large firms. As greater efficiency would be stimulated in both sectors, the net outcome should be consistent with the three goals of growth, fuller employment, and a reduction in the numbers below a basic-needs poverty line. The Republic of South Korea can be cited as one example where these results have been achieved in this way.

TECHNOLOGICAL RESEARCH

It would, however, be misleading to infer that the problem is exclusively one of incentives and opportunities, and that the appropriate technological response would be immediately forthcoming and applied. National pride and prestige considerations are certainly non-economic barriers to the more widespread use of technologies which are considered outmoded but objectively remain the best available for the circumstances. But no country would wish to rely entirely on techniques developed elsewhere, whether currently or in the past.

Innovation which incorporates the full extent of scientific knowledge, but translates it into more appropriate forms, holds out the prospect of yielding optimum solutions. Yet the costs and difficulties in pursuing this goal should not be underestimated. Those countries which have pushed back the frontiers of technological and scientific knowledge have incurred heavy costs and waste (through following false leads and through duplication) as well as gaining substantial rewards.

How can developing countries minimise the costs of innovative research and maximise the rewards? Various studies of research institutions in selected countries indicate that the most successful formulas include the following elements:

(i) A fairly high degree of specialisation by product group or sector (e.g. the International Rice Research Institute); technological know-how is rarely interchangeable between products except at a very general level of engineering or scientific principles.

(ii) Close links with similar institutions in other countries which over the years have acquired a profound knowledge of the materials and processes involved if not of the particular socio-economic setting in which they need to be combined by the more recent institution. The UNDP has proposed sponsorship of such " twinning " arrangements to encourage an exchange of know-how and personnel.

(iii) Close relationships with the users of the technology developed; this may best be stimulated by including representatives of user industries on the governing boards and by charging a levy on member firms of employer associations to ensure their financial interest in the institution's work.

(iv) An appropriate salary and incentive structure for the staff which rewards the development of practical applications rather than theoretical investigations.

If these research institutions can add to the stock of appropriate technology in this manner, there remains the problem of communication. Sufficient funds should be available for demonstration activities and for the training of key personnel from user industries. But the need for widespread diffusion applies to existing as well as new technologies.

As noted earlier, engineering firms can be vital disseminating agents, as they convert prototypes into tested, refined machinery and have a commercial interest in their propagation. For these reasons the machinery development division of the International Rice Research Institute, for example, has worked closely with selected engineering firms in the Philippines, Thailand and Singapore. But information has also to reach the multitude of scattered workshops. And potential users may need more objective data before making their selection. There is ample scope for information clearing-houses, instructional and self-help manuals, trade journals, newsletters from employers' associations, extension services of small industry institutes, etc.

INTERNATIONAL CO-ORDINATION

Arrangements need to be made to co-ordinate and maintain an over-all perspective for the diverse work under the label of appropriate technology which is going on within the United Nations system. The need for this co-ordination has been recognised in various UN resolutions. The resolution on science and technology in relation to industrial development, adopted by the 51st Session of the Economic and Social Council, recommends that UNIDO, the ILO and the FAO undertake a joint project to provide more information on alternative technologies in selected industries of interest to developing countries. It also requests UNESCO, UNIDO and the ILO to examine with the educational and training authorities of member States ways of including the appropriate technology concept in the curricula for engineers and managers. More recently the Second General Conference of UNIDO (Lima, March 1975) called for the adoption of a co-operative programme of action by UNIDO, the ILO, UNCTAD and the WIPO relating to " appropriate industrial technology ". Finally, Resolution 3362 (S-VII) adopted by the Seventh Special Session of the United Nations General Assembly called for a " strengthening . . . of the technological infrastructure " and " the creation of suitable indigenous technology ", " the establishment of an international centre for the exchange of technological information for the sharing of research findings relevant to developing countries " and " the establishment of an industrial technological information bank ".

The proposals outlined below are inspired by the conclusions and recommendations of the United Nations General Assembly.

CONSULTATIVE GROUP ON APPROPRIATE TECHNOLOGY

No mechanism for mobilising multilateral and bilateral resources and determining research priorities in appropriate technology as yet exists. However, it is equally clear that if the resolution of the Seventh Special Session of the United Nations General Assembly to the effect that the developed countries should " increase substantially the proportion of their research and development devoted to specific problems of primary interest to developing countries, and in the creation of suitable indigenous technology " is to be implemented, the creation of such a mechanism would be highly desirable as a matter of priority. The ILO, with its tripartite structure, should be in a particularly good position to play an active role in this respect since it can involve non-governmental organisations which are becoming more active in this area, particularly as regards rural and small-scale technology development and dissemination. The Conference may therefore wish to consider recommending the establishment of a Consultative Group on Appropriate Technology.[1]

---

[1] A recent ILO Technical Meeting on Adaptation of Technology (organised in collaboration with UNIDO and ESCAP with UNDP financial support) gave the highest priority to the establishment of such a consultative group. See ILO: *Policies and programmes of action to encourage the use of technologies appropriate to Asian conditions and priority needs*, Report of

This group would concentrate primarily on the secondary and tertiary sectors, since research on agricultural technology is already being promoted through the Consultative Group for International Agricultural Research (CGIAR), established by the UNDP, the World Bank and the FAO.

Some experience with such Consultative Groups has already been gained. The CGIAR, founded in 1971, was designed mainly to mobilise funds from international funding agencies, governments (bilateral donors) and private sources, and for promoting agricultural research through the establishment of international agricultural research centres. Participation of major regions of the developing world is ensured through country representatives. The Rockefeller and Ford Foundations and international and bilateral donors were instrumental in financing the establishment of various agricultural research centres. All the research programmes supported by the CGIAR have international governing bodies and international staffs. Most of the programmes have so far concentrated on biological research although some institutes like the International Rice Research Institute have already made some beginnings in the design of farm equipment.

The Consultative Group on Food Production and Investment proposed by the World Food Conference is another example of an institution designed to promote internationally agreed objectives. Unlike the CGIAR, however, this Group is not aimed so much at financing the establishment of international institutions as at making a critical examination of investment flows and resource transfers for food production, investment strategies and rural development.

It would seem that for the implementation of the resolution of the Seventh Special Session of the United Nations General Assembly the Consultative Group on Appropriate Technology would be better modelled on the CGIAR than on the Food Production and Investment Group.

The principal donor organisations concerned with the utilisation of more appropriate technologies would form the Consultative Group on Appropriate Technology. Both international and bilateral organisations and private foundations would be invited to participate.

The priority responsibility of the Consultative Group would be to suggest programmes of action taking into account other programmes under way or being planned, and to provide for their adequate financing. The priority problem areas could be identified from among candidates by small task forces. Once a candidate problem area had been given a priority by the Consultative Group, it could be entrusted to an appropriate international or regional

---

the Technical Meeting on Adaptation of Technology to suit Special Market Conditions of Developing Countries, Bangkok, 3-14 November 1975 (doc. ILO/TMAT/75/R.1/Rev.; mimeographed).

institute. If such institutions did not exist, the Consultative Group might sponsor feasibility studies on their creation. Such studies and other supporting services could be provided to the Group by an International Appropriate Technology Unit.

AN INTERNATIONAL APPROPRIATE TECHNOLOGY UNIT

This Unit would have the following tasks: first, to identify areas in which technological innovation can have a significant impact; second, to achieve concentrated, co-ordinated research and development in these areas; third, to remove the barriers to widespread dissemination of the results of research.

This new mechanism should closely co-ordinate its work with the " UNIDO Clearing House on Industrial Information ", the " FAO International Information Systems for the Agricultural Sciences and Technology ", and the proposed UNCTAD " Technology Transfer and Development Centres ", all of which have important specialised roles to play. The proposed Unit is not meant to be a clearing-house or an industrial data bank. It is envisaged as being different from a normal international or national institute: hence the use of the term " Unit ".

The Unit would concentrate on four to six broad areas and a limited number of issues in each. These might include, for example, food processing; solar power and other small-scale sources of power; simple modes of transport; the development of equipment for lifting and moving water, brick-making and other building materials.

The need for selectivity implies that efforts should be concentrated on certain areas, at least initially. The Unit should be alert to switch to new areas when existing priority has developing its own momentum, at national or regional levels, or when technological barriers suggest that the effort was premature or misdirected.

The International Unit should build up national research and development capacity as closely linked to users as possible and not carry on research of its own. The technologies developed are much more likely to be adapted to local conditions if research and development are done mainly in national and regional institutions; similarly, the learning effects would be most likely to accrue to those who would most benefit from them.

The Unit should be a catalyst—identifying areas, mobilising interest, exchanging basic data, co-ordinating research and development, assisting in channelling flows of finance and technical personnel, and communicating results. This requires that it operate through and within a network of national and regional institutes. This approach should have the advantage of increasing the Unit's flexibility both in selecting its areas of emphasis and in switching to new topics as the need arises. It will also promote research and development in developing-country institutions and by their nationals.

The main objective of the Unit would be the promotion of technologies appropriate for the needs of the urban and the rural poor in developing countries. It is important that a single institution be concerned with both these functions because of the obvious links between the two. Adequate world communications, for instance, may reveal that in a particular area of activity the problem is not so much one of research and development as of lack of information about appropriate techniques developed elsewhere. Quite often communications gaps result in duplication by many research institutes in developing countries of work which has already been done elsewhere.

The Unit would collect information on countries and areas in which the technology sought was known to be in use, how this technology was employed and the extension programmes established to encourage its adoption. Such information would make it possible for the clients of the Unit to decide which institutions should be visited or contacted for more detailed data. Because of the integral relationship of development and extension to the actual use of technology, data from such non-institutional sources of information as domestic consultancy and design services, trade information brokers and productivity institutes might also be collected and communicated.

Agencies such as India's Appropriate Technology Cell and Pakistan's Appropriate Technology Development Unit, and the national and regional centres of technology transfer and development proposed by UNCTAD [1] would supply information on existing techniques and would identify needs among potential users for the International Unit. On the other hand, the International Unit would transmit information about existing technological alternatives to other developing countries with similar needs. Once the local institutions had received from the Unit information on research gaps and sponsorship of high priority research and development, the results of such research would be transmitted back to the Unit for communication to the rest of the world, and to the users through national governmental and non-governmental agencies. It is not envisaged that all information will go through the International Unit. Indeed, it would be preferable to bypass the Unit whenever possible in order to avoid centralisation. The Unit could simply put an institution in one country in contact with another elsewhere.

The Unit's role in promoting research and development could take a number of different forms. It may simply provide information to those national

---

[1] See UNCTAD: *Report of an informal group of experts on the establishment of centres for the transfer and development of technology* (Geneva, 8-12 December 1975) (doc. No. TD/B/595); and idem: *Establishment of centres for the transfer and development of technology: progress report,* by the UNCTAD secretariat (doc. No. TD/B/C.6/9/Add.3, 12 Nov. 1975).

or regional research institutions which are anxious to undertake appropriate research and development but would like advice as to the precise areas of activity on which to concentrate. It may also contract out particular projects of research with financial assistance. In between these two extremes there are variations of support to research and development institutes in the form of information, finance and technical manpower. The Unit could provide finance from its own resources, or might simply act as an intermediary, putting together donors who wish to support appropriate technology and require research and development facilities. Finance for these activities could be mobilised through the Consultative Group on Appropriate Technology discussed earlier. The Unit could second international expertise to research institutes of the developing countries to participate in and reinforce work on appropriate technology.

The Unit could provide consultancy and advisory services on request, not only to specialised national and regional institutions, as discussed above, but also to national governments seeking assistance in formulating policies and programmes for appropriate technology. In countries without a national infrastructure for appropriate technology the Unit could provide advice on how best to create national technological capabilities and encourage their development.

The Unit—in close collaboration with other institutions such as the Turin Centre, CINTERFOR, etc.—could contribute to training for appropriate technology in a number of ways. Work on appropriate technology is hampered by the lack of suitable training materials for schools, technical centres and universities. One of the functions of the Unit could be to promote systematic " packaging " of appropriate training materials for supply to educational and training institutions in developing and advanced countries. This would broaden the research and development base for appropriate technology.

It is essential for the successful functioning of the Unit that it be linked to existing and proposed national and regional institutions on appropriate technology through a well defined system of affiliation. Such an arrangement is also in line with the UNDP " new dimensions " of technical co-operation.

TRANSFER OF TECHNOLOGY

Whatever arrangements may be made for promoting the study and dissemination of information on technologies, a further problem which needs to be considered is the mechanism by which technology is transferred. Among the problems to be tackled here are the following:

(a) excessively broad packages are offered to developing countries, preventing both selectivity and cost reduction through negotiation;

(b) adequate control over the use and adaptation of technology is often not obtained;

(c) inappropriate purchases are made even where better options exist;

(d) costs of transfer are high and rising.

To tackle one problem alone may not be very efficient. For example, lowering the direct costs of technology transfer without greater control over use and adaptation could increase the imports of inappropriate technology and the incentives for domestic producers to employ it. However, this is a case for joint action on several fronts, not for total inaction.

There is growing experience of systematic national and regional efforts to negotiate and regulate in respect of costs, control over the use and adaptation of acquired technology, and " unpackaging ". The experience of Mexico and the Andean Pact countries shows that this is feasible. The question at the global level is how to support, complement and generalise national and regional initiatives. Four possibilities, some of which are already under consideration by UNCTAD, seem to have practical potential:

(a) creation of small, specialised data-collection and analysis units to provide both (i) information on existing technology-transfer contracts and their terms, and on national regulatory systems, and (ii) analysis directed to identifying strengths and weaknesses of existing contracts and institutions, and possible directions and procedures for national action;

(b) provision of more effective technical assistance to countries seeking to develop institutional frameworks, train the personnel to man them and carry out important negotiations. This function might be combined with data collection and analysis or undertaken regionally by pooling national resources, as in the operations of the Andean Pact Secretariat;

(c) joint purchase of technology-use rights for several firms in several developing countries (either on a cost-sharing basis or by a single initial purchase followed by sub-licensing); this might reduce transfer costs significantly in some cases;

(d) revision of the national and international patent system to make it more responsive to the needs of developing countries and to the attainment of the aims and objectives of a basic-needs strategy.

INFLUENCING RESEARCH AND DEVELOPMENT BY MULTINATIONAL ENTERPRISES

Multinational enterprises also have a potentially important role in the transfer of technology. In general the research and development undertaken by the multinational enterprises is highly centralised, although some efforts have been made to transfer research to their subsidiaries in developing countries. This seems to make their research less likely to be of benefit to developing host countries.

Concentration of research and development in the departments of the parent company at its headquarters implies that the learning effects of research are limited; that the spread of such research and of technologies does not take place outside the areas covered by the firm. As discussed earlier, and in the following chapter, in some cases multinational enterprises have done significant work in adapting technologies or designing more suitable products.

One idea recently promoted is that the developing countries should require multinational enterprises to include and locate research and development efforts in their territory. However, care needs to be taken to ensure that this does not simply contribute to the "internal" brain drain leading to the employment of local scientists and engineers on research on technology inappropriate for the host countries.

One way in which the research and development of multinationals could be located in host countries and directed to their benefit is to stipulate that a certain proportion of the net revenue of subsidiaries of foreign firms be used for local scientific and technological research.

However, the most effective manner to influence multinational research, adaptation and development would be by altering the opportunities and incentive patterns open to them. Changes in demand patterns resulting from a shift to basic-needs oriented development would have this effect in and of themselves. In addition, the changes in relative factor prices already discussed would give incentives to multinational enterprises to adapt technologies to suit local conditions prevailing in developing countries. For example, an appropriate incentives structure is likely to attract multinational engineering firms to establish local machine fabrication facilities in the host countries.

It is unlikely in the near future that it will be possible to impose international taxes and regulations to influence the choice of technology by multinational enterprises. But co-ordinated action, particularly at the regional level, would be more effective than isolated national initiatives. The more countries impose similar charges and requirements, the greater will be the incentive to modify research and development and the less the potential for relocating activities in less strict countries. There are some encouraging examples of co-ordination of fiscal measures in respect of multinationals among some groups of neighbouring States (e.g. the Kenya, Uganda and Tanzania treasuries) and of the joint regulation of technology transfer and use in the context of the relationship of foreign to local enterprise.

These are, however, aspects of the much wider problem of the role of multinational enterprises in a basic-needs strategy. This broader subject is dealt with in the next chapter.

MULTINATIONAL ENTERPRISES

10

Multinational enterprises cover a wide spectrum of economic activities. Their ownership pattern is varied: the bulk of them are private, but they can also be state-owned. A high and increasing proportion of international transactions in goods, services, capital and expertise takes place under the auspices or through the mediation of such firms. These enterprises are major suppliers of advanced technology, management expertise, marketing information and assistance, and capital to the developing countries.

For a number of years now, criticisms, some severe, have been levelled against the activities of multinational enterprises, particularly in developing countries. At the same time the study of their behaviour and of the new problems which their activities may create has burgeoned. From the research carried out so far by the ILO and others the conclusion has emerged that it is very difficult to generalise about their effects on employment, technology, labour skills, etc.[1] The multinational enterprises are active in primary production for export (both in agriculture and in mining), in import-substituting manufacturing, in manufacturing for export, in banking and finance, and in other service activities. The key issues surrounding their activities not surprisingly vary with the sector. While most of the discussion has been concerned with their " direct investments " in which they offer their capital, management technology and marketing in a total " package " (one which they have typically preferred), they have shown themselves increasingly willing to engage in relations which only involve particular elements of this package. Their flexi-

---

[1] United Nations: *Multinational corporations in world development* (New York, doc. ST/ECA/10, 1973); ILO : *Progress of ILO activities on multinational enterprises*, document GB/198/5/6, 198th Session of the Governing Body of the ILO, 18-21 November 1975; idem: *Multinationals in Western Europe: the industrial relations experience* (Geneva, 1976); idem: *Social and labour practices of some European-based multinationals in the metal trades* (Geneva, 1976); idem: *Wages and working conditions in multinational enterprises* (Geneva, 1976).

bility and adaptability in this respect has been considerable, not least in the case of their relations with socialist States and nationalised industries. The multinationals appear willing to operate in countries which have tough rules, provided the rules governing their conduct are stable. Other factors which make it difficult to generalise about multinationals are the very great differences in their size, differences associated with their national origins, differences in the degree to which they compete with one another, and differences in the attitudes and proclivities of their managements. It should hardly be surprising that some multinational enterprises have had more positive effects upon employment and the meeting of basic needs in poor countries, and are consequently more welcome there, than others. Nor should it be surprising, in the light of their enormous importance in the Western world, that there should be such concern for the development of appropriate policies for dealing with them—not only in the poor countries but in rich ones as well.

Early in 1975 the ILO initiated a programme concerning multinational enterprises and their effects on employment and social policy. This programme, which is being undertaken in collaboration with other United Nations bodies, is focused on three main areas, namely employment and training, conditions of work and life, and industrial relations. Its objective is to collect and analyse as much factual information on the activities of multinational enterprises as possible in order to provide a sounder basis for the elaboration of appropriate policies. A meeting of experts to consider the results of the studies so far undertaken by the ILO will be held in May 1976. It will recommend what further action the ILO should take. Some of the views and suggestions made in this chapter may therefore need to be reconsidered in the light of the conclusions of that meeting.

MULTINATIONAL ENTERPRISES AND EMPLOYMENT

Developing countries

An estimate of the number of employees of the multinationals suggested a total of 13 to 14 million of direct employment for all market economies. Out of this total, the share of developing countries has been estimated at approximately 2 million persons, or roughly 0.3 per cent of the active population, all of whom are in the " modern " or " formal " sectors.[1] But such a figure has little meaning, for the employment is concentrated both by industry and by country, and it takes no account of indirect employment effects or the jobs created

---

[1] United Nations: *Multinational corporations in world development,* op. cit.; and ILO: *L'impact des entreprises multinationales sur l'emploi et la formation* (Geneva, 1976).

through activities of multinational enterprises other than direct investments. Moreover, employment effects vary enormously from sector to sector.

For example, in 1960 in Chile, Argentina, Brazil and Mexico [1] direct employment creation in extractive industries represented only 4.1, 0.6, 2.5 and 1.2 per cent respectively of total employment. This is mainly the result of two factors: both foreign and domestic firms in these industries use highly capital-intensive processes, and generally very little transformation of the raw material on the spot takes place. In the case of agriculture, however, direct employment creation by the multinational enterprises is much larger, since production techniques in agriculture are traditionally labour-intensive. In 1968, in Zaire, the large foreign agricultural companies (especially Unilever) had 230,000 employees plus 200,000 " independent contractors ", that is, 10 per cent of the active population.[2] In the case of manufacturing, direct employment in the multinational enterprises has increased sharply in recent years although the number of jobs created is still quite small when compared with the rest of the economy. For example, in countries such as Brazil and Mexico the multinational enterprises employ less than 10 per cent of the workers in manufacturing compared with a share of 30 per cent of investment.[3] This is partly because they are investing increasingly by taking over existing firms rather than by creating new ones. There is indeed a risk that multinationals may in some cases undertake a reorganisation of firms leading to a fall in the number of jobs.[4]

The aggregate employment impact of the activities of multinational enterprises can only be understood in the context of the national and international economy in which they play a major role. The multinational enterprises affect employment indirectly through their consumption of intermediate goods, through their competition with local firms and through the use of the earnings resulting from their operations.

Among the criteria for evaluating the role of particular multinational enterprises (particularly when engaged in direct investments) in the creation of employment or the meeting of basic needs are the following: the adaptability of their production technologies to local environments, the appropriateness of the products which they promote for local mass consumption, their performance in the training of workers and managers, their behaviour with respect to

---

[1] C. V. Vaitsos: " Employment effects of foreign direct investment in developing countries ", in *Technología para el desarrollo* (Mexico, Fondo de Cultura Económica, forthcoming).

[2] ILO: *Mémorandum au Gouvernement de la République du Zaïre de la mission exploratoire du BIT* (Geneva, 1972).

[3] US Senate Committee on Finance: *Implications of multinational firms for world trade and investment and US trade and labor*, 1973.

[4] ILO: *The multinational enterprises and social policy*, Studies and reports, New series, No. 79 (Geneva, 1973), p. 51.

social policy and wage rates, and the extent to which they have developed local subcontracting for inputs.

The technologies used by multinational enterprises and the appropriateness of their products present a mixed picture. Many studies have shown that the technologies adopted by the multinationals in the host country are the same as those used in the home country. The reasons for this situation include the need for standardisation of production techniques, the small size of domestic markets, the scarcity of supervisory skills and distortions in factor prices. This is not to minimise the importance of the adaptations to existing capital-intensive technologies and the introduction of labour-intensive ones which some firms have undertaken or the marketing efforts in the field of important agricultural inputs which others have conducted.[1]

Also very few of the applied research and development activities of the multinational enterprises have been undertaken in the developing countries. In 1966 only 6 per cent of the total research and development expenditure of American multinational enterprises in the manufacturing sector took place abroad. And of this, the amount done in subsidiaries in developing countries was negligible.[2]

In the sphere of social and wage policies, ILO studies suggest that multinational enterprises typically abide by local laws and customs and, if anything, tend to pay higher wage rates than local firms in similar lines.[3]

By importing advanced management and productive techniques, the multi-nationals can also contribute to training in developing countries. While skill formation occurs almost automatically for the production personnel, the position need not be the same for the management cadre. Localisation of skilled labour and management posts has taken place at a steady pace but it is not yet clear to what extent the training efforts which made it possible have yielded benefits to the host countries outside the firms.

While there are many instances in which multinational enterprises subcontract locally for the provision of particular inputs, there appears to be room for further improvements in this regard. The demand for the maintenance of quality standards in their final branded products and the integrated character of their international operations tend to generate a degree of rigidity in the input mix, and an unnecessary reliance upon imports at the expense of local suppliers.

---

[1] For empirical evidence on transfer and adaptation of technology by the multinational firms, see R. H. Mason: *The transfer of technology and the factor proportion problem: The Philippines and Mexico* (New York, UNITAR, 1972); ILO: *Technology and employment in industry*, op. cit., Ch. 4; and A. S. Bhalla: " Technology and employment: some conclusions ", in *International Labour Review*, op. cit., Mar.-Apr. 1976.

[2] United Nations: *Multinational corporations in world development*, op. cit.

[3] ILO: *Wages and working conditions in multinational enterprises*, op. cit.

Developed countries

As multinational enterprises rapidly expanded investments in developing countries in the 1950s, trade unions in the developed countries became concerned with what they saw essentially as export of jobs. Their fears proved unjustified, however, as an increasing flow of capital goods and intermediate product exports replaced the export of finished products. In the enormous growth of trade among the industrialised countries in the late 1950s and 1960s this did not become a major issue. While there were some shifts in the composition and destination of exports and some temporary adjustment problems, buoyant economic conditions ensured that any displaced workers were rapidly absorbed in new industrial and service jobs, often in the same firms.

As manufactured exports from developing countries began to flow into the markets of the rich countries in increasing quantities in recent years, however, the employment issue became a matter of increasing concern. Multinational enterprises now both purchased more of these products in low-income countries on the open market and began increasingly to invest in their own production facilities there. To some extent these new purchasing and investment patterns were encouraged by special tariff provisions (such as items 806.30 and 807.00 in the United States tariff schedule) which permitted import duties to be paid only on the value added abroad when materials originated in the importing country. (Similar provisions are also found in other countries' tariff schedules.) In support of their new international trading arrangements the multinationals championed the virtues of free trade in goods and technology while some trade unions in the rich countries turned increasingly protectionist. The pressures were exacerbated in the United States by its stricter limits on immigration and by the overvaluation of the United States dollar.

In Japan, where immigration was even more strictly regulated than in the United States, investment in low-cost sources in the manufacturing sector grew at particularly rapid rates. But the over-all Japanese rate of growth was so high that the employment effects there were scarcely noticed. Moreover, the Japanese multinationals were expected by the Government to ensure that alternative employment was available either in their own plants or elsewhere in the neighbourhood for any workers displaced by investment abroad. Thus much of this type of overseas Japanese investment was found in expanding industries or where more highly skilled jobs could replace those which were " lost " to overseas plants. In the case of textiles, however, the Government assisted in the phasing out of the most labour-intensive segments of the industry through an adjustment assistance programme for both firms and workers.

In Western Europe there were similar labour market developments as multinational enterprises increasingly bought from and invested in the Mediterranean countries and Eastern Europe. In this case, as has been seen in Chapter 8, the extensive migration of labour from low-income countries into Europe possibly delayed some of this reallocation, and, in any case, added a further dimension to these structural changes.

Although the employment impact in developed countries of the multinational enterprises' shifts of purchasing and production to low-cost countries has been extensively studied, particularly in the United States, there are wide differences of opinion on its size. Trade union estimates of job displacement in the United States are quite substantial whereas business-sponsored studies suggest that the net employment impact may have been positive. These differences stem partly from different assumptions as to what would have taken place in the absence of these plant relocations, and partly from the different interests of the parties most concerned. What is beyond dispute is that these new patterns imply significant readjustments in production patterns and labour markets in the rich countries. Chapter 7 has dealt with some of the efforts which have been made or might be made by governments to assist in smoothing the adjustment process.

MULTINATIONAL ENTERPRISES AND A BASIC-NEEDS STRATEGY

The introduction in the developing countries of a development strategy along the lines proposed in this report implies, as has been seen in Chapter 3, a major restructuring of incentives. Like other firms, multinational enterprises can be expected to respond to the new incentives by altering the products they sell and produce and by shifting their production technologies. Indeed, there is evidence to suggest that their superior managerial skills and wider experience might lead them to be more responsive than local firms, at least in the first instance. But the same restructuring of income distribution and incentives which reduced the bias in favour of import- and capital-intensity would also reduce some of the special advantages possessed by the multinational enterprises. Their particular strength in the manufacturing sector is, after all, the advanced technologies and branded Western-style consumer-goods which would often be relatively disadvantaged in the proposed restructuring.[1]

A basic-needs strategy implies that the demand for simple consumer goods would increase, as would the market for intermediate and capital goods related to the production of basic goods and services. New profit opportunities would

---

[1] For empirical support of this argument, see ILO: *Employment, incomes and equality: a strategy for increasing productive employment in Kenya*, op. cit., Ch. 9 and Technical Paper No. 16.

arise in the spheres of agriculture, transportation, housing and urban services, health, educational services and product design. Flexible and innovative firms capable of developing efficient technologies appropriate to local resource endowments would also encounter increased opportunities. Some of these new opportunities may generate the creation of new multinational enterprises, perhaps some quite small ones. Some multinational enterprises are already active in the provision of goods which are consumed largely by the poor categories of the population (for example agricultural inputs, sewing-machines, bicycles) and their activities will undoubtedly expand.

All things considered, local firms should be more capable of competing with the multinationals in the provision of these basic-needs oriented goods and services than in the sectors which require the use of advanced technologies. The proposed strategy would undoubtedly create new opportunities for developing countries to co-operate with one another in the fields of trade, investment, technology, development and planning. Third World-based multinational enterprises, private or public, might well be encouraged to emerge—supplying different types of products and different types of technologies.

Increased standardisation of products may generate further efficiencies by reducing the degree to which over-differentiated manufacturing products are produced in too many excessively small-sized plants. Moreover, the resulting increased (because concentrated) local market size will enhance the bargaining position of the host country vis-à-vis the multinational enterprises which want the market in question.

Generally speaking, the less complex and more standardised technologies tend to be more readily available through licensing and technology sales on the open market than are more " advanced " and rapidly changing ones. This is likely, therefore, to reduce the dependence of developing countries on the traditional direct investment package which multinationals provide. While international manufacturing enterprises embarking upon production for export from low-income countries do seem to have a preference for wholly owned subsidiaries, the existence of independent trading houses and other buyers and technology suppliers somewhat reduces the significance of this preference.

An important element in the restructured incentives which are part of the proposed new development policies is the encouragement which they will offer to manufacturing for export. The combination of altered relative factor prices, altered exchange rates and more uniform trade barriers will make production for export much more attractive than previously. Indeed incentives may be restructured in such a way as to favour this type of activity even without a complete shift to a basic-needs strategy; many developing countries have already shifted in this general direction. Except in very small countries, such partial restructuring cannot be expected to reduce significantly the over-all problem of meeting basic needs, but it may be politically less difficult to undertake such partial measures first.

Multinational enterprises' knowledge of or control over markets in the developed countries and the large numbers of developing countries competing to enter them place individual developing countries in particularly weak bargaining relationships in the case of manufacturing for export. Assembly of imported components for re-export, as part of a vertically integrated multinational enterprise, must be the most dependent type of trade yet observed. Multinational enterprises' influence upon trade policies in the developed countries is likely to be such as to favour relatively free trade in the products which they themselves are producing. Protectionist pressure is therefore disproportionate on those sectors in which weaker national firms are found and in which more independent developing-country exporters are emerging. This bias in the structure of trade barriers tends to make developing-country exporters more dependent on the multinational enterprises for the purpose of gaining market access. However difficult it may seem, there is therefore a particular need for developing countries to agree on joint policies towards the multinational enterprises in this sphere.

Host country environment

The effects of particular multinational enterprises' direct investments or other activities upon employment and basic needs considered earlier can in the final analysis only be assessed in terms of the environment in the host countries in which they operate. Unfortunately, complete information which would make it possible to undertake concrete empirical analyses of costs and benefits is not always available, and it would help to dispel the atmosphere of distrust and uncertainty which surrounds the activities of multinational enterprises if more information were made publicly available by the firms themselves.[1] Independent data collected by the United Nations new Commission on Transnational Enterprises should assist in these assessments, as will the studies undertaken by the ILO.

There are, in any case, many dimensions to such calculations of benefits and costs. On the benefits side, it is necessary to consider the indirect employment and income effects (both positive and negative) as well as the direct ones. The effects of training of labour and management, assistance with lobbying for access to foreign markets and other less quantifiable benefits also need to be considered. In assessing the costs, in addition to measuring the

---

[1] The trade unions have already begun to demand legislation obliging multinationals to disclose detailed financial information and other data. Specific proposals are contained in ICFTU: *Charter of trade union demands for the legislative control of multinational companies*, Mexico City, 17-25 October, 1975.

opportunity cost of local capital inputs, labour and government subsidies, allowance should also be made for the extra cost of unnecessary and expensive imported inputs. Again assessment is required of less quantifiable matters such as possible effects upon local businesses, or stimulation of too import-intensive tastes, or the creation of a pattern of demand which is inappropriate to the strategy proposed in this report.

It is, ultimately, the host country government's responsibility to ensure that the terms under which the enterprises operate are such as to generate net national gains. In this regard it is very important that countries are sufficiently equipped to negotiate with multinational enterprises and to take decisions in full knowledge of the implications.

The behaviour of profit-seeking enterprises is governed, above all, by the structure of incentives. If, for example, the structure of trade barriers and exchange rates, the cost of local capital and the local income distribution are such as to favour the erection of import-using, capital-intensive luxury goods industries of less than efficient scale, then those are the industries which they will erect. And if large " modern " firms are particularly favoured, whether consciously or through the working of market forces, by credit schemes, tax incentives and licensing arrangements, one can expect to see multinational enterprises reaping disproportionate success relative to small, local firms. Product mix, choice of technology and the role of foreign enterprise are, in mixed economies, strongly influenced by the pattern of local incentives.

Needless to say, multinational enterprises are particularly interested in the development of markets for the final products, intermediate inputs and technologies which they themselves have for sale; these tend to be final products (and consequent inputs) which cater to higher income tastes and more capital-intensive technologies. They therefore engage in vigorous marketing efforts on their behalf and seek to obtain incentive systems which favour their use. They may tend to do so for a variety of reasons; for example, lack of known alternatives (sometimes there are none), response to existing local incentives, preference for " modernity ", or dominant influence of engineering rather than economic advice.

Performance is not governed exclusively by the incentive structure. Once that structure is established, the benefits and costs of any particular relationship between a poor host country and a multinational enterprise is the product of a complex and multidimensional bargaining process. Among the elements of the bargain are local ownership or participation provisions, tax treatment, prices to be paid for local labour and material inputs, training obligations, local content requirements, rights with respect to repatriation of profits and capital, provisions with respect to exporting, terms of technology contracts, location, etc.

The capacity of particular countries' governments, trade unions or firms to bargain effectively with multinational enterprises is the product of many influences, not the least of which is the relative power of the parties involved. In the case of resource-based ventures, the scarcity of the relevant resource to a large extent sets limits on the outcome. In the case of import-substituting manufacturing, it is the size of the relevant local market that is the prime determinant of bargaining strength. This clearly argues for economic co-operation among developing countries and joint bargaining for access to wider markets where possible. On the other hand, the degree of competition among foreign firms and sources of technology, marketing or management also influences the multinational enterprises' bargaining strength. Poor countries' bargaining strength is undoubtedly at its weakest in the case of negotiations over the export of unskilled labour-intensive products since there are many alternatives open to the foreign firms.

A key element in the formulation of national policies towards multinational enterprises, and therefore in the preparation for bargaining, is a decision as to what exactly is desired from them. Individual firms understandably seek to supply as much of what they have to offer as possible. On the other hand, some elements of their technologies, some inputs, some services and, of course, capital may be available at lower cost from alternative sources or otherwise be more desirable. A certain amount of " shopping around ", which is itself costly, is therefore desirable in order to ensure that reasonable agreements are being struck.

The future role and performance of multinational enterprises in assisting in the provision of basic needs to the world's poor will be determined in part by the environment created by host countries (government, employers and labour), in part by developed countries and international action, and in part by their own initiatives and those of employers' associations. It can be expected to vary from one host country to another, from one time period to another, and from one firm to another.

Developing countries

The most important determinant of the multinationals' role in a particular developing country is the development strategy adopted by the government and people of the country in question. If a basic-needs strategy is adopted and pursued, multinational enterprises can be encouraged or controlled in such a way as to support it. In particular, if existing incentive systems which favour the use of capital and imported inputs at the expense of labour and local inputs are altered, their behaviour can be expected to some extent to change accordingly.

Whatever the development strategy, more effective bargaining on the part of host countries (government, firms and unions) can be expected to improve their share of whatever total gains are achieved through the multinational enterprises' activities. This has been particularly evident in the minerals and petroleum industries in recent years. Effective bargaining is the product of the existence of relevant skills in the fields of law, economics and administration, the existence of alternative sources of skills, technology or markets, the availability of relevant information (on alternative sources of capital and technology, the terms of analogous contracts and agreements in other countries, the true total rate of return to the foreign firm, and so forth), and the existence of co-ordinated positions with other potential host countries on the key elements of the bargain (for example tax treatment, terms of technology contracts, and repatriation rights and obligations). The development of joint policies is of particular importance. There is now a wide consensus, for example, that special tax incentives to encourage foreign investment in import-substituting manufacturing, when offered by all developing countries simultaneously, are mutually offsetting and therefore not only unnecessary but counter-productive.

The highest priority must therefore be attached to the development, within the developing countries, of the technical capacity to bargain and to administer policies with respect to foreign business—through training programmes and, in the case of particularly weak countries, short- to medium-term technical co-operation agreements for the purpose. While programmes in international business abound in developed countries' business schools, there do not at present exist training institutions in developing countries which offer an equivalent for those planning careers in negotiations with multinational enterprises on behalf of developing countries. Such programmes should be developed, if possible with international support, as a matter of urgency.

Bargaining between trade unions or local firms and multinational enterprises may also be assisted by governmental rules or conditions setting certain minimum conditions for contracts. Moreover, there is evidence that better bargains are struck by local trade unions and national firms where there are strong federations of trade unions and employers, respectively, in host countries. Host governments ought therefore to encourage the development of strong local institutions of this kind.

Developed countries

Individual developed countries may introduce policies in support of the developing countries' basic needs. The governments of developed countries have traditionally offered incentives for direct investments (and for goods exports) by home-based enterprises. As increasing experimentation develops with the unpackaging of the direct investment package, such incentives should be extended so as not to discriminate in favour of this particular institutional form of multinational enterprise activity. Access to developed countries' capital markets should be eased and even encouraged, and management and technology agreements unaccompanied by capital flows should normally qualify equally for whatever incentives or insurance programmes are offered to direct investors. Developed country governments may find it advantageous to arrive at some agreements among themselves as to the appropriate terms of such encouragements. Access to these incentives, instead of remaining almost automatic, could also be restricted to firms which abide by stipulated codes of conduct or even to firms or projects which are assessed by the relevant agency as making a positive development contribution. At a minimum, counter-productive restrictions which forbid assistance to certain types of firms should be eliminated. Developed countries could also formulate common policies, for example within the framework of the European Communities and OECD.

Labour

Workers' organisations are concerned with the activities of multinational enterprises not only because of their direct interest in the extent, nature and terms of employment but also because of their long-run interest in the improvement of the world's use of productive resources. However, workers also need to have some assurance that they will not be forced to bear a disproportionate share of any costs of adjustment and structural change resulting from efforts to attain these long-term objectives. To this end, organised labour in the developed countries will legitimately insist on working with the managements of multinational enterprises and with governments to minimise dislocations associated with structural changes of whatever kind, but specifically those associated with the new geography of world industrial production. Programmes for retraining, relocating or otherwise redeploying labour and for compensating workers for the costs of dislocation need to be jointly planned if they are to be acceptable and as useful as possible.

At the international level, organised labour can be expected to strengthen its existing arrangements for the exchange of information and co-operation at the industry and firm level so as to reduce a possible imbalance in knowledge and bargaining strength between multinational enterprises and individual national unions.

Multinational enterprises

Multinational enterprises can be expected to respond primarily to incentives rather than to exhortations to improve performance. It is worth emphasising to their managements, in whatever ways are possible, the potentially productive role which they may play in developing new products or adaptations of old ones, conducting research in the field of appropriate and efficient technologies geared to greater labour intensity and smaller scale, accelerating training programmes, employing local sources and subcontracting where feasible, and pursuing appropriate social and wage policies.

" Good citizenship " is of course in their own joint long-run interest.[1] When a single multinational enterprise abuses its rights by engaging in political interference, by disregarding local laws and customs or international Conventions, by failing to comply with agreements, by promoting harmful products and so forth, all will suffer by association. It is for this reason that many of them, individually and through employers' associations, are anxious to co-operate in the development of codes of behaviour for multinational enterprises (such as that on advertising, recently adopted by the international baby-food makers) to support relevant in-house or independent research in such fields as agro-business and to improve the flow of information concerning their activities. The interests of both the multinational enterprises and the host countries are served, in the long run, by the creation of an atmosphere of mutual trust and respect in which the rules for inter-relationships are known in advance and are strictly observed, relevant information is available to the parties concerned, and negotiation is conducted in the flexible and arm's-length manner characteristic of commercial exchange under law. Far-sighted multinational enterprises will recognise their long-run interests in minimising unnecessary conflicts and assisting the weaker developing countries to deal effectively and fairly in international capital, skill and technology markets.

" Good citizenship " is also called for in the countries in which the multinational enterprises are based. In this case, labour and government should be brought into discussions of structural changes, plant relocations and closures well in advance so that they can play a role in the planning process. Here too, disclosure of more information would ease some of the areas of friction. In this connection it must be stressed that most multinational enterprises are members of local employers' organisations in both industrialised and developing countries. Where and when they participate actively, this has a positive effect in that the multinationals adapt themselves to the local situation. Their active participation in employers' organisations can be expected to make them accept increasingly national objectives such as employment creation and the satisfaction of basic needs. Full participation of multinationals in national employers' organisations must therefore be encouraged.

---

[1] See International Chamber of Commerce: *Guidelines for international investment:* " The investor should respect the national laws, policies and economic and social objectives of the host country in the same way as would a good citizen of that country . . . " (p. 12).

International action

Reference has already been made to the need for building, within the developing countries, the technical capacity for assessment, for bargaining and for administration of policies with respect to multinational enterprise activities. This is an area in which technical co-operation agreements have a potential role to play. To minimise the possibility or the appearance of bias in training programmes and consulting services, this area of technical co-operation is best organised and financed by international agencies, such as UNCTAD and the ILO. On a limited scale, through its Turin Centre, the ILO already acts as an intermediary between trainees from the developing countries and the multinational enterprises which offer these trainees their in-plant facilities for a certain duration of their training courses. The Conference might wish to consider whether the ILO should undertake specialised training programmes in collaboration with UNCTAD and with the support of the multinational enterprises.

Scope also exists for international action in promoting smaller multinational enterprises in developing countries catering mainly for their markets. The ILO, UNCTAD and other United Nations agencies should also support the efforts of developing countries to form themselves into regional bodies for the purpose of research, co-ordinating policies vis-à-vis multinational enterprises, exchanging information and developing their own multinational enterprises.

The development of a code of conduct relating to multinationals has been included in the work programme of the United Nations Commission on Transnational Corporations. Similarly, the OECD Secretariat is working on the preparation of a comprehensive draft code of behaviour for multinational enterprises. Following the instructions of the Governing Body, the ILO has undertaken a study of the usefulness and feasibility of various approaches to international principles and guidelines relating to activities of multinational enterprises within its competence, and this is among the subjects on which the meeting of experts mentioned above is to give further advice to the ILO.

Consideration might be given to including in such a code a number of items such as the employment implications of international subcontracting, the utilisation and adaptation of technologies and the provision of training to production workers and management staff by the multinational enterprises. The arrangements for information exchange and consultations between the enterprises and governments and workers' organisations might also be included.

Although such a code need not be as rigid and binding as a Convention which calls for ratification, it could still act as an instrument of moral persuasion. With the endorsement of international organisations and of public opinion, such a code could offer good prospects of wide acceptance and actual implementation.

CONCLUSIONS

SOME SUGGESTED MAJOR ISSUES FOR DISCUSSION

11

The World Employment Conference is different from other recent world conferences in at least three respects.

First, it is a tripartite conference, at which not only governments but also representatives of the workers and employers of the world will express their views. Changes and adaptations in international economic and social relations are of direct major interest to trade unions and employers' associations, and the ILO's Constitution therefore makes the Organisation responsible for examining and considering " all international economic and financial policies and measures in the light of [its] fundamental objective ".[1] To the extent that the Conference succeeds in reaching a consensus on future orientations of development, and on the scope and nature of necessary adjustments to be brought about in both industrial and developing countries, its conclusions would have considerable weight because they would have behind them the backing of the main productive forces in the world. Thus, any conclusions that the Conference might reach on adjustments to changes in international trade flows, or on social criteria of international aid and investment, should receive serious consideration by the international bodies concerned with negotiations about trade and the transfer of resources, such as UNCTAD, GATT, the World Bank, and the Paris Conference on International Economic Co-operation.[2]

Secondly, the World Employment Conference has a specific mandate to discuss not only international issues but also national ones. It is suggested in this report that the Conclusions of the Seventh Special Session of the General

---

[1] Annex to the Constitution (Declaration of Philadelphia), article II *(d)*.

[2] " The need to establish a relationship between the United Nations system and the Conference on International Economic Co-operation " is stressed in the United Nations General Assembly Resolution of December last year, relating to that Conference.

Assembly of the United Nations regarding the development of international economic co-operation need to be complemented by conclusions (which might perhaps be reflected in revision of the International Development Strategy) regarding measures to be taken within States, particularly in the areas of employment and poverty. It is a major assumption of this report that growth *per se*, and international action to facilitate and accelerate it, do not in themselves reduce the employment and poverty problems. The proposed shift towards a basic-needs strategy implies a vigorous change in national policies, supported by reform of the arrangements and institutions governing international economic relations.

Thirdly, the World Employment Conference is called upon to discuss issues of employment, income distribution and social progress as a one-world problem. All too often discussions are limited to developing countries and to how the developed part of the world can help. This no doubt reflects a correct sense of priorities. But it is not easy to see how developed countries can do more to support developing countries without taking into account their own problems and constraints; they have structural and employment problems and the way in which they tackle these problems could influence the success of a basic-needs approach in developing countries.

This Conference should therefore permit a more representative and more balanced discussion of some of the main issues now confronting the world: more representative because of its tripartite composition; more balanced because of its emphasis on national as well as international issues, and on developed as well as developing countries. It should also be a comprehensive discussion, in that the employment and income distribution problems are at the very centre of economic and social decision making and cannot, therefore, be examined out of the over-all development context.

The issues that have been raised in this report are so numerous that to attempt to summarise and recapitulate them all would be tedious and repetitive. The following brief, and by no means exhaustive, list of key policy issues may nevertheless help the Conference to focus its attention on the major points that are dealt with in the report in Chapters 3, 4 and 5 as well as in Chapters 7, 8, 9 and 10. The more detailed proposals made are not recapitulated here.

The *central issue* is whether the Conference would agree that national and international development efforts should be directed at the satisfaction within the next generation of basic needs, as that term is defined in Chapter 2 and further elaborated in Chapter 3. On the assumption that there would be a consensus on that proposal, the following points relating to each of the five items on the agenda of the Conference deal with some of the major national and international policy issues raised by a basic-needs approach.

Item 1 : National employment strategies and policies, with particular reference
to developing countries

1. Even on the assumption that changes are made in international trade
and other aspects of economic relations between States to support national
development efforts, this report stresses that nearly all developing countries
will need to undertake a thorough reappraisal of their economic and social
development policies in order to satisfy the basic needs of the poorest members
of their population. In essence, this approach implies that developing countries
will need to set targets not only for increased output but also for increased
consumption by the very poor, and to adjust their development policies and
strategies accordingly. The International Labour Conference already agreed on
the need for far-reaching national action of this nature when adopting in 1964
the instruments on employment policy (for instance, the clear and public
definition of the aims of employment policy, " wherever possible in the form of
quantitative targets for economic growth and employment " [1]). In 1971, the
Conference urged member States to apply these instruments " as speedily as
possible ", and, to this end, to orient all aspects of development policies
towards full employment and to " review immediately national legislation,
policies and practices that may limit the employment of workers ", while
industrial countries should review their trade, aid and investment policies with
a view to adjusting them to the needs of increasing employment.[2] The present
Conference may not only wish to confirm these earlier conclusions, but
complement them with conclusions regarding the orientation of policies
towards a basic-needs strategy for the remainder of this century—a strategy
which would require as an essential element a more labour- or employment-
intensive growth path.

2. While basic-needs targets will vary from country to country, the report
invites the Conference to consider whether it would not be desirable and feasible
to establish a minimum level of basic needs, as targets to be achieved by the
world community within the next generation. This level might, for instance, be
embodied in internationally agreed policies, or inter-agency agreements. It
might also be taken into account in the revision of existing ILO standards.

3. The report stresses that one major element in a reorientation of
development policies to meet basic-needs targets is to increase the productive
income-earning opportunities of the working poor by means of a significant
redirection or redistribution of investments. This would imply that, throughout
the next 25 years or so, as growth proceeds, the resources becoming available
for investment are, to a much larger extent than at present, channelled to the

---

[1] Recommendation No. 122, Para. 2.
[2] *Official Bulletin* (Geneva, ILO), 1971, No. 3, pp. 273 and 274.

working poor, enabling them to increase employment and productivity and, hence, their incomes. This in itself should lead to important changes in income distribution. Will it be politically feasible to initiate such a change immediately and to sustain the effort over such a long period of time? How could the organisation of poverty groups, for instance, along the lines of the instruments concerning the organisation of rural workers adopted at last year's session of the International Labour Conference, be made to facilitate the process?

4. The further question arises as to whether the effort will be sufficient if the specific basic needs proposed in the report are to be met in one generation. It may be necessary to go beyond the " incremental approach " of redistributing additions to a country's resources resulting from economic growth, and to redistribute also some of the present, " initial ", incomes so that basic needs can be met faster. In some countries this might imply a redistribution of land ownership; in many countries it will be necessary to redistribute land utilisation by changes in conditions of tenancy. In many countries drastic educational reform will be required.

5. Over and above the crucial issues raised above, what other major changes and adaptations in priorities and policies are required for a basic-needs oriented development strategy? The report suggests changes in various fields including incomes and price policies, role of the public sector, choice of production techniques and population policies.

6. How should basic needs be defined for the more developed countries? While poverty does not exist in these countries in anything like the breadth and depth that it does in the less developed world, first priority should no doubt be given to raising the standards of living of those whose incomes fall below nationally defined " poverty lines ". Beyond that, and in addition to attaining or maintaining levels of full employment, consideration should be given to:

— facilitating structural changes that make possible further growth, higher standards of welfare and increased assistance to, and trade with, developing countries;

— establishing adequate levels of social security and other benefits for the sick, the disabled, the unemployed and the aged;

— setting targets for attaining more qualitative goals, such as greater participation, better balance between work and leisure, improved working conditions, a safer and more satisfying environment in life and work.

Item 2: International manpower movements and employment

1. In the longer term, international manpower movements may diminish because of orderly changes in the international division of labour. In the short

run, abrupt movements—for example return migration caused by economic difficulties in receiving countries—should be avoided.

2. How can the ILO contribute to the formulation of national and international policies to avoid the brain drain? The Seventh Special Session of the General Assembly of the United Nations established " an urgent need " for such policies.[1] How can the adverse effects of the brain drain be kept to a minimum, by means that do not infringe on basic freedoms, and what effects would the introduction of a basic-needs strategy have on this?

3. The easy access to a manpower reservoir which many developed market economies have outside their borders, may have delayed structural adjustments in the receiving countries by maintaining industrial activities that otherwise would no longer be viable. If this is so, can it be said that this is not only to the disadvantage of developing countries because of the implications for their industrial development, but also against the longer term self-interest of the developed countries because of the implications for their industrial structure and competitiveness?

4. Regional arrangements to facilitate manpower movements are important and consideration may be given to the establishment of a " clearing-house " or a skilled manpower pool.

5. Priority attention should be given to improved welfare of migrants, for example by making sure that they reap the full benefits from their social security and pension payments.

Item 3 : Technologies for productive employment creation in developing countries

1. The debate on appropriate technology often tends to become polarised as between the views expressed by the protagonists of capital-intensive techno-logies, on the one hand, and of labour-intensive technologies on the other. But should not the problem be posed somewhat differently? The real issue is the decision about the pattern of growth to be pursued. If a basic-needs strategy is adopted, this will require, over-all, a more balanced combination of a labour- or employment-intensive growth path with the adoption, as appropriate, of capital-intensive technologies in certain sectors of the economy.

2. The report invites the Conference to examine the possibility of setting up a Consultative Group and an International Appropriate Technology Unit which should look into the possibility of channelling more resources into research and development to stimulate the adaptation of technologies to the

---

[1] Resolution 3362, Ch. III, para. 10.

circumstances of the developing countries, and to ensure their widespread dissemination. This proposal should be seen in the light of the conclusions of the Seventh Special Session of the United Nations General Assembly on issues of technology.[1]

Item 4: The role of multinational enterprises in employment creation in the developing countries

1. How flexibly can multinational enterprises adapt to a basic-needs strategy and how can they further employment creation in this context? Will a code of conduct and rules of " good citizenship " be helpful in this respect? Should one consider different types of measures of a more legal character?

2. Building up the technical capacity in developing countries for assessing the impact of multinational enterprises on national development, including employment, and for negotiating with them is of great importance. To what extent could regional co-operation and training programmes assist in meeting these urgent requirements?

3. Could multinational enterprises do more in the field of research and development to stimulate the adaptation of their technologies and products to the needs of the countries in which they operate?

Item 5: Active manpower policies and adjustment assistance in developed countries

Adjustment assistance

1. What further research and consultation are required to identify industries or lines of industrial or agricultural production in industrial countries that are, or may become, less competitive with developing countries, and for which adjustment measures are therefore needed?

2. Could the creation of an International Reconversion Fund stimulate trade adjustment programmes in the industrial countries? What role could the ILO play in furthering this proposal?

3. What measures can European socialist countries take with respect to the above points?

4. What role should the ILO's Industrial Committees play in these matters? Could their advice be a significant input in the sectoral consultations called for by the Seventh Special Session of the United Nations General Assembly?

---

[1] The Assembly decided, among other things, that a United Nations Conference on Science and Technology for Development should be held in 1978 or 1979 and that the work of the relevant United Nations bodies, including the International Labour Organisation, to facilitate the transfer and diffusion of technology " should be given urgent priority " (Resolution 3362, Ch. IV; Ch. V, para. 2).

Active manpower policies

5. Workers and their families should not bear the burden of adjustment to changes in trade patterns and technology. What possibilities could be explored with a view to making more effective the various measures of active manpower policies now widely accepted in principle—training and retraining, income maintenance, assistance in moving to new areas, special assistance to backward or depressed regions?

6. Would it be useful to promote and provide for exchanges of views and experiences between industrially advanced countries on these matters?

7. To what extent, and in what circumstances, is government assistance to declining industries and firms justified in an attempt to protect jobs?

A NOTE ON THE
WORLD EMPLOYMENT CONFERENCE

A NOTE ON THE WORLD EMPLOYMENT CONFERENCE

Charles Paolillo

The World Employment Conference that met in Geneva from June 4 to June 17, 1976, under the sponsorship of the International Labour Organisation (ILO) dealt with one of the most important and most complex questions facing the world today: How can development be carried out in a way which can satisfy the basic needs of all people in the shortest possible time? Formally called the Tripartite[1] World Conference on Employment, Income Distribution and Social Progress and the International Division of Labour, the Conference dealt with a range of topics related to employment problems in both industrialized and developing countries. Among the items on the agenda were international migration, technology, the role of multinational corporations, manpower policies and trade adjustment assistance. But the centerpiece of the Conference was the proposal for developing countries to shift to a "basic-needs" strategy of development presented in the document prepared for the Conference by the International Labour Office, *Employment, Growth and Basic Needs: A One-World Problem*, which is reproduced in entirety as the main part of this volume. This basic-needs strategy was endorsed in principle as part of the final resolution of the Conference, the Declaration of Principles and Programme of Action (reproduced as Annex B of this volume), which the Conference adopted by acclamation.[2]

On the subject of the basic-needs strategy, the Conference concluded that rapid growth in GNP has not automatically reduced poverty and inequality in many countries. Therefore, major shifts in development strategies are urgently needed to ensure full employment and adequate income for all people in the shortest possible time. The Conference declared itself committed to the attainment of an equitable distribution of income and wealth through appropriate strategies to eradicate poverty and promote full, productive employment to satisfy basic needs. In developing countries, the Conference decided, satisfaction of basic needs cannot be achieved without both acceleration of economic growth and measures aimed at changing the pattern of growth, as well as access to the use of productive resources by the lowest income groups.

This Note is excerpted and adapted by the author from his report to the US House of Representatives Committee on International Relations, entitled A Basic Human Needs Strategy of Development: Staff Report on the World Employment Conference *(Washington, D.C., US Government Printing Office, September 1976). Mr. Paolillo is Staff Consultant to the Committee, for which he conducted a special staff study mission to the World Employment Conference. The observations and findings in this Note (and in the just-cited report on which it is based) are those of the staff study mission, and do not necessarily reflect the views of the Committee on International Relations or any of its members.*

[1]The word "tripartite" in the name of the Conference refers to the International Labour Organisation's tripartite (governments, employers and workers) representation and voting structure. The Conference was attended by 1,271 delegates—including 121 delegates of governments, 112 of employers, and 116 of workers, as well as 921 advisors to the three groups.

[2]Statements on the final resolution were expressed by representatives of several governments in the Conference Committee of the Whole or submitted in letter form for inclusion in the Conference final record. These statements are reproduced in this volume as an appendix to Annex B.

The Conference stated that a basic-needs-oriented policy implies the participation of the people in making the decisions which affect them through organizations of their own choice. It requires effective mass participation of the rural population in the political process in order to safeguard their interests. In this connection, the Conference supported a policy of active encouragement to small farmers' and rural workers' organizations to enable them to participate effectively in programs of land reform; access to credit, inputs, markets and other needed services; and rural works and rural industries.

Finally, the Conference urged that policies required to meet basic needs become an essential part of the UN Second Development Decade (1970s) and form the core of the Third Development Decade Strategy (1980s).

The final resolution of the Conference, therefore, represents a formal acceptance by governments, employers and workers from developing and developed countries alike, of the need to focus development efforts explicitly on the needs of the poor. It states unequivocally that major shifts in development strategies are urgently needed. And it recognizes that such "major shifts" would require fundamental change in the internal policies of most developing countries.

Differences of View

A conference made up of delegates from all over the world cannot escape a certain ambiguity in its final results. The words of the resolution of the Conference supporting the principle of a basic-needs strategy naturally mask considerable differences of view and varying understandings of meaning and implication.

With respect to the issue of the basic-needs strategy itself, there were several related issues over which delegations expressed widely differing perspectives. Among the most discussed were:

(1) The importance of changes in the international economic order compared to changes in the domestic economies of developing countries;

(2) The extent to which a basic-needs strategy might tend to perpetuate backwardness and weakness of poor countries and their continued dependence on rich countries;

(3) The importance of agriculture as opposed to industry, labor-intensive production as opposed to capital-intensive production, intermediate technology as opposed to advanced technology, and small-scale production methods as opposed to large-scale production methods; and

(4) The degree to which individual developing countries could subscribe to policy changes implied by a basic-needs strategy without reserving explicitly the right to pass on the applicability of each for their own country.

In general, those countries which most vehemently asserted the importance of changes in the international economic order rather than in internal policies were those who also saw a basic-needs strategy as a means of keeping poor countries weak and helpless, who favored large-scale, capital-intensive industry and the most advanced technology and who most strongly insisted on the sovereign right of each country to decide its own policies.

For example, some developing countries took the view that the primary, or even the sole, cause of poverty in the developing world is an international economic order favoring the rich countries. At least one country soundly criticized the Director-General's Report for ignoring the real causes of poverty and misery in the world, which are to be found in the inequities of the international economy, and specifically in the exploitation of poor countries by industrialized countries. The remedy is a restructuring of the international economy along the lines called for by the developing countries in their formal proposals for a "New International Economic Order".

In this view, the real solutions to poverty are political, rather than technical or econometric. Therefore, creation of jobs in order to keep social or political peace is to be avoided. And while growth for growth's sake, or growth for profit, should give way to growth for the production of goods to satisfy basic needs, that growth must not be based on small-scale agriculture and small-scale industry, but on an "authentic" industrial base, without which poor countries will remain forever dependent on industrialized countries.

Other countries, while not taking the position that poverty stems solely from international inequities between rich and poor countries or that rich countries want to keep poor countries down, did stress their belief that a restructuring of the international economic order to be more favorable to poor countries was a prerequisite for poor countries to carry out a basic-needs strategy—that a national basic-needs strategy cannot be achieved without changes in the international order as well. Still other countries recognized a need for changes in the international order as an aid to adoption of national basic-needs strategies, but without asserting that basic-needs strategies could not be adopted without such changes. A few of these countries also stressed their belief that rapid industrialization and large-scale production units are preferable to emphasis on agriculture and on many small productive enterprises.

Some of the industrialized countries, including the United States, appeared to take the position that there is at best a tenuous or indirect link between basic-needs strategies and a new international economic order. It is hard to say if this position was founded on substantive analysis or was merely a procedural attempt to keep the discussion (and the resolution) away from international economic order issues, in an attempt to deflect such matters to past and future forums where delegations are prepared to deal with them in detail.[3]

The position stated by the Soviet Union, and echoed by other East European countries, was that the Director-General's Report is based on a number of "dangerous doctrines". Among these are (1) that food production should be emphasized (whereas it is clear that the best road to development lies through rapid capital formation, industrialization and modern production techniques); (2) that multinational corporations can help developing countries by improving technical levels (whereas it is certain that these corporations simply want profits from cheap labor); and (3) that more labor-intensive technology should be used (whereas it is known that such a path is not realistic and is merely a way for the rich countries to push the people of developing countries into docility and keep them at a lower stage of development).

Thus the Soviets and their East European allies (along with a few developing countries), while supporting the thesis contained in the Director-General's Report that the goal of development is the satisfaction of basic human needs through full employment and an equitable distribution of wealth, totally disagreed with the methods proposed for achieving that goal. (The Soviet answer was for developing countries simply to copy the policies of the Soviets and other East Europeans.)

On the other hand, most of the delegates at the Conference, from both developing countries and industrialized market economy countries, did favor the proposed methods, in general, as indicated by their support for the essential elements of the basic-needs strategy. At the same time, it was clear that developing-country delegates had a natural reluctance to pin themselves down in a binding way to particular courses of action, and the final resolution contains many provisions which seek to maintain flexibility in this respect.

------

[3]For a detailed commentary on the US position at the Conference on the issue of the basic-needs strategy, see *A Basic Human Needs Strategy of Development: Staff Report on the World Employment Conference* (Washington, D.C., US Government Printing Office, September 1976).

For example, the resolution softens many of the recommendations with references to "some countries", "most developing countries", "often", "in many cases" and general statements affirming each nation's sovereignty, such as, "Obviously, each country must democratically and independently decide its policies in accordance with its needs and objectives". Not content with those formulations, some of the developing countries —finding it ultimately difficult, even with the existing qualifiers, to subscribe to a resolution calling on them to adopt a series of specific policy measures which the resolution itself calls essential for a basic-needs strategy—succeeded in the final draft of the resolution in modifying a key provision setting forth such policy measures by stating that a basic-needs-oriented strategy should include them as essential elements "to the extent that countries consider them to be desirable".

The tendency to avoid emphasizing the specific measures implied by a basic-needs strategy was reflected also in a draft resolution put forth by a large number of developing countries which was considered along with other documents and positions by the working groups dealing with the various agenda items. That resolution was considerably less detailed in spelling out such measures than either the Director-General's Report or the final resolution adopted by the Conference.

The desire of countries to avoid the imposition of universal guidelines was manifest also in the absence from the final resolution of any reference to a suggested world-wide standard of minimum basic needs, in addition to relative standards to be determined by each country.

Similarly, in dealing with appropriate technology, the Conference approved the need to measure technologies against the available factors of production and to adopt labor-intensive technologies where indicated. But the resolution also stresses the need for a balance between labor-intensive and capital-intensive production, the right of each country to choose the technology it wishes and a disclaimer of any intention to rule out advanced technology for developing countries.

Finally, it is worth mentioning in this connection an example which cuts across the entire range of agenda items, including trade adjustment assistance and the international division of labor. The Conference, while adopting the principle of a basic-needs strategy and favoring increased attention to labor-intensive methods of production in the developing world, clearly wished to stop somewhere short of the proposals in the Director-General's Report calling in effect for a world division of production into more labor-intensive for developing countries and more capital-intensive for industrialized countries.

While such a grand international division of labor and production methods might result in the greatest theoretical efficiency, neither the poor nor the rich countries are prepared to accept such a scheme in anything like a pure form. While most of the developing countries do not (though a few do) regard proposals of that sort as capitalist plots to keep the developing countries in a state of perpetual dependence on the industrialized West, they clearly want to retain and expand a "modern" sector based on the latest, most sophisticated, most advanced, and if need be most capital-intensive technology. At the same time, the industrialized market economies are not prepared to transfer all labor-intensive production to the developing world—no matter how much more cheaply the products of labor-intensive manufacture can be produced there—as long as such a transfer is believed to aggravate problems of unemployment in the rich countries.

Implications for the Implementation of a
Basic-Needs Strategy

In sum, the results of the Conference indicate a major move in the direction of acceptance of a basic-needs strategy. It is particularly noteworthy that the strategy was adopted by a world conference heavily dominated by delegates from the developing world itself. The stage has been set for its incorporation into the UN Second and Third Development Decade Strategies and its adoption throughout the UN system.

But implementation of a basic-needs strategy would require profound changes in the internal policies of most developing countries. Their commitment is largely rhetorical at this stage. And, as noted, the final resolution of the Conference leaves considerable room for flexibility in interpretation and implementation. Accordingly, and in light of the variety of views expressed at the Conference, it seems fair to wonder how fast the poor countries can be expected to move to make a basic-needs strategy of development a reality. And to the extent that the rich countries are prepared to support such a strategy, what might they do to make it easier for poor countries to put a basic-needs strategy into practice?

The internal changes necessary to implement a basic-needs strategy can obviously be undertaken only to the extent that a developing-country government possesses the motivation and political will and sees the practical possibility of carrying the changes through. While each situation must be judged on its own facts, it seems likely that the process might be facilitated in some cases by a favorable external environment. The Conference has created a rhetorical momentum which may be carried forward by discussions of the strategy at the UN General Assembly and in other forums. Economic and political support by industrialized countries and international agencies for governments undertaking such changes might often be helpful. Aid programs and other instruments available to rich countries to help promote development can be used to ease the way. But each developing country clearly must decide for itself the steps it feels prepared to take; outsiders can only help those countries which themselves determine to follow a basic-needs strategy.

The speed with which, and extent to which, any developing country may wish to move toward a basic-needs strategy is also, naturally, up to that country. Again, the industrialized countries and international agencies can help countries move faster and farther, if the countries are so minded. But many countries may well want to take steps toward a basic-needs strategy while at the same time expanding the modern sector, increasing the use of advanced technology and strengthening the heavy industrial base. Their reasons may include politics, prestige, psychology, security and self-reliance.

Finally, the impact of adoption of a basic-needs strategy on the total relationship between rich countries and poor countries is bound to complicate the matter. A basic-needs strategy, even in its pure form, need not be viewed as a formula for keeping the poor countries in their place, as a few of them asserted at the Conference. In the long run, the strategy should result in higher GNP growth and form a broad and solid base for expansion of more modern and more capital-intensive production as time goes on. In the very short run, however, it does not decrease the existing vulnerability of the developing countries to the industrialized countries; it does not redress the economic power balance between them.

Viewed in this fashion, the basic-needs strategy can take on the appearance of yet one more attempt by the rich countries to impose on the developing countries what the rich countries believe is right for them—in which their problems are defined and solutions proposed not by themselves, but by planners from the North. The growing acceptance of some form of basic-needs or participation strategy of development among both development experts and political leaders in the poor countries makes this problem less acute than it might otherwise be. But the fact remains that many developing countries are likely to find the short-run dependency implications of the basic-needs strategy difficult if not impossible to accept. Unless some way is found to overcome these implications, therefore, a basic-needs strategy is likely to be adopted only to a limited degree in many poor countries.

The way out may lie in simultaneously restructuring the international economic order in ways which reduce dependency of developing countries on industrialized countries. If a new set of international economic rules were to permit developing countries to make overall economic gains, to have a larger voice in making international economic policy and to obtain a more equitable share of the benefits of global economic growth, they would be less likely to regard adoption of a basic-needs strategy as dooming them to perpetual weakness and dependence on the rich countries.

A healthier overall economic situation would also make it easier in purely economic terms for developing countries to make the changes required by a basic-needs strategy. As noted above, the feeling was widespread at the Conference that carrying out national basic-needs strategies in the poor countries would be very difficult, if not impossible, without accompanying changes in the international economic order.

The developing world is quite clearly united on the need for a new international economic order. But no redistribution of wealth among countries is going to solve the problem of world poverty, without measures also to redistribute wealth within countries; that was the message of this Conference. Thus, while some countries place great emphasis on the internal changes necessary to a basic-needs strategy of development, and a few focus almost entirely on the necessity for a new international economic order, the consensus—reflected in the final resolution of the Conference—is that both are needed and that they can be mutually reinforcing.[4] Indeed, it is entirely possible that neither will happen without the other.

---

[4]An effort to restructure domestic economies in support of a basic-needs strategy in conjunction with a restructuring of the world economy to provide greater opportunities for economic progress would be, in many ways, the equivalent on a global scale of arrangements made under many development aid programs whereby internal economic measures are taken in conjunction with the provision of external assistance.

DECLARATION OF PRINCIPLES AND PROGRAMME OF ACTION

DECLARATION OF PRINCIPLES AND PROGRAMME OF ACTION[1] ADOPTED BY THE 1976 WORLD EMPLOYMENT CONFERENCE

DECLARATION OF PRINCIPLES

The Tripartite World Conference on Employment, Income Distribution and Social Progress and the International Division of Labour held in Geneva from 4 to 17 June 1976 in accordance with the resolution adopted by the International Labour Conference during its 59th Session (1974):

Aware that past development strategies in most developing countries have not led to the eradication of poverty and unemployment; that the historical features of the development processes in these countries have produced an employment structure characterised by a large proportion of the labour force in rural areas with high levels of underemployment and unemployment; that underemployment and poverty in rural and urban informal sectors and open unemployment, especially in urban areas, has reached such critical dimensions that major shifts in development strategies at both national and international levels are urgently needed in order to ensure full employment and an adequate income to every inhabitant of this One World in the shortest possible time;

Aware that industrialised countries have not been able to maintain full employment and that economic recession has resulted in widespread unemployment;

Noting that the Conference is a major initiative on the part of the International Labour Organisation towards the efforts that many of the member countries are making to establish a more equitable international economic order, and that it is consistent with the deliberations of the important world conferences of recent years;

Recalling further the conclusions of the Sixth and Seventh Special Sessions of the United Nations General Assembly, in particular Resolution 3202 (S-VI) concerning the Establishment of a New International Economic Order, and Resolution 3362 (S-VII) concerning Development and International Economic Co-operation;

Noting that underemployment, unemployment, poverty, malnutrition and illiteracy are caused by both national and international factors; that at the national level they are caused by structural factors emanating from underdevelopment and, at the international level, they are due mainly to the deteriorating situation in developing countries, which is partly the consequence of cyclical and structural imbalances in the world economic situation;

Recognising that one of the primary objectives of national development efforts and of international economic relations must be to achieve full employment and to satisfy the basic needs of all people throughout this One World;

---

[1]World Employment Conference Document WEC/CW/E.1.

Committed to the attainment of an equitable distribution of income and wealth through appropriate strategies to eradicate poverty and promote full, productive employment to satisfy basic needs;

Noting:

(a) that unemployment, underemployment and marginality are a universal concern and affect at least one-third of humanity at the present time, offending human dignity and preventing the exercise of the right to work;

(b) that the experience of the past two decades has shown that rapid growth of gross national product has not automatically reduced poverty and inequality in many countries, nor has it provided sufficient productive employment within acceptable periods of time;

(c) the current unsatisfactory international economic situation and the discussions of problems affecting unemployment and related issues in UNCTAD IV;

(d) that the existence of an informal urban sector which has grown out of proportion during the past decades in the developing countries and the chronic lack of jobs in rural areas burden the labour markets and hinder the sectoral and regional integration of national development policies;

(e) that it is necessary to replace the current international division of labour wherein the participation of developing countries in international trade is mainly the exportation of raw materials, semi-processed products and highly labour-intensive manufactured goods and the importation of highly capital-intensive industrial products, so as to enable all countries to engage in other types of production in accordance with their national priorities;

Recalling the Universal Declaration of Human Rights, in particular Article 23, adopted by the General Assembly of the United Nations in 1948;

Considering that only productive work and gainful employment, without discrimination, enable man to fulfill himself socially and as an individual, and reconfirming that the assured opprotunity to work is a basic human right and freedom;

Considering that the growth of productive employment is one of the most effective means to ensure a just and equitable distribution of income and to raise the standard of living of the majority of the population;

Convinced that the establishment and modernisation of small and medium-sized enterprises in rural as well as in urban sectors will increase the volume of employment and therefore play an important part in a basic-needs strategy, and that the private sector has an important role to play in development and employment creation;

Considering that integrated development of developing countries can be achieved only insofar as equal priority is attached to the social, economic and political aspects of development;

Affirming that the problems of underemployment, unemployment and poverty must be attacked by means of direct, well coordinated measures at both national and international levels;

Recognising that in most developing countries, the government is the principal promoter of development and employment and the competent instrument to achieve a just and equitable distribution of income, with the effective participation of trade unions, rural workers' organisations and employers' associations;

Recognising that international relations should be based on cooperation, interdependence, national sovereignty, self-determination of peoples, and nonintervention in the internal affairs of countries;

Reconfirming the importance of regional and subregional cooperation as a major instrument to achieve the expansion of domestic markets, to facilitate the use of modern technologies, efficient industrialisation, better integration into the world economy, and to give greater weight to the positions of developing countries in international relations, with a view to accelerating the development of Third World countries;

Noting the firm commitment of the developing countries and of some developed countries to implement the New International Economic Order, based on the principles contained in the Charter of Economic Rights and Duties of States;

Noting that a review and appraisal of the strategy for the Second Development Decade (Resolution 3517 of the United Nations General Assembly) are taking place and that preparations for the Third Development Decade have commenced;

Convinced that the strategy for the Second Development Decade needs to be complemented by a programme of action to guide international and national development efforts towards fulfilling the basic needs of all the people and particularly the elementary needs of the lowest income groups;

Recalling that the ILO, particularly through its World Employment Programme, has a direct responsibility for elaborating such a strategy with regard to the achievement of full productive employment in decent working conditions, and ensuring respect for the freedoms and rights of association and collective bargaining laid down in Conventions Nos. 87, 98 and 135;

The Conference hereby adopts and requests the Governing Body of the ILO to implement the Programme of Action where appropriate in co-operation with other international organisations.

PROGRAMME OF ACTION

I. Basic Needs

1. Strategies and national development plans and policies should include explicitly as a priority objective the promotion of employment and the satisfaction of the basic needs of each country's population.

2. Basic needs, as understood in this Programme of Action, include two elements. First, they include certain minimum requirements of a family for private consumption: adequate food, shelter and clothing, as well as certain household equipment and furniture. Second, they include essential services provided by and for the community at large, such as safe drinking water, sanitation, public transport and health, educational and cultural facilities.

3. A basic-needs-oriented policy implies the participation of the people in making the decisions which affect them through organisations of their own choice.

4. In all countries freely chosen employment enters into a basic-needs policy both as a means and as an end. Employment yields an output. It provides an income to the employed, and gives the individual a feeling of self-respect, dignity and of being a worthy member of society.

5. It is important to recognise that the concept of basic needs is a country-specific and dynamic concept. The concept of basic needs should be placed within a context of a nation's over-all economic and social development. In no circumstances should it be taken to mean merely the minimum necessary for subsistence; it should be placed within a context of national independence, the dignity of individuals and peoples and their freedom to chart their destiny without hindrance.

Strategies and Policies to Create Full Employment and to Meet Basic Needs in Developing Countries

6. In developing countries satisfaction of basic needs cannot be achieved without both acceleration in their economic growth and measures aimed at changing the pattern of growth and access to the use of productive resources by the lowest income groups. Often these measures will require a transformation of social structures, including an initial redistribution of assets, especially land, with adequate and timely compensation. Land reform should be supplemented by rural community development. In some countries, however, public ownership and control of other assets is an essential ingredient of their strategy. Obviously, each country must democratically and independently decide its policies in accordance with its needs and objectives.

7. Any national employment-centered development strategy aiming at satisfying the basic needs of the population as a whole should, however, include the following essential elements, to the extent that countries consider them to be desirable:

Macro-economic policies

(a) An increase in the volume and productivity of work in order to increase the incomes of the lowest income groups;

(b) strengthening the production and distribution system of essential goods and services to correspond with the new pattern of demand;

(c) an increase in resource mobilisation for investment; the introduction of progressive income and wealth taxation policies; the adoption of credit policies to ensure employment creation and increased production of basic goods and services;

(d) the control of the utilisation and processing of natural resources as well as the establishment of basic industries that would generate self-reliant and harmonious economic development;

(e) developing inter-regional trade, especially among the developing countries, in order to promote collective self-reliance and to ensure the satisfaction of basic import needs without depending permanently on external aid;

(f) a planned increase in investments in order to achieve diversification of employment and technological progress and to overcome other regional and sectoral inequalities;

(g) reform of the price mechanism in order to achieve greater equity and efficiency in resource allocation and to ensure sufficient income to small producers;

(h) reform of the fiscal system to provide employment-linked incentives and more socially just patterns of income distribution;

(i) safe-guarding ecological and environmental balances;

(j) provision by the government of the policy framework to guide the private and public sectors towards meeting basic needs, and making its own industrial enterprises model employers; in many cases this can only be done in a national planning framework;

(k) the development of human resources through education and vocational training.

Employment policy

8. Member States should place prime emphasis on the generation of employment, in particular to meet the challenge of creating sufficient jobs in developing countries by the year 2000 and thereby achieve full employment. Specific targets should be set to reduce progressively unemployment and underemployment.

9. The following policies should be adopted to encourage employment creation:

(a) Member States should ratify ILO Convention No. 122 and should ratify, implement and safeguard fair labour standards, such as the right to organise and to engage in collective bargaining, as laid down in ILO Conventions No. 87, 98, and 135.

(b) In the criteria for project selection and appraisal, employment and income distribution aspects should have adequate emphasis in development planning and in the lending policies of international financial institutions.

(c) Member States should implement active labour market policies of the type set forth in the ILO Human Resources Development Convention, 1975 (No. 142), and the accompanying Human Resources Development Recommendation, 1975 (No. 150), and adjust enterprise-level policies, especially with regard to recruitment, work organisation, working conditions and work content, so as fully to absorb under-utilised labour resources.

(d) Wage policies should be such that:
  (i) they ensure minimum levels of living;
  (ii) the real wages of workers and the real incomes of self-employed producers are protected and progressively increased;
  (iii) wage levels are equitable and reflect relative social productivity;
  (iv) anti-inflationary incomes and price policies, where introduced, take these objectives into account.

(e) Equality of treatment and remuneration for women should be ensured.

Rural sector policies

10. Governments should give high priority to rural development, and increase the effectiveness of their policies, including those to reorganise the agrarian structure. Rural development involves the modernisation of agriculture, the development of agro-based industries, and the provision of both physical and social infrastructure. It should encompass educational and vocational training facilities, the construction of main and feeder roads, the provision of credit facilities and technical assistance, especially to small farmers and agricultural labourers.

11. Co-operatives should be promoted in accordance with ILO Recommendation No. 127 and extend not only to the use of land, equipment and credit, but also to the fields of transportation, storage, marketing and the distribution network, processing and services generally. More emphasis should be placed on the development of co-operatives in national policies, especially when they can be implemented so as to involve the lowest income groups, through their own organisations.

12. In most of the developing countries, agrarian reform, land distribution and the provision of ancillary services are basic to rural development. A minimum requirement is to provide house sites for rural and plantation workers and other landless labourers

so as to assist them in building their homes and making them independent, especially in case of loss of employment.

13. The main thrust of a basic-needs strategy must be to ensure that there is effective mass participation of the rural population in the political process in order to safeguard their interests. In view of the highly hierarchical social and economic structure of agrarian societies in some developing countries, measures of redistributive justice are likely to be thwarted unless backed by organisations of rural workers. A policy of active encouragement to small farmers and rural workers' organisations should be pursued to enable them to participate effectively in the implementation of:

(a) programmes of agrarian reforms, distribution of surplus lands and land settlement;

(b) programmes for developing ancillary services such as credit, supply of inputs and marketing; and

(c) programmes concerning other employment generation schemes, such as public works, agro-industries and rural crafts.

As specified in ILO Convention No. 141, Governments should create conditions for the development of effective organisations of rural workers.

Social policies

14. Social policies should be designed to increase the welfare of working people, especially women, the young and the aged.

Women

15. Since women constitute the group on the bottom of the ladder in many developing countries in respect of employment, poverty, education, training and status, the Conference recommends that special emphasis be placed in developing countries on promoting the status, education, development and employment of women and on integrating women into the economic and civic life of the country.

16. Specifically, the Conference recommends:

(a) the abolition of every kind of discrimination as regards the right to work, pay, employment, vocational guidance and training (including in-service training), promotion in employment and access to skilled jobs;

(b) that more favourable working conditions be ensured so that women may perform their other functions in society and married women may be able to return to either full-time or part-time productive employment;

(c) that the work burden and drudgery of women be relieved by improving their working and living conditions and by providing more resources for investment in favour of women in rural areas.

The young, the aged and the handicapped

17. In the implementation of basic-needs strategies, there should be no discrimination against the young, the aged or the handicapped. Every effort should be made to provide the young with productive employment, equal opportunity and equal pay for work of equal value, vocational training and working conditions suited to their age. Exploitation of child labour should be prohibited in accordance with the relevant ILO standards.

Participation of organised groups

18. Governments must try to involve employers' organisations, trade unions and rural workers' and producers' organisations in decision-making procedures and in the process of implementation at all levels. These are the organisations which represent

the vast majority of the population and, therefore, they must be the ones to help define the basic needs and apply the necessary strategies.

19. Employers' and producers' organisations, trade unions and other workers' organisations such as rural workers' organisations have an important role to play in the design and implementation of successful development strategies. They must be encouraged to participate effectively in the decision-making process. Workers' organisations are also of great importance in the search for a reform of the existing international economic structures and they have a major role to play in the achievement of a fairer distribution of income and wealth.

Education

20. Education is itself a basic need, and equality of access to educational services, particularly in rural areas, is therefore an important ingredient of a basic-needs strategy. Lack of access to education denies many people, and particularly women, the opportunity to participate fully and meaningfully in the social, economic, cultural and political life of the community.

21. Educational and vocational training systems should be adapted to national development needs and should avoid an élitist bias; priority should be given to adult and primary education, especially in the rural areas.

Population policy

22. High birth rates in poverty-stricken areas are not the cause of under-development but a result of it. They may, however, jeopardise the satisfaction of basic needs. It is only through the fulfillment of these needs, with special emphasis on the development of the position and status of women, that couples will be in a better position to determine the size of their family in a manner compatible with the aims of their society. The Conference is of the view that population policies consistent with the culture and the societies involved, as recommended by the 1974 World Population Conference, should be strongly encouraged. It recommends that information on population programmes should be made available to people in a form and language that they can understand.

International Economic Co-Operation

23. The satisfaction of basic needs is a national endeavour, but its success depends crucially upon strengthening world peace and disarmament and the establishment of a New International Economic Order. The World Employment Conference fully supports the efforts being made by the United Nations General Assembly in its resolution as adopted at the Seventh Special Session and through the relevant agencies of the UN system to introduce international reforms in trade and finance in favour of developing countries and thus to contribute to the creation of a New International Economic Order. The Conference recognises that the basic-needs strategy is only the first phase of the redistributive global growth process.

24. In particular, the Conference, recognising the primary objectives of national development, urges ILO member States to continue their efforts through the appropriate UN agencies to:

(a) stabilise developing countries' exports of primary products and improve their terms of trade through financing an integrated commodity programme;

(b) secure expanded access for developing countries' manufactured exports to the markets of rich countries through trade liberalisation measures on a non-reciprocal basis;

(c) increase the net transfer of resources to developing countries, including the mitigation of their debt burden;

(d) increase mutual economic co-operation between countries with different social and economic systems.

25. The Employers' group wished it to be placed on record that they regarded the section on international economic co-operation as being outside the proper competence of the ILO and as being inappropriate for comment by employers. They agreed, however, that the ILO should co-operate with relevant UN organisations, wherever appropriate, in implementing its policies throughout the developing world.

26. A number of Western industrialised countries wished it to be placed on record that they regarded the section on international economic co-operation (paras. 23 and 24) as being outside the proper competence of the ILO. They took the view that, within its area of competence, the ILO should co-operate with other UN organisations, wherever appropriate, in implementing its policies throughout the developing world.

Recommendations

27. The ILO should co-operate with other UN agencies in bringing about these desired reforms in order to give meaning and reality to the expressed commitment of the world community to assist national basic-needs strategies. It should work through, in particular, the World Employment Programme, including its regional components, and its recognised instrumentalities, such as the existing standard-setting activities, technical assistance and industrial activities.

28. The ILO should, in particular, undertake promotion of short-term and quick employment-generating programmes for making an immediate impact on the prevailing levels of poverty and massive waste of human resources. The Conference recommends that a portion of the $1,000 million International Fund for Agricultural Development should be used for the generation of employment in the rural sector.

29. The Governing Body of the ILO is urged to recommend the review of research programmes, operational activities and organisational structures of the UN family so as to focus them more sharply on the contribution they can make to meeting the basic-needs targets, particularly of the lowest income groups. The Administrative Committee on Co-ordination (ACC) should be requested to review, monitor and report on the work of the different agencies and regional commissions of the UN system.

30. The ILO should, in co-operation both with other UN bodies and with interested national governments, consider the feasibility of initiating a world-wide programme in support of household surveys to map the nature, extent and causes of poverty; to assist countries to set up the necessary statistical and monitoring services; and to measure progress toward the fulfillment of basic needs.

31. Member States should, to the extent possible, supply the ILO, before the end of the decade, with the following information:

(a) a quantitative evaluation of basic needs for the lowest income groups within their population, preferably based on the findings of a tripartite commission established for the purpose;

(b) a description of policies, existing and in preparation, in order to implement the basic-needs strategy.

32. The ILO is requested to prepare a report for an annual conference before the end of the decade and to include the following information:

(a) an elaboration of more precise concepts defining basic needs on the basis of national replies;

(b) a survey of the entire range of national replies received and an analysis of the national situations with respect to the levels of basic needs as well as policies to attain them.

33. The Governing Body of the ILO is urged to place the question of the revision of Convention No. 122 on the agenda of an early session of the International Labour Conference.

34. The Conference finally requests that policies required to meet basic needs become an essential part of the United Nations Second Development Decade Strategy and form the core of the Third Development Decade Strategy.

II. International Manpower Movements and Employment

General objectives of national and international policies

35. The aim of national and international policies in this field should be threefold: (i) to provide more attractive alternatives to migration in the country of origin; (ii) to protect migrants and their families from the difficulties and distress which sometimes follow migration; (iii) to take care that neither migration nor its alternatives are prejudicial to the rest of the population or harmful to economic and social development in either the country of origin or the country of employment.

Measures designed to avoid the need for workers to emigrate

36. The development strategy in the countries of origin should include in particular an employment policy which would give workers productive employment and satisfactory conditions of work and life.

37. This strategy should be implemented in the framework of multilateral and bilateral co-operation which would make it possible through such means as encouragement of appropriate intensified capital movements and transfers of technical knowledge to promote a reciprocally advantageous international division of labour; this calls for necessary readjustments in countries of employment.

Measures against migrations in abusive conditions and in favour of the promotion of equality of opportunity and treatment

38. Governments, employers and workers of the countries of employment should ensure that all migrants are protected against any exploitation and effectively enjoy equality of opportunity and treatment. These principles and the means of implementing them are stated in detail in the international standards of the ILO and more specifically in the Migrant Workers (Supplementary Provisions) Convention, 1975 (No. 143), and in the complementary Migrant Workers Recommendation, 1975 (No. 151). A special effort should be made to ratify and apply the Convention and give effect to the provisions of the Recommendation, especially with regard to:

(a) the fight against migrations in abusive conditions, particularly through sanctions in conformity with Article 6 of the Convention;

(b) the promotion of equality of opportunity and treatment in respect of employment and occupation, of social security, of trade union and cultural rights and of individual and collective freedoms and especially the encouragement of the efforts of migrant workers and their families to preserve their national and ethnic identity as well as their cultural ties with their country of origin, including the possibility for children to be given some knowledge of their mother tongue;

    (c) the elaboration and implementation of a social policy which emphasises:
        (i) reunification of families;
        (ii) protection of the health of migrant workers;
        (iii) establishment of adequate social services;
    (d) minimum guarantees as regards employment and residence.

39. In order to combat discrimination and illegal trafficking in manpower, governments, employers and workers should strengthen their action to ensure the application of national legislation and collective agreements and to initiate the early introduction of appropriate penal sanctions against all who organise or knowingly take advantage of illegal movements of manpower.

Multilateral and bilateral agreements

40. Multilateral and bilateral agreements should be drawn up to deal with the migration of workers and problems concerning migrant workers and their families. Such agreements should be in accordance with the principles established in ILO standards. As far as possible, representative organisations of employers and workers should participate in their preparation and implementation.

41. Such agreements should be based upon the economic and social needs of the countries of origin and the countries of employment; they should take account not only of short-term manpower needs and resources, but also of the long-term social and economic consequences of migration, for migrants as well as for the communities concerned.

42. One of the principal objectives of mutually accepted policies in the framework of these agreements should be to even out fluctuations in migration movements, return migration flows and remittances and make them as far as possible predictable, continuous and assured so as to facilitate the implementation of long-term programmes of economic and social development.

43. Taking into account the economic and social circumstances in the countries and regions concerned and the characteristics of the migration movements concerned, these agreements should in appropriate cases:

    (a) facilitate the co-ordination of employment policies, especially in the framework of efforts for economic and social integration on a regional basis;

    (b) regulate the recruitment of migrant workers without discrimination and according to their free choice under the auspices of the employment services of the countries concerned;

    (c) provide for periodic exchange of information between the countries concerned on the occupational categories and the number of workers to whom contracts could be offered and who would be ready to emigrate or return to their country of origin; for this purpose skilled manpower pools or data banks should be established to provide reliable information on the supply of and demand for skilled, professional and technical manpower;

    (d) reinforce co-operation between the employment and other services dealing with migration and migrant workers in the countries concerned;

(e) give priority to the recruitment of workers who are underemployed or unemployed;

(f) provide that countries of origin should adopt appropriate measures so as to avoid the departure of skilled workers, including adaptation of education and training schemes to national needs and offering highly trained personnel conditions permitting them to remain and serve their own country;

(g) provide that countries of employment should refrain from recruiting skilled and highly skilled workers when there are recognised or potential shortages of such workers in the country of origin;

(h) provide that the countries of employment could take complementary measures to aid the developing countries to minimise their loss of qualified manpower, for example, by increasing training possibilities for their own nationals in those fields where skills are scarce and by eliminating any part of their immigration laws and regulations which have the effect of encouraging the entry of professional and other highly qualified migrants;

(i) provide ways of limiting losses in countries of origin, particularly developing countries, which may result from the departure of skilled personnel whose education and training they have provided;

(j) establish training facilities, where these do not already exist, making possible:
   (i) suitable preparation, documentation and training of candidates for emigration;
   (ii) vocational training and advancement of migrant workers in the country of employment;
   (iii) training of workers wishing to return to the countries of origin, taking account of the aptitudes of such workers and the needs of their countries;

(k) adopt the necessary measures to facilitate the voluntary return to their countries of origin of migrant workers and their resettlement;

(l) provide for social security benefits for families which have stayed in the country of origin and for suitable means of ensuring that migrant workers returning to their home countries enjoy continuity of social security benefits;

(m) take into consideration the need for financing the above measures by appropriate means.

The Role of the ILO

44. At their request, the ILO should provide technical co-operation to the countries concerned and technical support to regional organisations in order to make it possible to prepare and implement the above measures.

45. At the request of governments concerned, the ILO should study the possibility of setting up at regional or subregional levels a system designed with the collaboration of the representative employers' and workers' organisations concerned to improve information on the availability of job opportunities in certain industries and certain types of employment for the benefit of candidates for emigration or return to their country of origin.

46. The Office should:

(a) initiate studies on the economic and social effects of different kinds of migration for employment;

(b) make studies and organise meetings at regional or subregional levels on the problems of migrant workers who have not been regularly admitted or who lack official papers.

III. Technologies for Productive Employment Creation in Developing Countries

Policy Objectives

47. Technology has an important role to play in the process of development. Since technology is linked with the choice of products as well as with capital investment, labour and skills required to produce them, it has a bearing on the level of productive employment and the distribution of income. Technology, therefore, is an important element of the basic-needs strategy, which must be part of an over-all national, economic and social development strategy.

48. There is an urgent need for appropriate and optimal technology, that is, management and production techniques which are best suited to the resources and future development potential of developing countries. Such technology should contribute to greater productive employment opportunities, elimination of poverty and achievement of equitable income distribution.

49. The exclusive use of labour-intensive techniques will neither solve the problems of the developing countries nor reduce their dependence on industrialised countries. Likewise, the exclusive use of capital-intensive techniques will present the developing countries with serious problems: financial difficulties, lack of managerial staff and supervisory personnel and delays in the solution to employment problems. Thus developing countries should arrive at a reasonable balance between labour-intensive and capital-intensive techniques, with a view to achieving the fundamental aim of maximising growth and employment and satisfying basic needs. This strategy of equilibrium between the various types of technologies should also take account of the desire to adopt advanced techniques, with a view to reducing the existing technological gap between countries.

50. Choice, development and transfer of technology require that proper emphasis should be placed on the building up of national infrastructure for human resources development, particularly to promote training of workers, technicians and managers for appropriate technology selection.

51. In the selection of new technologies appropriate to their needs, the developing countries should take due account of the need to protect their ecology and natural resources. There is also a need to pay due attention to social aspects, working conditions and the safety of workers when introducing new technologies.

Action at the National Level

52. The choice of appropriate technologies is dependent on the conditions prevailing in each country and the characteristics of each economic sector. This choice must also be based on the full utilisation of national resources. Thus each developing country has the right and duty to choose the technologies which it decides are appropriate. To facilitate such a choice, it will be helpful to establish national subregional and regional centres for the transfer and development of technology and to promote co-operation both between developing countries and between the latter and developed countries. The ILO should help in the establishment of these centres in conjunction with other agencies of the UN system.

53. The promotion of research should be a fundamental priority in policies to increase the national technological capacity of developing countries and reduce their dependence on industrialised countries. This research should mainly be undertaken within, and under the direction of, the developing countries themselves or in corresponding regional or subregional bodies where these exist, with the technical and financial assistance of international and other agencies presently involved in such activities. Technological research should furthermore contribute towards the satisfaction of basic needs.

54. Each developing country should accelerate appropriate technological advancement in the informal urban and rural sectors, in particular, to eliminate underemployment and unemployment and raise productivity levels.

55. Foreign firms, in response to the national legislation of developing countries and in negotiation with them, and taking into account the national economic development plans, should:

(a) introduce technologies which are both growth- and employment-generating, directly or indirectly;

(b) adapt technologies to the needs of the host countries, and progressively substitute national for imported technology;

(c) contribute to financing the training of national managers and technicians for the better utilisation and generation of technology;

(d) supply resources and direct technical assistance for national and regional technology research; and

(e) spread technological knowledge and help in its growth by subcontracting the production of parts and materials to national producers, and particularly to small producers.

56. Each developing country should accelerate the formulation and implementation of a training plan at the following levels:

(a) middle-level technicians and skilled workers to be employed in the production technologies associated with the goods and services required to satisfy basic needs;

(b) professionals, technicians, managers and skilled workers to replace expatriate staff who presently apply advanced technology;

(c) professionals and technicians needed to manage research and studies undertaken by national and/or regional technological research bodies; and

(d) technicians, professionals and skilled workers, who should be assured of a measure of social status and incentives to prevent a brain drain, in order to promote the utilisation of technologies designed to achieve material and social objectives.

Action at the International Level

57. International agencies and bilateral and multi-lateral aid programmes should devote resources and technical assistance to complement developing countries' efforts.

58. At present several organisations of the UN system are engaged in work on appropriate technologies for developing countries. Better co-ordination of this work would ensure that the full potential benefits may be realised.

59. The UN Interagency Task Force on Information Exchange and the Transfer of Technology is working towards the establishment of a network for the exchange of technological information. At its second session in May 1976 it recommended that: "organisations of the United Nations system and other organisations having substantive

responsibility in the field of technological information and the transfer of technology should develop their relevant activities as components of the over-all network, and in mutual co-operation make available their own information bases and information-handling capabilities as appropriate".

The ILO should strengthen its activities in the field of the collection and dissemination of information on appropriate technologies, especially for the rural sector, and so make an important contribution towards the establishment of the information exchange network referred to above.

60. The ILO should reorient and strengthen its existing programme in order to provide more manpower training and human resources development in the developing countries.

61. The ILO should pursue its research and technical co-operation in the field of development and transfer of technology. It should set up a Working Group in which employers and workers would be represented to examine action on appropriate technology for employment, vocational training and income distribution. The developing countries should participate directly in this Working Group, which should not encroach upon the activities of other UN agencies.

62. The Group of 77 endorsed the establishment of a Consultative Group on Appropriate Technology and an International Appropriate Technology Unit, especially directed to research on the choice of alternative use of resources allowing a greater utilisation of labour per unit of investment, provided that such mechanisms are integrated with the ongoing activities of the UN system. The Workers' Group also endorsed these proposals but emphasised that these bodies should be tripartite in character. Most Western industrialised countries did not support these two proposals. The Workers' Group and the Group of 77 supported the UNCTAD proposal for an international code of conduct for technology transfer. This should be of a legally binding, not voluntary, nature. They further supported the suggestion that the Paris Convention of 1883 on industrial property should be drastically revised.

IV. Active Manpower Policies and Adjustment Assistance in Developed Countries

General Principles

63. Governments of developed countries should pursue a determined policy to achieve and maintain full employment, i.e. to provide employment opportunities for all those who want to work, and contribute to a fair distribution of income and wealth in these countries. Employment policy should be closely integrated with over-all economic policy and national planning. It has to be related to other social policies.

64. The success of active manpower policies pursued with this aim will facilitate adaptation to structural changes including those which result from expanding trade with developing countries, thereby supporting growth and increased employment in these countries. Employment policy should not exclusively be based on measures to influence general demand. It should also be based on a range of selective measures to create new job opportunities. Such selective measures should also make a contribution to the struggle against inflation. Governments in the industrialised countries should strengthen the co-ordination of economic policies to maintain full employment. Measures should also be taken to ensure close collaboration concerning the migratory movement of workers between countries of origin and reception.

65. This policy will contribute to a high level of economic activity and improvements in the international economic order as called for by the UN General Assembly, and will lead to increased trade with the developing countries, thus increasing growth and employment in these countries.

66. Structural changes resulting from modifications in the international economic order must not take place at the expense of workers. Such changes should contribute to job creation in both industrialised and developing countries, and assure suitable employment to all workers, involving countries of whatever social and political system. The governments concerned should provide adjustment assistance in order to facilitate the establishment of new economic relations between developing and developed nations. It is envisaged that such adjustment assistance would not diminish development aid.

Policy Measures

67. The priorities of national employment policies should be:
    (i) the maintenance of as high a demand for labour as is necessary in order to achieve full employment;
    (ii) measures and policies to promote stable economic growth, which should include both general and selective measures;
    (iii) the reinforcement of measures designed to provide protection against undesirable effects of cyclical evolution or structural change, such as those mentioned in ILO Conventions and Recommendations. These measures could include:
    — provision of maximum practicable notice of change for workers whose jobs are threatened;
    — provision of appropriate income levels for a reasonable period and the safeguarding of pension rights;
    — provision of retraining;
    — provision of special measures for women, migrants, young workers, and handicapped workers whose re-employment involves special problems.

These matters should be dealt with in close co-operation between governments, employers and workers.

68. Many of these features already exist in the policies of industrialised countries.

69. In implementing employment and manpower policies, the industrialised countries should continue to pursue and expand trade liberalisation policies in order to increase imports of manufactures and semi-manufactures from developing countries in an effort to increase their employment and incomes, while continuing to maintain employment in industrialised countries. Adjustment assistance is considered preferable to import restrictions.

70. Consistent with national laws and systems, adjustment assistance should start well before workers lose their jobs, when this can be clearly established, and not only when unemployment is imminent.

71. Regional or national readjustment funds could be set up by the industrialised countries or existing funds (for example the EEC Social and Regional Funds) could be adapted for the purpose of assisting in the adjustment of industries and workers affected by changes in the international economic situation. This ought not to reduce development aid.

72. The competitiveness of new imports from developing countries should not be achieved to the detriment of fair labour standards.

73. The World Employment Conference expresses the hope that the discussions in the Multilateral Trade Negotiations concerning the GATT safeguard clause, i.e. GATT Article 19, will lead to improvements in the international safeguard system.

74. Governments and employers' and workers' organisations shall work together to improve industrial life. Employers and workers should consider participation by workers in matters of recognised mutual concern.

Proposals for an ILO Action Programme

75. The traditional role of the ILO regarding labour standards should be continued in order to ensure respect for fair labour standards in developing and industrialised countries alike.

76. The ILO could contribute to the exchange of information and experience on the functioning and problems of active manpower policies and adjustment assistance. The Workers' members felt that the ILO could, within its special competence and in the context of multi-lateral trade negotiations, contribute to the improvement of an international safeguard system covering employment and income guarantees, fair labour standards and adjustment measures.

77. ILO Industrial Committees could provide a forum for discussing the problems of employment and working conditions resulting from structural change.

78. The Turin Centre, CINTERFOR and other regional vocational training centres have an essential role to play in training, a role which could usefully be widened into areas not currently covered.

V. The Role of Multinational Enterprises in Employment Creation in the Developing Countries

The Conference was unable to reach a consensus on the role of multinational enterprises in developing countries. The following paragraphs reflect the position of the different parties.

Declarations of Government Members

79. Some governments stressed the positive aspects of the activities of multinational enterprises in developing countries, which they saw as direct employment creation, the linkage effects on the economy, the firms' contribution to an improvement of training, the creation of social services, etc.

80. Some governments stressed that multinational corporations had a role to play in the implementation of a basic-needs strategy. However, it is necessary first to identify the different types of corporation according to their objectives in order to determine which ones could be expected to contribute to the implementation of a basic-needs strategy.

81. Some governments on the other hand underlined the negative effects of the activities of multinational corporations in developing countries, which they saw as the creation of an international division of labour unfavourable to these countries, the control of raw

materials, the lack of respect for the sovereign rights of States, the insecurity of the employment provided, the lack of respect for trade union rights and notably the expatriation of profits.

82. Some governments felt that efforts should be made to try to reinforce co-operation between host countries and multinational enterprises, especially through the creation of a favourable climate for private foreign investments. In addition, according to these governments, multinational corporations should not be treated less favourably than local companies.

83. Other governments expressed the opinion that the application of discriminatory measures with regard to multinational enterprises as opposed to local enterprises was one of the sovereign rights of States.

84. The Government members of countries belonging to the Group of 77 based their position on Resolution 3201 adopted by the General Assembly of the United Nations on 1 April 1974 on the establishment of a New International Economic Order based on equity, equality, sovereign rights, interdependence, common interests and co-operation between all States regardless of their economic and social systems, as well as on the conclusions and recommendations adopted by the Fourth Conference of Non-Aligned Countries in Algiers. These countries stated that transnational enterprises were responsible for the worldwide economic imbalance, that they infringed the sovereignty of States, and that they sometimes tended to constitute monopolies and to engage in market sharing and fixing prices. These governments maintained that all action vis-a-vis transnational enterprises must be taken within the framework of a global strategy conceived to bring about quantitative and qualitative changes in the present system of economic and financial relations. They recalled the sovereign rights of States and condemned all interference in the internal matters of the countries in which transnational enterprises invested.

85. The member countries of the Group of 77 recommended strengthening national enterprises to enable them to take necessary steps with a view to preventing the negative effects of the activities of transnational corporations (TNCs). They also recommended that member States and the ILO continue to provide full support to the activities of the UN Commission on Transnational Corporations to regulate the activities of such enterprises particularly in relation to the Code of Conduct which TNCs should observe, containing the following basic principles:

  (i) TNCs must be subject to the laws and regulations of the host country and in the event of a dispute accept the exclusive jurisdiction of the courts of the country in which they operate;
  (ii) TNCs should refrain from all interference in the internal affairs of the States in which they operate;
  (iii) TNCs should refrain from interference in their relations between the government of the host country and other States, and from influencing these relations;
  (iv) TNCs should not serve as an instrument of the external policy of another State nor as a means of extending to the host country juridical regulations of the country of origin;
  (v) TNCs should be subject to the permanent sovereignty which the host country exercises over all its wealth, natural resources and economic activities;
  (vi) TNCs should comply with national development policies, objectives and priorities and make a contribution to their implementation;

(vii) TNCs should supply the government of the host country with relevant information on their activities in order to ensure that those activities are in accordance with the national development policies, objectives and priorities of the host country;

(viii) TNCs should conduct their operations in such a way that they result in a net inflow of financial resources for the host country;

(ix) TNCs should contribute to the development of the domestic, scientific and technological capacity of the host countries;

(x) TNCs should refrain from restrictive trade practices;

(xi) TNCs should respect the socio-cultural identity of the host country.

86. The Group of 77 also recommended that developing countries adopt measures at the national, regional and international levels in order to ensure that transnational enterprises should reorient their activities so as to undertake further manufacturing processes in developing countries and processing in those countries of raw materials for national or foreign markets. They also recommended that the ILO and member States co-operate with a view to bringing the UN Commission on Transnational Corporations to consider among the points to be included in the compulsory Code of Conduct of TNCs those concerning the obligation of these enterprises to hire local labour, not to discriminate against local workers in respect of salaries, conditions of work, training, promotion and access to different levels of seniority. And lastly they recommended that developing countries take steps in order to regulate and control the activities of transnational enterprises so as to ensure that they would act as a positive factor supporting the efforts of developing countries to expand their exports, through the direct impact which the diversification and expansion of such exports can have on the generation of productive employment.

87. The Group of 77 considered that, in conformity with the policies laid down in national development plans, and adhering to the national laws and priorities, and fully respecting the sovereignty of the host countries, the transnational corporations should:

(i) introduce technologies which are both growth- and employment-generating, directly or indirectly;

(ii) adapt technologies to the needs of the host countries;

(iii) contribute to financing the training of national managers and technicians for the better utilisation of technology;

(iv) supply resources and direct technical assistance for national and regional technology research;

(v) spread technological knowledge and help in its growth by subcontracting the production of parts and materials to national producers and particularly to small producers;

(vi) disclose and fully make available to the host countries all the technical know-how and information involved in production maintenance, design, construction, research and development, etc.

88. The Group of 77 supported the proposals of the Workers' Group set out in paragraph 113 (i)-(vi) below, in particular the suggestion that the ILO Governing Body should place the issue of transnational enterprises and social policy on the agenda of the 1978 Session of the International Labour Conference in order that Conventions on TNCs should be adopted in the following areas: industrial relations, employment and training, conditions of life and work.

89. Government members of the European socialist countries supported in principle the position of the Group of 77 as well as that of the Workers' members, and endorsed the

proposal to place the issue of multinational enterprises and social policy on the agenda of the International Labour Conference in 1978. They felt that in the countries where multinational enterprises operated, they should contribute to employment creation without hindering either a just distribution of incomes or social progress. They underlined that States had an unconditional right to control the activities of multinational enterprises, and that these enterprises must respect the sovereign rights of States and must not interfere in their internal affairs.

90. Most Government members of industrialised market economy countries underlined the positive effects of the activities of multinational enterprises on the economic development of developing countries. These governments underlined the importance of the task of all countries concerned in assisting the economic development of the Third World. They were of the opinion that the multinational enterprises could contribute to the economic development of the host country, especially through the creation of employment. The governments of home countries of multinational enterprises, while considering their own national requirements, should continue to apply selective incentives for foreign investments in such a way as to encourage investments which met the basic needs of the host country. Countries which welcomed foreign investment should create a favourable and stable investment climate which encouraged multinational enterprises to adapt their activities to the economic needs of the country. For this purpose the governments of the host countries should avoid introducing or maintaining inequalities of treatment between multinational enterprises and domestic enterprises in social matters affecting their respective workers.

91. Most Government members of industrialised market economy countries expressed the hope that such policies would help in taking full advantage of the positive aspects of the activities of multinational enterprises. In this spirit these Government members noted the recommendations of the ILO Tripartite Advisory Meeting on the Relationship of Multinational Enterprises and Social Policy, held in Geneva from 4 to 13 May 1976, that appropriate arrangements be made with a view to preparing an ILO Tripartite Declaration of Principles concerning Multinational Enterprises and Social Policy, which would provide the ILO's input into the much broader Code of Conduct which is currently considered by the United Nations Commission on Transnational Corporations. The interests of both the host countries and multinational enterprises were best served, in the long run, by an atmosphere of mutual trust, in which the rules for inter-relationship were known in advance and strictly observed, relevant information was available to all parties concerned, and negotiations were conducted in a flexible manner.

92. In the light of the above, the Government members of industrialised market economy countries were of the opinion that the present contributions of multinational enterprises to the creation of employment in the developing countries could be further increased through various measures such as:

    (i) local subcontracting when this was technically possible;
    (ii) a progressive increase in the local processing of raw materials;
    (iii) local reinvestment of profits to the greatest extent possible;
    (iv) replacement of expatriates and maximum utilisation of local personnel;
    (v) training and promotion of local production workers and of local management personnel;
    (vi) co-operation on matters of training between the multinational enterprises and the various local institutions providing training.

    It should be understood, however, that the role the multinational enterprise could play in employment creation varied from one host country to another, from one time-period to another, and from one firm to another. On the other hand, the contribution of multinational corporations could only be partial since the reduction of unemployment in developing countries was a global task, the responsibility for which lay primarily with governments. It was therefore up to them to ensure that the contribution of multinational corporations to employment creation was maximised. The multinational enterprises should respect the sovereign rights of States as well as the relevant laws, rules and national practices and recognised international obligations, it being understood that it would be desirable to refer to Conventions and Recommendations of the ILO when legal, political and economic considerations so permitted Multinational enterprises should adapt the activities of their subsidiaries to the development programmes and economic objectives of the countries where they were established. This adaption should take into account all the economic and social factors of these countries.

93. Government members of the industrialised market economy countries considered that it was necessary to reinforce the technical negotiating capacity of developing countries vis-a-vis the multinational corporations. For this purpose:

    (i) it recommended that the ILO should study regulations in the employment and training fields, adopted by developing countries, regarding foreign investment and multinational corporations;

    (ii) it would be desirable to clarify the need for training in developing countries for the purpose of dealing with foreign investment and to establish corresponding training programmes which would assist governments in negotiating with multinationals on matters relating directly or indirectly to employment creation and the improvement of training;

    (iii) it was desirable that the ILO, to the extent of its competence, should be ready to provide technical assistance as required in those fields to governments which requested it.

Also it would be desirable to ask the ILO to carry out studies on employment, training and wage policies adopted by developing countries regarding multinational enterprises. Research should equally be strengthened in the field of appropriate technology and labour-intensive goods, the production of which should be promoted in developing countries.

94. Certain Government members of developing countries associated themselves with most of the proposals in paragraphs 92 and 92 above.

95. Government members of industrialised market economy countries felt that multinational enterprises should so far as possible devote themselves to stepping up research and development in the field of appropriate technology and to the development of products to further employment creation. And that, lastly, for their part, governments should be able, before accepting the investment of multinationals on their territory, to be sure that the techniques proposed were those most suited to employment creation, taking account also of other factors affecting production and marketing.

96. Certain representatives of industrialised market economies, whilst in agreement with certain general points made in paragraphs 90 to 93 above, nevertheless expressed their sympathy vis-a-vis the declaration of the Group of 77. They also expressed their agreement with the procedures proposed in the Tripartite Advisory Meeting of May 1976, as well as with the proposal for research which the ILO could undertake in collaboration with the United Nations Commission on Transnational Corporations, without this implying, however, an acceptance of all the conclusions of that meeting. In addition they stated that it was necessary to co-ordinate the ILO's activities on

multinational enterprises with those of the UN Commission on Transnational Corporations.

97. Certain governments, while recognising the importance of a Code of Conduct regulating the activities of multinational enterprises, put the stress on relations of a bilateral character which can exist between host countries and multinational enterprises and on the importance of national regulations for controlling the activities of these enterprises.

Declarations of the Employers' Members

98. The Employers' members stated clearly that the relevant agenda item as determined by the Governing Body at its 196th (May 1975) Session, called for a discussion of "the role of multinational enterprises in employment creation in the developing countries" and that they were prepared to discuss this specific question. They considered that companies in general, including multinational enterprises, as well as governments and trade unions, had a responsibility to bring about a better balance in the distribution of the world's products and knowledge. Multinational enterprises in conjunction with home and host governments and trade unions had an important role to play in advancing social progress. It was not possible for multinational enterprises to solve the problem of employment and to meet the basic needs of the world, but they had a contribution to make in this field; nevertheless, the responsibility of this task lay primarily with governments.

99. The Employers' members stressed that the discussion of the problem should concentrate on which kind of employment opportunities multinational enterprises could create. These enterprises did concern themselves with developing new activities important for employment, for example in agriculture. Although direct creation of employment by multinational enterprises was limited, the indirect effects were significant and could stimulate national economic development and know-how.

100. They believed that it was up to each government to decide what kinds of industrial activities and technologies were best suited to meet the development needs of its country. New activities of multinational enterprises in developing countries should fit into national plans. Agriculture should be given priority attention in developing countries, and multinational enterprises could provide assistance in developing the production of industrial inputs to agriculture and in building up industries processing agricultural outputs.

101. The Employers' members stressed that multinational enterprises were a significant vehicle for the transfer of advanced technology, that choice of technology was often dictated by governments and that governments of developing countries generally insisted upon the most sophisticated kinds of technology.

102. They further expressed the view that multinational enterprises had beneficial effects on wages and working conditions. It was for host governments to define the social obligations under which multinational enterprises should function. It was the general practice of multinational enterprises to recognise workers' rights as well as the maintenance of labour standards and working conditions. In general, multinationals were responsible, did train local staff, had good industrial relations, had pay scales as good as, or better than, those of national companies, and worked within national regulations. Multinational enterprises were entitled to a fair remuneration for their efforts.

209

103. The Employers' members pointed out that multinational enterprises were free not to invest and that foreign investors needed a stable investment climate. Tough rules were acceptable as long as they were not arbitrarily changed. Moreover, multinational enterprises objected to regulations which were not applicable also to national companies. The Employers' members insisted on equal treatment on social matters.

104. Taking cognisance of the five reports prepared by the ILO at the request of the Tripartite Meeting on the Relationship between the Multinational Corporations and Social Policy which met in Geneva from 26 October to 4 November 1972 and of the agreed conclusions reached at the Tripartite Advisory Meeting on the Relationships of Multinational Enterprises and Social Policy of 4-12 May 1976, the Employers' members believed that it was not the mission of the World Employment Conference to discuss the content of principles to govern multinational enterprises. A voluntary code of conduct could be helpful.

105. The Employers' members considered that the ILO study on international principles and guidelines was a clear and comprehensive survey of possibilities in the ILO context. The ILO studies had shown that the multinational in general behaved responsibly. They had failed to reveal the existence of problems of the kind referred to by the Workers' members. The multinationals had been shown in the ILO studies to be a force for economic development. Indeed, they were the most effective means yet found for reducing the time-span for producing the management skills needed to organise resources and muster finance. It was necessary to be careful that any action taken would not have adverse implications for the future. The Employers' members were therefore unconvinced of the need for international action in regard to multinationals in the social field. In particular, they considered that any move towards the adoption of an international labour Convention in this area risked creating an impossible situation through the variations in the extent of ratification or acceptance in different countries— a risk mentioned in the ILO study. There was also a question of discriminatory treatment. The bulk of the existing Conventions were of general application, the exceptions to this being so narrow in scope that there was no analogy between them and the wide range of enterprises and industries covered by the term "multinational", with their varying degrees of foreign and national ownership. A Convention applying to all employees of any enterprise under any degree of foreign ownership would place these employees under special regulations that might well be more favourable than those in the prevailing industrial economy of the country, with adverse effects on the orderly conduct of industrial relations. Having regard to the variety of industrial relations patterns and behaviour in different countries, the Employers' members believed that such matters must primarily be determined by the governments of the country concerned and the ordinary law and practice of the country.

106. Another approach that had been suggested was the preparation of a tripartite declaration of principles which could eventually be embodied in more comprehensive United Nations guidelines. The Office study had pointed to the guidance given in Conference resolutions and conclusions of Industrial Committees and other advisory meetings as indicating the feasibility of such a procedure. The Employers' members were not against guidelines in principle, as shown by those published by the International Chamber of Commerce as long ago as 1972 and the active participation of their organisation in OECD's work on a code. The Employers' members were however convinced that such a declaration would not be useful and might well be harmful unless the guidelines met the following points:

(a) that they ensure that the operations of multinational enterprises can continue effectively to the benefit to society as a whole;

(b) that they are non-mandatory but mutually agreed through a tripartite declaration of principles on responsible behaviour for multinational enterprises, governments and trade unions;

(c) that they ensure in social matters that all parties respect the laws and regulations of the host country;

(d) that they recognise the principle of equal treatment for foreign-owned and for national enterprises in matters of industrial relations and social policy;

(e) that they do not bind multinationals to observance of ILO standards not ratified or accepted by the host country, or introduce a system of standards making existing ILO Conventions and Recommendations applicable only to multinational enterprises;

(f) that they are flexible enough to permit application to very different national situations and national objectives and in regard to widely different types of companies and industries;

(g) that they apply effectively to enterprises with public or mixed ownership as well as to privately-owned companies.

Restrictive legislation would only slow down employment creation in developing countries by multinational enterprises. Multinational enterprises were already subject to many regulations and governments had adequate powers of their own, any of which could frustrate a company's expectations of a reasonable return.

107. The Employers' members stated that, following the proposal in paragraph 106 above, the Tripartite Advisory Meeting had recommended that a small tripartite group should be established to draft a voluntary declaration of principles applying to multinational enterprises, governments and trade unions. In view of this, the Employers' members did not consider it appropriate to place the question of multinational enterprises and social policy on the agenda of the International Labour Conference in 1978.

108. The Employers' members, after two weeks of discussion, were reluctantly forced to accept that no consensus existed in the group because the differing views of Government, Workers' and Employers' members were irreconcilable.

109. The representatives of employers of European socialist countries fully supported the point of view of the Government members of the European socialist countries with regard to the role of multinational enterprises in employment creation in developing countries.

Declarations of the Workers' Members

110. The Workers' members expressed the concerns and preoccupations of trade unions and workers with regard to the effects of the activities of multinational enterprises on employment and more generally on development. They declared that the questions raised under item 4 in Chapter 11 of the Director-General's Report were not exhaustive and therefore should not limit the discussion. Consequently, the discussion ought to include other questions which were just as important. The Workers also underlined the fact that consideration of the problem should not be restricted by the conclusions of the Tripartite Advisory Meeting held in May 1976. Under these circumstances, the three international trade union federations asked that, on the international and national levels, steps should be taken to strengthen control of multinational enterprises. This control should be exerted by the countries in which they operated. The areas in which international and national action should take place were, in particular, as follows:

(i) in all the countries where multinational enterprises operated, the existing Conventions of the ILO ought to be applied, in particular Conventions Nos. 87 on trade union liberties, 98 on collective bargaining, 100 on equal remuneration, 122 on employment, 135 on representation of workers, 140 on paid education leave and 143 on migrant workers. In addition, reference to ILO Conventions must include working conditions for multinational enterprises in countries which had not yet ratified these ILO standards and in those countries where they were persistently violated;

(ii) employment of local workers and non-discrimination should be guaranteed. Non-discriminatory working conditions should be established on a democratic basis and should correspond to the highest wages, salaries, working conditions and standards of hygiene and safety in all the branches and units of multinational enterprises;

(iii) multinational enterprises ought to guarantee that the enterprises supply the representatives of the workers with essential information, especially on the composition of capital, the general organisation of the company at the level of the parent company and the branches, the evolution of the company with respect to workers' participation, detailed investment plans, current and former agreements, conditions of work, wages and recruitment of personnel in each factory, data on financial management and results, etc.;

(iv) in addition, the right of trade unions to take solidarity action at the level of each factory and of the multinational organisation as a whole, and the right of trade unions to decide freely on any action designed to enforce economic sanctions;

(v) the transfer of activities following labour conflicts should be prohibited. In the case of a transfer of production, workers should be provided with new jobs with equivalent working conditions, and a compensation fund should be created to support workers losing their jobs;

(vi) furthermore, in a more general economic context, the profits of multinational enterprises should remain in the countries in which these enterprises operated in order to contribute to the creation of productive employment and to a healthier balance of payments situation.

111. The Workers' members felt that in order to achieve this, several convergent paths should be followed at both national and international levels. On the one hand, it would be desirable to strengthen legislative and executive powers to provide the possibility of prohibiting certain economic concentrations, to integrate the activities of the companies in national planning and to provide for real public control over exchange, prices, monetary movements, investments, taxation and credit. On the other hand, the sovereign rights of States to nationalise in order to control their development and their sovereignty over natural resources should be respected. The right to nationalise should apply particularly when the interests of the workers or the country were threatened. Finally, it was necessary that a code of conduct should be elaborated at the international level defining the obligations of multinational enterprises. This code should take into account notably the principles and measures presented by the Workers' members. It should have a legal and binding form.

112. The Workers' members recognised the importance of the principle of nondiscrimination between multinational enterprises and national companies in industrialised countries, but stressed that the very nature of multinational companies and the problems relating to them necessitated the possibility of making exceptions to this principle. In developing countries it was permissible and in some cases even necessary, in the interest of the development of these countries, to take measures which were discriminatory.

113. All foreign investments should be undertaken under the general conditions set out in paragraphs 110-112 and 118. In this context the multinational corporations should abide by the following principles:

    (i) local subcontracting when this is technically possible;

    (ii) a progressive increase in the local processing of raw materials;

    (iii) local reinvestment of profits to the greatest extent possible;

    (iv) replacement of expatriates and maximum utilisation of local personnel;

    (v) training and promotion of local production workers and of local management personnel;

    (vi) co-operation on matters of training with the various local institutions providing training.

114. Multinational enterprises should be required to study the manner in which they could adapt the activities of their subsidiaries to the development programmes and economic objectives of the countries where they were established. The multinational enterprises must respect the sovereign rights of States and take into consideration the legislation, regulations and relevant national practices as well as internationally recognised obligations. They must also recognise the rights of workers and should not undermine but contribute to progress in the field of standards and conditions of work in the host country.

115. As to future action of the ILO, a majority of the Workers' members insisted on the need to strengthen the technical capacity of developing countries to negotiate with multinational enterprises. In this field it was desirable that the ILO, to the extent of its competence, should be ready to provide the required technical assistance to governments desiring to strengthen their bargaining power vis-a-vis multinational enterprises.

116. A large number of the Workers' members thought that it would also be desirable to request the ILO to carry out studies on policies concerning employment, training and wages followed by developing countries in relation to multinational enterprises. It would also be desirable to step up research in the field of appropriate technology and on products with a high employment content, the production of which it would be desirable to promote in the developing countries. For their part the multinational enterprises, so far as possible, should devote themselves to stepping up research and development in the field of appropriate technology and the development of products for furthering employment creation.

117. The Workers' members stressed that the ILO should deal with all the areas relating to the social aspects of the activities of multinational enterprises. The work of the ILO in these fields should be closely co-ordinated with the activities of the UN Commission on Transnational Corporations.

118. The Workers' members finally considered that:

    (i) the ILO should continue its current work concerning multinationals and social policy on the basis of the conclusions of the Tripartite Advisory Meeting of 4-12 May 1976, but without confining itself to those conclusions;

    (ii) the ILO should contribute in the field of its competence and within the United Nations to the elaboration of an international instrument (Code of Conduct) with a binding character permitting the control of multinational companies;

    (iii) the ILO, within the framework of a reform of the mechanisms for examining questions concerning the violation of trade union freedom, should provide for a procedure to be applied to multinational corporations;

(iv) the ILO Governing Body should at its next meeting give consideration to the respective positions of the governments, the Employers' Group and the Workers' Group at the World Employment Conference;

(v) the ILO Governing Body should place the issue of multinational enterprises and social policy on the agenda of the 1978 Session of the International Labour Conference, in order that Conventions on multinational enterprises should be adopted in the following areas: industrial relations, training for employment, conditions of life and work.

119. The Workers' members expressed their profound dissatisfaction that it was not possible to reach any common points of agreement on this crucially important subject. They moreover wished to point out in this context that a number of individual points of agreement were recorded between the Workers' members and several governments. The Workers' members expressed their support for the proposals of the Group of 77, in particular the basic principles covered by paragraph 85. They also supported points (i)-(vi) in paragraph 92 as proposed by the Government members of industrialised market economy countries.

APPENDIX. STATEMENTS CONCERNING THE DECLARATION OF PRINCIPLES AND PROGRAMME OF ACTION ADOPTED BY THE WORLD EMPLOYMENT CONFERENCE[1]

Statement by the Government Delegate of Luxembourg on Behalf of the Member States of the European Community

I would like to make a statement on behalf of the European Community and its member States.

We are very grateful for the efforts which have gone into the production of the Declaration of Principles and of the Programme of Action which we are considering. In particular, Mr. President, we are appreciative of the contribution made by the Chairman of the Committee of the Whole, Dr. Subroto of Indonesia.

The Governments for which I speak wish to emphasise their support for the "basic needs" approach. The result of our work constitutes a compromise which includes for everyone, as the discussion in the Committee of the Whole demonstrated, some acceptable elements and some unacceptable elements. Taking into account the compromise nature of the document, I am glad to be able to state that the nine members of the European Community can associate themselves with the consensus achieved on the Declaration of Principles and the Programme of Action for submission to the Governing Body of the ILO.

In thus associating themselves with the general consensus, the Community and its member States are conscious that the Declaration of Principles and the Programme of Action are wide-ranging and ambitious and that they contain proposals of concern to many international bodies. In so far as these proposals fall within the competence of the ILO, we accept that they will be considered by the Governing Body and we hope that the programmes of the ILO will in large measure take them into account. In so far as the proposals fall within the competence of other UN bodies or international organisations, the European Community and the Governments for which I speak wish to emphasise that their views on many of these issues have been made clear in other fora, most recently in the course of UNCTAD IV. The European Community and its member States approved important resolutions in Nairobi and confirm that they stand ready to implement them. At the same time, the fact that they are associating themselves with the consensus achieved today does not of itself imply acceptance of proposals going beyond those resolutions.

Moreover, Mr. President, it goes without saying that nothing in this document can affect existing international agreements or can be invoked in order to weaken them.

Finally, Mr. President, we hope that the work begun at this Conference will be followed up within the ILO and other appropriate bodies. We are confident that this Conference will be considered as having made an important contribution to world-wide employment strategies.

Statement by the Government Delegate of Switzerland

By participating in the consensus by which the text was adopted by the Conference, the Government delegation of Switzerland wished to demonstrate its comprehension

---

[1]These statements, while not formally part of the Declaration of Principles and Programme of Action adopted by the Conference plenary by acclamation and reprinted in the preceding pages of this Annex, were made by governments in the Conference Committee of the Whole or submitted in letter form for inclusion in the final record of the Conference.

and its support for the preoccupations of the developing countries with problems of employment and more particularly underemployment.

In connection with the references to the ratification of certain ILO Conventions, the Swiss Government delegation wishes, however, to recall that the autonomy of the competent authorities of States must be respected, in conformity with the Constitution of the Organisation.

Regarding the points in the text which fall within the field of responsibility of other international organisations, particularly UNCTAD and GATT, Switzerland's participation in the consensus implies no change in the positions which it took in these organisations on the subjects in question, and most recently at the Fourth Session of UNCTAD.

Letter of 18 June 1976 from the Ambassador and Permanent Representative of Mexico to the Director-General of the International Labour Office

I have the honour to refer to the statement made by the Chairman of the Group of 77 at the closing sitting of the Tripartite World Conference on Employment, Income Distribution and Social Progress and the International Division of Labour.

I hereby inform you that, in conformity with the above-mentioned statement, my Government has decided to request you to arrange for official publication of the following reservation in the appropriate section of the Final Record:

The Government delegation of Mexico to the Tripartite World Conference on Employment, Income Distribution and Social Progress and the International Division of Labour reserves the position of its Government with regard to paragraph 18 of the Declaration of Principles adopted by the Conference, the text of which is as follows:

"Noting the firm commitment of the developing countries and of some developed countries to implement the New International Economic Order, based on the principles contained in the Charter of Economic Rights and Duties of States; . . ."

The Government delegation of Mexico refrained from submitting amendments to this Declaration of Principles—notably with respect to the paragraph quoted—in view of the fact that the final stages of parliamentary debate required that all delegations should refrain from formulating suggested texts or submitting amendments in order that a consensus should be reached on the Declaration of Principles and in order to avoid the submission of a large number of amendments which would have had the effect of preventing the adoption of any document.

For this reason the spokesman of the Group of 77, speaking on behalf of the Group, made it clear that the Governments which were members of the Group reserved their right to express their reservations once the Declaration of Principles and Programme of Action of the Conference had been approved.

The Government delegation of Mexico wishes to state, subject to any position which the Governments belonging to the Group of 77 might adopt on this question, that in its opinion the resolutions adopted by international bodies in accordance with their constitutional provisions are applicable not only to the countries which vote in their favour but to all the members of the organisation in which they are adopted especially where such resolutions enshrine standards of conduct covering the activity of the international community as a whole, as is the case of the Charter of Economic Rights and Duties of States.

The suggestion that standards of conduct which should be followed by all States which are members of the international community only govern the conduct of those States which supported them is equivalent to a denial of the existence of an organised international community and amounts to an incitement to anarchy at the international level.

The Government delegation of Mexico cannot support the implication in the paragraph in question that the New International Economic Order applies only to the developing countries and to some developed countries, particularly in view of the fact that the General Assembly of the United Nations, at its Seventh Special Session, recognised by consensus that the Charter of Economic Rights and Duties of States lays down the foundations of the New International Economic Order; that it should be the basis of greater cooperation among States to contribute to strengthening peace and security in the world; and that the economic and social system of the United Nations should be more responsive to the requirements of its provisions".

I should be grateful for your prompt attention to this request which I am making on the instructions of my Government.

Letter of 22 July 1976 from the United States Ambassador to the Director-General of the International Labour Office

The United States Government wishes to confirm the following reservations it took during the World Employment Conference on the final document (WEC/CW/E.1).

1. In general, the United States reserves position on any part of the final document that could be construed to indicate a deviation from positions taken by the United States at the Sixth and Seventh Special Sessions of the General Assembly and UNCTAD IV.

2. The United States agrees fully with the reservation of western industrialised countries expressed in paragraph 26.

3. Along with "most western industrialised countries", the United States does not support the establishment of a Consultative Group on Appropriate Technology and an International Appropriate Technology Unit, as indicated in paragraph 62, for the reasons stated in the United States delegate's speech to the Committee of the Whole on June 9 and by the Government representative in Working Group III.

ABOUT THE ILO AND
THE INTERNATIONAL LABOUR OFFICE

Originally established in 1919 under the Treaty of Versailles that created the League of Nations, the International Labour Organisation in 1946 became the first of the specialized agencies of the United Nations. The ILO's broad mandate is to advance social justice, thereby helping to ensure universal and lasting peace. The membership of the ILO had grown from 45 nations to 132 nations by 1976; the United States has been a member since 1934. A unique feature of the ILO's structure is that representatives of workers and employers take part with government representatives in the International Labour Conference—which is the Organisation's supreme policy-making body—in the Governing Body, its executive council and in many of its regional and other meetings.

The International Labour Office is the ILO's secretariat, operational headquarters, research body and publishing house. The present Director-General of the International Labour Office is Francis Blanchard of France, who was appointed by the ILO Governing Body in February 1974 for a term of five years.

Since its establishment, the ILO has built up a code of international standards in the form of a vast number of Conventions and Recommendations relating to certain basic human rights (such as freedom of association, the abolition of forced labour and the elimination of employment discrimination); employment and training policy; conditions of work; social security; and a host of other social matters. Through ratification by member States, Conventions are intended to create binding obligations to put their provisions into effect. Recommendations provide guidance on policy, legislation and practice.

A major part of the ILO's work consists of the provision of expert advice and technical assistance to individual countries. Much of this operational activity lies in such fields as training, employment promotion, development of co-operatives, social security, occupational safety and health, workers' education and industrial relations. An International Institute for Labour Studies also operates in Geneva as an autonomous centre for advanced studies; and, in Turin, an International Centre for Advanced Technical and Vocational Training provides courses for instructors, supervisors and managers from developing countries.

The ILO's World Employment Programme—of which the report reprinted in this volume, *Employment, Growth and Basic Needs*, is an integral part—was launched in 1969 as the ILO's principal contribution to the International Development Strategy for the Second UN Development Decade (1970s). Under the Programme, the ILO gives practical assistance to countries in selecting employment policies designed to lead to more work in industry, rural development, public works and other schemes, and to choose the technologies and the training programmes which will use human resources to the full in achieving economic and social progress. Comprehensive employment planning missions under the World Employment Programme have been a particularly effective means of diagnosing problems and proposing solutions at the national as well as regional level.

The publishing work of the ILO aims to facilitate objective study as well as to spread knowledge and stimulate discussion of the major social and economic problems and trends throughout the world and to promote concrete national and international action in furtherance of the aims of the organisation. Research is published in the form of studies, comparative surveys, practical handbooks and reports for conferences and meetings. The ILO also issues a number of periodicals, including such well-known journals as the *International Labour Review*, the *Social and Labour Bulletin* and the *Bulletin of Labour Statistics*, as well as the *Year Book of Labour Statistics*.

Since the launching of the World Employment Programme (with the issuance of a major report of the same name) at the 1969 International Labour Conference, some seven comprehensive employment mission reports have been published; these studies focus specifically on Colombia, Sri Lanka, Kenya, Iran, the Philippines, the Dominican Republic and Sudan. Numerous employment mission reports, monographs on the international division of labour, technology and employment, urbanisation, education and population have been issued, and further studies are in preparation. The policy conclusions presented in the report to the 1976 World Employment Conference which forms the major part of this volume were also supplemented by the publication of two volumes of Background Papers. A further recent study, *Planning Techniques for a Better Future*, provides the conceptual and information framework for a "growth with redistribution" development policy.

Further details about the activities of the ILO and its publishing programme as well as a complete catalogue of ILO publications may be obtained free of charge upon request.

International Labour Office
ILO Publications
CH-1211 Geneva 22
Switzerland

International Labour Office
Washington Branch
1750 New York Avenue, N.W.
Washington, D.C. 20006
Tel. (202) 634-6335

⊄⊃ ABOUT THE
OVERSEAS DEVELOPMENT COUNCIL

The Overseas Development Council is an independent, nonprofit organization established in 1969 to increase American understanding of the economic and social problems confronting the developing countries, and of the importance of these countries to the United States in an increasingly interdependent world. The ODC seeks to promote consideration of development issues by the American public, policy makers, specialists, educators and the media through its research, conferences, publications and liaison with US mass membership organizations interested in US relations with the developing world. The ODC's program is funded by foundations, corporations and private individuals; its policies are determined by its Board of Directors. Theodore M. Hesburgh, CSC, is Chairman of the Board, and Davidson Sommers is its Vice Chairman. The Council's President is James P. Grant.

Research, seminars and publications on the interrelated subjects of employment, growth and the meeting of basic needs have been an important part of ODC's program since the Council's establishment. Among the many publications that reflect the Council's concerns and work in this area are the ODC monograph, *Jobs and Agricultural Development*, by Robert d'A. Shaw (1970); and the ODC development papers, "Rethinking Economic Development", by Robert d'A. Shaw (1972), and "Growth from Below: A People-Oriented Development Strategy", by James P. Grant (1973). Books focusing on major aspects of this field published by the Council in collaboration with other publishers include *Development Reconsidered*, by Edgar Owens and Robert d'A. Shaw (D.C. Heath Lexington Books, 1972); *In the Human Interest*, by Lester R. Brown (W.W. Norton, 1974); *By Bread Alone*, by Lester R. Brown with Erik P. Eckholm (Praeger, 1974); and *Women and World Development*, edited by Irene Tinker, Michèle Bo Bramsen and Mayra Buvinić and published in cooperation with the American Association for the Advancement of Science (ODC and Praeger, 1976).

In addition, the issues of growth, employment, income distribution and alternative development strategies have been a major feature of the Council's annually published book-length assessment of US policy, *The United States and World Development: Agenda for Action*—known as the ODC's *Agenda* series. Within that series, these issues received a particularly comprehensive analysis in the 1975 *Agenda* in the essay by Roger D. Hansen entitled "The Emerging Challenge: Global Distribution of Income and Economic Opportunity". (A complete listing of ODC publication titles and prices can be obtained by writing to Publications, Overseas Development Council, at the address shown below.)

In the 1977-1979 period, ODC's work program includes analysis, discussion and publications on several major aspects of the "employment, growth and basic needs" cluster of issues. Prominent among these efforts is the Council's work on alternative development strategies that are both a) designed to combine growth more effectively with meeting basic needs than was true of past approaches; and b) more closely linked to local values, objectives, initiatives and participation. A second line of ODC work in this area aims to speed up progress in identifying effective alternative strategies by helping to create an active exchange of views and collaboration among developed- as well as developing-country research groups that are formulating such strategies. A third related

ODC program area is the development of a "physical quality of life index" (PQLI), to supplement the per-capita-GNP indicator and thus permit better measurement of progress made in addressing basic human needs. A technical note on ODC's preliminary work on the PQLI index is included in the Council's 1977 policy assessment, *The United States and World Development: Agenda 1977.* The PQLI index is shown for all countries in the comprehensive statistical annexes that are part of the 1977 *Agenda*'s survey of development progress.

Overseas Development Council
1717 Massachusetts Ave., N.W.
Washington, D.C. 20036
Tel. (202) 234-8701

BOARD OF DIRECTORS

222

RELATED TITLES
Published by
Praeger Special Studies

Titles published in cooperation with the
Overseas Development Council:
*THE UNITED STATES AND WORLD
DEVELOPMENT: AGENDA 1977
John W. Sewell and the Staff of the
Overseas Development Council

WOMEN AND WORLD DEVELOPMENT
edited by Irene Tinker, Michèle Bo Bramsen,
and Mayra Buvinić

BEYOND DEPENDENCY:
THE DEVELOPING WORLD SPEAKS OUT
edited by Guy F. Erb and Valeriana Kallab

Other related titles:
*THE MULTINATIONAL CORPORATION
AND SOCIAL CHANGE
edited by David E. Apter and
Louis Wolf Goodman

*PLANNING ALTERNATIVE WORLD FUTURES:
VALUES, METHODS, AND MODELS
edited by Louis Rene Beres and
Harry R. Targ

*THE MAKING OF U.S. INTERNATIONAL
ECONOMIC POLICY: PRINCIPLES,
PROBLEMS, AND PROPOSALS FOR REFORM
Stephen D. Cohen

*PATTERNS OF POVERTY IN THE THIRD
WORLD: A STUDY OF SOCIAL AND
ECONOMIC STRATIFICATION
Charles Elliott, assisted by
Françoise de Morsier

THE NATION-STATE AND TRANSNATIONAL CORPORATIONS IN CONFLICT: WITH SPECIAL REFERENCE TO LATIN AMERICA
edited by Jon P. Gunnemann

EQUITY, INCOME, AND POLICY: STUDIES IN THREE WORLDS OF DEVELOPMENT
edited by Irving Louis Horowitz

DEVELOPMENT IN RICH AND POOR COUNTRIES: A GENERAL THEORY WITH STATISTICAL ANALYSIS
Thorkil Kristensen

INTERNATIONAL LABOR AND THE MULTINATIONAL ENTERPRISE
edited by Duane Kujawa

*DEVELOPMENT WITHOUT DEPENDENCE
Pierre Uri

THE WORLD FOOD CONFERENCE AND GLOBAL PROBLEM SOLVING
Thomas G. Weiss and
Robert S. Jordan

Also available in paperback as a PSS Student Edition.

PRAEGER PUBLISHERS
200 Park Avenue
New York, N.Y. 10017